Henry V, Hol

Henry V, Holy Warrior

The Reign of a Medieval King in Context

Timothy M. Thibodeau

McFarland & Company, Inc., Publishers

Jefferson, North Carolina

This book has undergone peer review.

ISBN (print) 978-1-4766-8708-7
ISBN (ebook) 978-1-4766-4620-6

LIBRARY OF CONGRESS AND BRITISH LIBRARY
CATALOGUING DATA ARE AVAILABLE

Library of Congress Control Number 2022001730

King Henry V by Unknown artist, oil on panel, late 16th or
early 17th century (National Portrait Gallery, London) NPG 545

Printed in the United States of America

*McFarland & Company, Inc., Publishers
Box 611, Jefferson, North Carolina 28640
www.mcfarlandpub.com*

Table of Contents

Table of Contents

Acknowledgments

I am especially grateful to Richard Kaeuper for his collegial encouragement and friendship over the many years that I have known him. His expertise in chivalry provided a scholarly foundation upon which to build some of the most critical aspects of my analysis of chivalry and violence during the late medieval period. In each stage of my research, my friend and colleague Greg Foran enthusiastically shared his expert knowledge of the historical plays of Shakespeare, especially *Henry V*. I deeply appreciate our many conversations and his careful commentary on early drafts of several chapters of this book. I would also like to thank Gary Mitchem from McFarland for supporting the publication of this work and offering timely and helpful feedback on its production. My student assistant Emmarae Stein provided invaluable service when she helped proofread the final drafts of the book.

My most enduring source of inspiration for bringing this book to life is my best friend, wife of thirty-five years, and mother of our two amazing children, Susan Corazza Thibodeau. Her passion for the study of the American Civil War, though far removed from the battlefields of medieval France, has been a constant source of motivation for my own work as a historian. Thanks to her, I did some of my best thinking about the historian's craft while bicycling or hiking with her across the vast battlefields of Gettysburg, Antietam, Chickamauga, and Shiloh. Sue diligently read and edited every part of this book and provided comments and suggestions of inestimable value. She also created the maps that accompany the text. This book is dedicated to her.

List of Maps and Illustrations

Maps

Illustrations

Timeline

1328—Coronation of French King Philip VI; beginning of the French
        Valois dynasty
1337–1453—Hundred Years War
1337—English King Edward III claims the French crown
1346—English victory at the Battle of Crécy
1356—English victory at the Battle of Poitiers
1377—Death of Edward III; Richard II becomes king of England
1380–1422—Reign of mad French King Charles VI
1381—The Great Revolt against Richard II
1386—Birth of the future Henry V
1398—Exile of Henry Bolingbroke, Duke of Lancaster, by Richard II
1399—Deposition of Richard II; coronation of Henry Bolingbroke
        as Henry IV
1403—Battle of Shrewsbury
1407—Murder of Louis, Duke of Orléans, brother of Charles VI
1413—Death of Henry IV; coronation of Henry V
1415—Henry V invades Normandy; Siege of Harfleur and Battle of Agincourt
1417—Henry returns to Normandy
1418–19—Siege of Rouen
1419—Murder of John the Fearless, Duke of Burgundy
1420—Treaty of Troyes; marriage of Henry V and Catherine Valois
1421—Siege of Meaux; birth of future Henry VI
1422—Death of Henry V; death of Charles VI; coronation of Henry VI
        as king of England
1429—Victory of Joan of Arc at Orléans; coronation of Charles VII
        as king of France
1431—Coronation of Henry VI as king of France; trial and execution
        of Joan of Arc
1435—Treaty of Arras
1437—Paris captured from the English by Charles VII; death of Catherine
        Valois

Timeline

1453—Capitulation of Bordeaux; French victory in the Hundred Years War

1455–87—Wars of the Roses

1461—Overthrow of Henry VI by Edward, Duke of York; crowned as
Edward IV

1471—Murder of Henry VI

1599—William Shakespeare's *Henry V*

The Central Characters

English

Edward III (1312–77), King of England (r. 1327–77)
  Son of Edward II and Isabella of France
  Great-grandfather of Henry V
Edward, the Black Prince of Wales (1330–76)
  Son of Edward III and father of Richard II
John of Gaunt, Duke of Lancaster (1340–99)
  Son of Edward III and father of Henry Bolingbroke
Richard II (1367–1400), King of England (r. 1377–99)
  Son of Edward, the Black Prince of Wales
Henry Bolingbroke, Duke of Lancaster (1367–1413)
  Cousin of Richard II
  Crowned Henry IV, King of England (r. 1399–1413)
Henry V (1386–1422), King of England (r. 1413–22)
  Son of Henry IV and Mary de Bohun
Henry VI (1421–71), King of England (r. 1422–61, 70–71)
  Son of Henry V and Catherine Valois of France
  Crowned King of France (1431)

French

Philip VI (1293–1350), first Valois King of France (r. 1328–50)
Jean II (1319–64), King of France (r. 1350–64)
Charles V (1338–80), the "Wise," King of France (r. 1364–80)
Charles VI (1368–1422), "the Mad," King of France (r. 1380–1422)
Catherine Valois (1401–37)
  Daughter of Charles VI
  Wife of Henry V and mother of Henry VI

The Central Characters

Louis Valois, Duke of Orléans (1372–1407)
   Younger brother of Charles VI; assassinated by John the Fearless
John the Fearless, Duke of Burgundy (1371–1419)
   Assassinated in a plot involving the Dauphin Charles
      (the future Charles VII)
Philip III, Duke of Burgundy (1396–1467)
   Son and successor of John the Fearless; ally of Henry V
Isabeau of Bavaria (c. 1370–1435), wife of Charles VI
   Mother of the Dauphin Charles
Yolande of Aragon [also of Sicily] (1381–1442)
   Mother-in-law of the Dauphin Charles
Joan of Arc (1412–31)
   English nemesis; advocate of the Dauphin Charles
Charles VII (1403–61), King of France (r. 1422–61)
   Disinherited by Treaty of Troyes (1420); crowned king with
      the aid of Joan of Arc (1429); victorious in the Hundred
      Years War (1453)

Preface

For nineteenth-century English Romantics, the Hundred Years War (1337–1453) yielded its share of gallant warriors and iconic battles. At the top of that list is Henry V (r. 1413–22), who created an enduring legend when he put forward his audacious claim to the French crown and mounted a massive invasion of Normandy to make good on that claim. After a long and difficult siege that ended with the capture of the port city of Harfleur, Henry and his beleaguered men were forced to do battle by a numerically superior French army. But owing to the king's personal courage, his skill as a commander, and the relentless, deadly volleys of his archers and their longbows, the English slaughtered the flower of French chivalry at the Battle of Agincourt (October 25, 1415). Henry immediately promoted this victory as a miraculous triumph that validated both his new Lancastrian dynasty in England and his ancestral right to the French throne.

When he returned to France in 1417, for the next five years, Henry and his forces pummeled Normandy with a string of sieges, forcing the mad French king Charles VI (r. 1380–1422) to concede the French monarchy to him and his male heirs when Charles died. The Treaty of Troyes (1420) recognized Henry's dynastic claims and marked the legal extinction of Charles' Valois dynasty. His son and successor the Dauphin (the French term for the crown prince), also named Charles, was formally disinherited. But Henry died of dysentery before he could ever wear the French crown, preceding Charles VI in death by only a few months. Fortunately for the English, Henry's marriage to the king's daughter Catherine Valois (1401–37) produced a son and successor named Henry VI (r. 1422–61, 70–71). He became the youngest monarch in English history and the only English king ever crowned king of France, in what turned out to be a meaningless ceremony when he was nine years old. Henry VI would never effectively govern France and through his incompetence as a ruler, he eventually lost all of his father's conquests in Normandy before being dethroned in England, then imprisoned and murdered.

Preface

After Henry V's untimely death, anti–English fervor replaced the shame and humiliation of the French forces that he had defeated. The electrifying career of an illiterate teenage peasant named Joan of Arc (1413–31) revived resistance to the foreign conqueror, turned the tide of the war, and provided Romantic French nationalists with their own iconic hero from the Hundred Years War. After Joan helped to lift the English siege of Orléans (May 8, 1429), she encouraged and attended the coronation of the disinherited Dauphin, Charles VII (r. 1422–61). His long and successful reign led to the defeat of the English and the bona fide end of the Hundred Years War. Though they had covered themselves with glory on the battlefield, the English eventually recognized that they could not control a vast colonial empire in France, especially during the turbulent reign of their own mad king, Henry VI. Bit by bit, the French won a war of diplomacy and attrition that culminated with the capitulation of the English-allied city of Bordeaux in 1453.

The Hundred Years War defies easy categorization and it does not naturally produce a simple, continuous narrative. It began with arcane disputes over feudal hierarchies, vassalage, and fiefdoms that are difficult for modern people to comprehend. Because of the intermarriage of the English and French princes and princesses of the royal blood, these quarrels eventually escalated into a full-blown war for the crown of France. Henry V was a direct descendant of his great-grandfather Edward III (r. 1327–77), who began the Hundred Years War when he invaded France in 1337. Edward's French mother Isabella was the sister of the last Capetian king of France, Charles IV (r. 1322–28). After his uncle Charles died without a male heir, Edward registered his claim for the French crown and was eventually willing to wage war against the founder of the new Valois dynasty, Philip VI (r. 1328–50), to enforce his right to dynastic succession. When Henry's invasion force landed in Normandy in August of 1415, he revived an ancient dispute over the origins of the Valois dynasty that he believed could only be settled on the battlefield.

This book offers a contextual and thematic analysis of Henry V's career as a holy warrior and conqueror. When Henry put his nation on a war footing, rallying his countrymen around the unifying principle of war against a foreign enemy that deprived him of his just rights, he dramatically embodied the ideals of late medieval kingship. Virtually everything that he did as king was informed by a well-crafted religious ideology which envisioned his reign and military campaigns in France as an extended holy war. Henry's monarchy successfully fused political authority, religious piety, and martial prowess. He was without a doubt one of the most ambitious rulers

2

in medieval English history, anxious to validate his father Henry IV's (r. 1399–1413) new Lancastrian dynasty after his tumultuous reign and to earn the respect of the crowned heads of Europe for his war against the French.

My presentation focuses on three constituent, interconnected components of Henry's nine-year reign as king of England: the establishment of his authority in England and France (chapters 1–3); his concept of holy war for the French crown (chapters 4–5); and his successful promotion of Agincourt as a miraculous victory (chapter 6). The chapter on Agincourt offers extensive coverage of the battle and its aftermath since it was a paradigmatic event for the duration of Henry's reign and has long been viewed as a defining moment for English national identity. For the victorious English king and his court, Agincourt provided palpable evidence that God's favor rested on the English monarchy and that his war in France was just. Shakespeare's play *Henry V* (1599) codified the king's interpretation of this great victory and immortalized a mythic presentation of the battle that has prevailed for more than four centuries.

The overall approach of this book is narrative and chronological, with a detailed consideration of the political, religious, and diplomatic forces that gave Henry's reign its unique character. A significant portion of this analysis focuses on the critical players in the drama of Henry's life and reign and their interconnections. Henry's monarchy and his war in France can only be understood within the framework of the tortuous relationship of his father, Henry IV, with his cousin Richard II (r. 1377–99), whom he deposed, imprisoned, and allegedly murdered. The overthrow and suspicious death of Richard left an indelible black mark on the Lancastrians and cast a long shadow over the younger Henry's reign. His ostentatious displays of piety when he became king, his articulation of a developed ideology of holy war for his just rights, and his military asceticism can only be fully appreciated by understanding the conflicted relationship between Richard II and Henry IV. The allegations of usurpation and regicide hung like a pall over the new Lancastrian monarchy and informed virtually every act of piety and religious benefaction of Henry V.

There are also disputed questions about Henry's conduct in war that will be addressed and debated. For example, was his order to massacre wounded and unarmed prisoners at the Battle of Agincourt a criminal act that defied the laws of war as they were understood by his contemporaries? Was the forced starvation of abandoned French civilians outside the walls of Rouen also a transgression of the medieval laws of war? The modern mischaracterization of chivalry, the problems associated with the application of just war theology to the Hundred Years War, and the danger of imposing modern legal definitions of criminality in war on Henry V and his contemporaries will all be analyzed and debated, especially in the final chapter.

This book is aimed primarily at advanced undergraduate or beginning graduate students who are new to the study of Shakespeare's *Henry V*, or who are enrolled in a course on medieval English history or the Hundred Years War. My presentation is predicated on a vast and deep academic literature (noted in the Suggestions for Further Reading and Bibliography). I have attempted to distill and represent the best research on the war and Henry's reign while also highlighting the ongoing debates over his actions as king and military commander. In the reconstruction and interpretation of Henry's life, I have consistently kept historiographic questions in the forefront of the analysis, reflecting a complex academic literature that oscillates between adulation and hero worship, and vilification for his arrogance and the supposed criminality of some of his acts. Despite his questionable motives for provoking a war with France, the brutality of his long campaigns in Normandy, and the religious language with which he cloaked his violence, if he is judged by the standards of his era, Henry V was undoubtedly a highly successful warrior king.

Introduction

Constructing and Deconstructing
the Legend of Henry V

The Measure of Greatness

As the Romantic revival and glorification of classical and medieval heroic figures unfolded, Scottish philosopher Thomas Carlyle (1795–1881) famously proposed that the study of world history is essentially the biography of "great men." In his work *On Heroes, Hero-Worship, and The Heroic in History* (1841), he proclaims: "Universal History, the history of what man has accomplished in this world, is at bottom the History of Great Men who have worked here."[1] Given his personal courage on the battlefield, his conquest of Normandy, and his attainment of the French crown, Henry V (r. 1413–22) certainly qualifies as "great" by Carlyle's definition. For a man whose reign only lasted nine years and who died unexpectedly at the age of thirty-five, he left behind a remarkable set of achievements.[2] And long after his death, Henry remained a larger-than-life figure, immortalized in Shakespeare's epic drama *Henry V* (1599), a work that did more to establish his reputation as a great warrior king than any contemporary chronicle or modern piece of academic literature. Nineteenth-century Romanticism could therefore easily embrace the young monarch as an enduring symbol of national pride for the English, inspiring awe and reverence among his countrymen. This adulation continued well into the twentieth century. In the dark days of the Second World War, Henry was promoted by Prime Minister Winston Churchill as a rallying point for British resolve and ultimate victory against the Nazi regime that terrorized Europe.

But the "hero worship" that affected the study of Henry in the nineteenth and mid-twentieth century has given way to a more sober and critical analysis of his military career in the twenty-first. Aside from objecting to his flagrant patriarchal bias, and contrary to his bold proclamations about a historiographic paradigm that can be applied to "universal history," Carlyle's critics contend that "greatness" is itself a subjective, even capricious term. In his forceful deconstruction of Henry V's legend, Ian Mortimer argues that the application of the label "great" or "greatest" to a long-dead historical figure is a meaningless exercise. Taking issue with British historian K.B. McFarlane (1903–66), who called Henry V "the greatest man that ever ruled England," Mortimer declares: "Greatness itself is absurd: an undefinable and distorting chimera."[3]

If we study the representation of Henry V in post-war scholarship up to the present, we encounter a polarity of interpretations.[4] A handful of modern detractors have harshly judged him for his supposed arrogance, vengefulness, and cruelty; some of his acts have even been viewed as morally reprehensible and verging on criminality.[5] For his critics, Henry was a ruthless opportunist who claimed the French crown to unify his tottering realm around the common cause of a foreign war. The glory of Agincourt so memorably celebrated in the verse of Shakespeare cannot mask the trail of death, destruction, and misery that Henry left behind in Normandy as he fought a costly and relentless military campaign to validate the Lancastrian monarchy and make good on his flimsy political claim in France. Yet despite recent attempts to dismantle his legend and diminish his overall character, on the whole Henry V's reputation as a "great" ruler and military commander remains largely intact. In popular culture, he continues to be imagined as the gallant warrior king in the tradition of Richard the Lionheart (r. 1189–99) and Edward III (r. 1327–77); the iconic embodiment of chivalry and nationalism for the English; the courageous commander who gave rousing speeches and led his badly outnumbered men to a stunning victory at Agincourt.

Taking into account these conflicting modern interpretations of Henry, and assessing his reign within his fifteenth-century context, we must conclude that he was far too complex a figure to evaluate and judge with simplistic binary categories of wholly "good" or "evil." The superb field commander who could inspire his men through his courage and iron will to win seemingly impossible victories was also responsible for the starvation, death, and deportation of thousands of helpless civilians. Henry often cloaked his violence with religious language and a well-developed ideology of holy war, calling himself "the scourge of God" sent to punish people for their sins.[6] He steadfastly believed that the righteousness of his cause and the obduracy of those who disobeyed his legitimate authority put him above any criticism for the consequences of his actions.

Although there were often political motives associated with his ostentatious displays of piety, we cannot completely dismiss Henry's public religiosity as a cynical attempt to manipulate public opinion. After his coronation, he became a deeply religious man by the standards of his era and went to great lengths to expiate the sins of his father Henry IV (r. 1399–1413), who had deposed Richard II (r. 1377–99) and was ultimately responsible for his death in captivity. At great personal expense, the younger Henry provided Richard II with a proper burial and endowed religious foundations to offer an impressive number of masses for his soul. Henry also worked indefatigably to establish an ethos of holy war for himself and the men he commanded: attending daily mass, regularly receiving communion, practicing celibacy, and banning prostitutes from his royal residence and military camp.

At the Battle of Agincourt (October 25, 1415), this ideology of expiation and martial asceticism was put to the most severe test. Henry in effect subjected himself to the *Judicium Dei*, or the Judgement of God, in a harrowing trial by combat in which he was nearly killed. He survived a sword blow to his head that broke the crown off his helmet as he protected his wounded brother, Humphrey, Duke of Gloucester (1390–1447).[7] This was, in fact, Henry's second near-death experience in combat. At the age of sixteen, he fought alongside his father Henry IV against a rebellious coalition at the Battle of Shrewsbury (July 21, 1403). The younger Henry was gravely wounded when an arrow struck his face. This injury and the excruciating treatment he endured to remove the deeply lodged arrowhead could have easily killed him.[8] Twelve years later at Agincourt, Henry immediately interpreted his second brush with death and his triumph against overwhelming odds as a miraculous sign of the justice of his war in France and his right to the French throne. The king and his acolytes masterfully exploited this remarkable victory, waging a highly developed and successful propaganda campaign to convince his countrymen and the crowned heads of Europe that God had judged his cause for war as just and that His favor now rested on the Lancastrian monarchy.

Despite his overall success as king and soldier, there are many parts of the story of Henry's nine-year reign that continue to be contested among modern scholars. Some of these discussions might appear trivial. For example, did the Valois crown prince, the Dauphin Louis of Guyenne, really send Henry a box of tennis balls to mock his demand for the French crown before his invasion of France? This provocation is dramatically presented in the opening scenes of Shakespeare's *Henry V*, and the young king's angry response to the French emissaries (1.2.281–88) turns this "mock" of balls into "gunstones."[9] Other debates focus on Henry's reputation as a military leader and also pose disturbing questions about his morality and overall character. Was Henry really outnumbered 3: or 4:1 at the Battle of Agincourt, or were his English forces more evenly matched with the French? Was Henry's order to kill the unarmed and wounded men who surrendered during the battle a criminal act? Did it violate the laws of war as they were understood by the combatants on both sides of the Hundred Years War? Can Henry's behavior while campaigning—including orders that caused the deaths of thousands of French noncombatants who suffered grievously during his war of conquest—be reconciled with the Romantic conception of chivalry and the late medieval Catholic theology of just war?

Ultimately, the conclusions we draw and the judgments we make about the justice of Henry's cause for war and the methods he used to achieve victory must be done with careful deliberation and proper historical context. Modern theories of just war and modern legal definitions of criminality in warfare should not be imposed anachronistically on medieval combatants. We should also be mindful of how Henry was judged by his contemporaries, including the French chroniclers who showed great respect and admiration for his abilities as king and warrior.[10] When they wrote about the ruthless killing of prisoners at Agincourt, these same chroniclers did not blame Henry for their deaths but rather castigated the French commanders for their vanity and incompetence. Still, we can question and criticize Henry's motives for some of his actions as both king and military commander; challenge the sincerity of some of his acts of pious benefaction; and judge some of his behavior on the battlefield as inhumane and morally questionable.

Debating Shakespeare's Warrior King: A Historiographic Overview

For the English-speaking world, the modern image of Henry V is almost entirely formed by the compelling historical play of William Shakespeare (1599), written and performed within a decade of Elizabeth I's stunning defeat of the Spanish Armada (1588).[11] At the beginning of his reign, her father Henry VIII (r. 1509–47) embraced Henry V as his alter ego. Imagining himself as a glorious warrior and conqueror of lost English territory in France, the Tudor monarch commissioned a widely read translation of an early Latin biography of the medieval warrior king: *The First English Life of King Henry the Fifth* (1513).[12] But Shakespeare's plays (*Henry IV*, 1 and 2, and *Henry V*) created the enduring literary myth of Henry V. In *Henry IV* (c. 1597–99), we are introduced to the frivolous adolescent Prince

8

Hal, who pursues a reckless life of pleasure until he finds himself seated on his dead father's throne. In *Henry V*, the warrior king who miraculously triumphs at Agincourt has been judged worthy of both the English and French crowns. The victor of Agincourt emerges as the "true" Henry for posterity, the model of Christian kingship and the courageous emblem of English nationalism. Unlike other historical plays about English kings, Shakespeare's Henry is not primarily focused on internal conflicts or struggles. In this nationalist epic, the young English monarch wages war against a treacherous, foreign enemy who mocks him with the gift of tennis balls and deprives him of his just rights. But Henry emerges victorious, to the honor and glory of the king and his countrymen. His vanquished foes live with the eternal shame of their loss to his vastly outnumbered but courageous forces.

That Shakespeare's play essentially created the modern view of Henry is beyond dispute. In his recent study of the Battle of Agincourt, Mortimer observes that Shakespeare's character essentially supplanted the real historical figure: "There are many biographies of Henry, and there are many books on Agincourt: but there are even more books on Shakespeare's play, *Henry V*."[13] The leading historian of the battle, Anne Curry, is equally emphatic: "The separation of truth and fiction proves difficult. Some believe that what Shakespeare has Henry say at the battle is actually what he said. This idea has affected our written culture for over 250 years."[14]

After a brief period of acclaim in Tudor England, Shakespeare's triumphant Henry was soon lost to the political tumult of the early Stuart kings, the catastrophic Civil War and Protectorate, the restoration of the monarchy, and the Glorious Revolution. Seventeenth-century England figuratively (and sometimes literally) provided little space for the glorification of a hyper-religious Catholic warrior king from the dying days of feudalism.[15] As a consequence of new conflicts and wars between France and England, the mid-eighteenth century witnessed a renewed interest in the play. As was the case with his legendary counterpart Joan of Arc (1412–31), it was the nineteenth century and its culture of Romanticism that supplied the most fertile ground for the revival of Shakespeare's heroic Henry V.[16] One glaring exception was the English essayist and philosopher William Hazlitt (1778–1830), who dismissed Henry as a warmongering hypocrite, an allegation that would be revived by the king's twentieth-first-century detractors.[17] But as James N. Loehlin notes, aside from such stinging criticism of the king by Hazlitt, the "conservatism and antiquarianism of the Victorian age brought *Henry V* back into popularity as a patriotic pageant."[18] Victorian Romanticism was also coupled with a renewed interest in the historical details of Henry's life and the Hundred Years War, marking the beginning of modern research for the staging of the play.

The warrior king was most noticeably restored as an iconic national figure during the Second World War, when *Henry V* was deployed by Winston Churchill as a rallying point for the battered British Empire. Laurence Olivier's 1944 screen adaptation of the Elizabethan drama—produced at the behest of the prime minister and dedicated to British soldiers fighting Nazi Germany—was designed to boost the sagging morale of the English, much as Henry V's St. Crispin's Day speech inspired his men to achieve ultimate victory in the bloody fields of Agincourt in October of 1415.[19] The speech that Shakespeare put in Henry's mouth on that fateful day (delivered just before the battle) is both transfixing and transcendent, guaranteeing him a permanent place in the pantheon of great motivational speakers and courageous battlefield commanders.[20]

Olivier's movie was also responsible for creating the most widespread interest in Henry V since the production of Shakespeare's play. As Curry observes, Olivier's film adaptation of the play "is the single most important shaper of modern perceptions of Agincourt"; it was also the first time that the battle was brought to a mass audience on the wide screen.[21] Film historian Harry Geduld argues that Olivier's interpretation of Henry V also provided historical proof and validation of the warrior ethos that had made England a global power in modernity: "[Olivier] apotheosizes most of the public school virtues that were supposed to have built the British Empire."[22]

In his monumental *History of the English-Speaking Peoples*, for which he won the Nobel Prize in Literature (1953), Churchill declares that Agincourt "ranks as the most heroic of all the land battles England has ever fought."[23] And according to the prime minister, after Agincourt, there was no greater figure in English history to rally his people to the cause of nationalistic sacrifice than the fabled warrior king: "Henry stood, and with him his country, at the summit of the world."[24] This idolization of the young king in film came only months after the Allied invasion of Normandy and the liberation of Paris from Nazi captivity. Less than six months after the film's premiere in the United Kingdom, the once seemingly invincible Nazi empire would lie in ruins. Churchill's own rousing "St. Crispin's Day speeches" to the Houses of Parliament had contributed to his countrymen's triumph.[25]

Henry V also had a loyal following among professional, post-war British academicians. The revered British historian, K.B. McFarlane (1903–66) in effect granted Henry the political equivalent of canonization when he

Laurence Olivier (1907–89) in *Henry V* (1944). Olivier's film version of Shakespeare's play was done at the request of British Prime Minister Winston Churchill. Designed to boost the morale of British troops waging war against Nazi Germany, the movie created widespread interest in Shakespeare's historical drama. It also featured the first depiction of the Battle of Agincourt on film (Ronald Grant Archive / Alamy Stock Photo).

declared him to be "the greatest man that ever ruled England."[26] These sentiments are echoed in a more tempered form in a recent biography, where John Matusiak states that Henry "was better prepared for kingship than any previous monarch since Edward I."[27] In his conclusion, Matusiak praises his "vision, vigour, fortitude and unremitting self-confidence," describing these qualities as being "so distinctive and impressive."[28]

A prominent authority on Henry's military career, Juliet Barker prefaces her study of Agincourt by describing Henry V as an "aggressor," while drawing analogies with the failures of western intervention in the Middle East in the post–9/11 world of the global war on terrorism.[29] Yet as her meticulous analysis of the fabled Battle of Agincourt progresses and then draws to a close, we feel the presence of Shakespeare's heroic king looming over the narrative. Prince Hal has become King Henry, and the sins of his father—the usurpation of the throne and the killing of Richard II—have been expiated in a trial by combat. The concluding words of Barker's book encapsulate the enduring legend of Henry's interpretation of his great victory over a superior French force: "Henry proved beyond all doubt that he was also the true king of England. God had chosen to bless him with victory at Agincourt despite the fact that he was the son of a usurper. There could have been no more effective demonstration to the world that the sins of the father would not be held against the son."[30]

Current scholarship on Henry V oscillates between poles of admiration and hypercriticism. But in the late twentieth and early twenty-first century, Henry still has more admirers than critics. In his magisterial biography of the king in the Yale English Monarch Series, Christopher Allmand argues against the "hero worship" that has affected the study of Henry V: "The reader anxious for emphasis on the Henry of contemporary legend may have been disappointed by this study. I make no apology for this. It has always seemed to me essential to demythologize the king, and to place him firmly within the context to which he belonged."[31] However, Allmand concludes his work by observing that despite Henry's shortcomings, his biography of the king preserves and enhances his "high reputation."[32] And in the preface to a collection of essays on Henry V's reign, published to commemorate the 600th anniversary of his coronation, Gwilym Dodd notes that Henry's lasting reputation still rests with his military victories: "The enduring image of Henry as the ideal late medieval warrior king is justly deserved."[33]

Henry has also drawn the criticism of select scholars. Jonathan Sumption, the premiere English historian of the Hundred Years War, is more circumspect about Henry's legacy. He argues that the nationalist myth of the warrior king rested on the "uncritical adulation of his contemporaries" and the nostalgia of future Englishmen who lamented the loss of his territorial and political gains in France.[34] Popular historian Desmond Seward goes much farther; he is convinced that the French populace suffered more under Henry V than at any other time between the Vikings and the Nazis, even comparing the young English ruler to Napoleon and Hitler.[35] But Henry V's most vehement modern critic is undoubtedly Ian Mortimer. Focusing only on his "year of glory" (1415), where the legend of the warrior king was born, he offers a blistering critique of the young monarch. In his telling, the king who won the lopsided and "miraculous" victory at Agincourt was a brooding, humorless, puritanical introvert; a man who was "undermined by his own pride and overwhelmed by his own authority."[36] Henry also had a cruel and vengeful streak that could be displayed even for the most minor offenses. Mortimer presents as evidence (without providing any of the details) a reference to a French trumpeter who was killed at the king's order because he made him angry.[37]

This incident took place during the surprisingly long and difficult siege of Meaux (October 1421–May 1422), about thirty miles due east of Paris. Meaux demanded Henry's attention because it was a large and well-fortified garrison that rejected his sovereignty and remained loyal to the Dauphin.[38] The Dauphin (the French term for crown prince) was, of course, Charles Valois (1403–61), whom Joan of Arc would one day help crown king of France after lifting the English siege of Orléans (1429). Charles had been exiled and disinherited from the French throne under the terms of the Treaty of Troyes (1420), which made Henry V regent of France and granted him and his legitimate male heirs the French crown after the death of the mad king, Charles VI (r. 1380–1422).[39] This miserable campaign occurred just five months before Henry fell ill and died of dysentery outside of Paris. Meaux had put up more of a fight than the English had expected, with the siege lasting a full seven months.[40] The weather had been brutally cold and wet, and English casualties were uncharacteristically high as dysentery and smallpox took their toll among Henry's shivering troops. The king had also faced a large number of desertions among his ranks. The only bright spot during that terrible winter campaign was news from London that his French wife Catherine Valois (1401–37) had given birth to a son, who was named Henry (December 6, 1421).

When Meaux finally capitulated in May of 1422, Henry subjected the defeated enemy to his wrath. The garrison commander was a supposedly notorious scoundrel named the Bastard of Vaurus, alleged to have perpetrated murderous crimes against some of the townspeople. The contemporary chroniclers record that Henry had him beheaded; his head was stuck on a pike and his body hung from an elm tree. Mid-fifteenth-century French writers later glorified the Bastard, presenting him as a heroic figure who put up valiant resistance against Henry and was therefore unjustly

13

executed.[41] Henry also demanded that a trumpeter named Orace (or Horace), who had taunted the king during the siege, be handed over for execution. Orace was publicly tortured to death in Paris for insulting Henry with trumpet blasts.[42] According to the early fifteenth-century French chronicler Pierre de Fénin (d. 1433?) and the Burgundian chronicler Jean de Waurin (c. 1400–74), other members of the garrison had taunted the English day and night. Some of them dragged an ass onto the town's ramparts and beat it until it brayed; then they cried out to the English that it was Henry and they should come rescue their king.[43] Henry had these poor fellows thrown into a particularly terrible prison as a punishment for their insult to the king.

Mortimer offers a microcosmic reconstruction of the king's 1415 campaign and he states that if he were doing a full-scale biography, he would devote much more space to criticism of Henry. Such a biography "would trace the development of his intoxication with his own power up to his death. Obviously he fell far short of the charming hero of Shakespeare's *Henry V*, and the overseer of murderous acts hardly deserves to be considered as a candidate for the title 'the greatest man who ever ruled England.'"[44] Mortimer is also quick to note that another respected scholar of Henry's reign, T.B. Pugh, contradicts McFarlane's glowing account of Henry. These criticisms come in his groundbreaking study of the purported plot to assassinate the English king before his invasion of France, the so-called Southampton Plot (August 1415). Pugh believes that no such plot to kill Henry and his brothers existed. And he dismisses McFarlane's judgment of the warrior king, calling it an "ill-considered verdict," while characterizing Henry as "a man of limited vision and outlook."[45]

From a modern perspective, it is easy to see why some of Henry's acts can be judged as needlessly vengeful and excessively cruel. But Rémy Ambühl convincingly argues that Henry's orders after the capitulation of Meaux fell within the bounds of "an accepted framework" for the end of a rebellious siege in the fifteenth century. By the terms of the Treaty of Troyes, rebellion against the regent of France was a treasonous, capital offense. And the rambunctious levels of disrespect that the rebels had shown to the person of the king—taunts with trumpet blasts and the beating of a donkey in the place of Henry—demanded proportionate punishment to repair his damaged honor. According to Ambühl: "The stout resistance of the besieged was an affront to the honour of the king and he was fully entitled to enact some form of retribution."[46] Without any contextual analysis, a presentist reading of Henry's administration of justice after the siege could lead us to characterize him as being thin-skinned, petty, and vindictive.[47]

Malcolm Vale also takes issue with the one-dimensional, negative portrayals of the king, arguing that the pejorative labels applied to Henry V by his modern detractors are excessive and unsubstantiated. In his compelling and provocative analysis of Henry's education and governance, Vale dismisses the gratuitous characterization of the king as a boorish warmonger. This myth began with Shakespeare's fictional construct in *Henry V*, a fabrication which nonetheless became the template for all future interpretations of the king. Despite its being a work of fiction, the play "continues to inform the popular image of the king as a warrior, if not a warmonger."[48]

Vale insists that we can only hope to arrive at an accurate understanding of Henry if we are familiar with his rather substantial library and his reading habits; if we comprehend the effectiveness of his government; and if we take note of his deep religious devotion, displayed through many costly acts of benefaction. In Vale's reconstruction, Henry emerges as a humane, thoughtful, pious, highly skilled, and efficient ruler of a troubled realm, in sharp contrast to the much touted warrior-king of Shakespeare.[49] In reflecting on Henry's impressive accomplishments in the administration of his realm, Vale proposes that it is better to think of Henry as "the first 'business-man king' or 'bureaucrat-king.'"[50]

Vale's work showcases a side of the young king that is often ignored by his modern critics. Few people know, for example, that Henry was a musician who probably composed parts of a mass (a Gloria and a Sanctus) and that he is largely responsible for the emergence of English as the language of politics and government in England.[51] The king was a far more complex historical figure than the fictional playboy turned holy warrior on display in Shakespeare. A disciplined and effective ruler, Henry excelled at an aggressive foreign policy, while moving the prestige of the English monarchy far beyond his father's damaged kingship. And despite the great divide between Henry IV and his son at the end of his reign, Henry V mirrored many of the same qualities that his father displayed before his notorious deposition of Richard II. The elder Henry was a natural athlete and champion jouster; he loved music and enjoyed the company of minstrels; and he was a bookish and learned man who could read and write in three languages (English, French, and Latin).[52]

While Vale makes a valid point about Henry's aversion to open field battles, this cannot negate the savagery of his long and systematic campaigns of siege warfare against the cities of Normandy. The destruction of property produced by his relentless artillery bombardments and the loss of civilian life were legendary, even prompting some of the king's supporters to question the cruelty and legitimacy of his methods. In the process of waging his protracted war in Normandy, Henry also bankrupted England, in effect mortgaging the future of his country for his immediate glory. Even as he hailed him as a national hero, and heaped praise on him for his military prowess, Churchill could still call Henry's imposing conquests "hollow," and his wars in France "wasteful" and "useless."[53]

Still, the undisputed modern authority on the Battle of Agincourt, Anne Curry, defends Henry's rightly earned reputation as a great warrior and ruler. While she is sometimes critical of him in various publications, Curry nonetheless views Henry as "the golden boy of fifteenth century history—strong, decisive, athletic, energetic, pious, and above all successful."[54] Despite the works of academics that have "whittled away at the king's reputation," she declares that considerably more good things can be said about Henry than bad and that McFarlane's judgment about Henry's greatness has yet to be disproven.[55] For Curry, Henry *should* be remembered as a warrior king, not a scholar-soldier whose character was molded and shaped by the peaceful arts. In her recent short biography of the king, she argues that Henry's "education" as future ruler of England really took place in military campaigns fought on behalf of his father during his turbulent reign. Henry's participation in the brutal suppression of the Welsh rebellion against Henry IV was, according to Allmand, "one of the formative influences" on his kingship.[56] And as Curry observes: "These uncertain, conflict-ridden years were also those of Prince Henry's royal apprenticeship. It was a time of almost constant military mobilization—something which is especially significant given that Henry would spend virtually his entire reign in active warfare; indeed, he knew no other way to rule."[57]

In summing up the conflicting interpretations of Henry in modern academic literature, we are best served by avoiding a simplistic "either/or" scenario in shaping our overall assessment of him. Combining Vale's exposition of Henry's life off the battlefield with Curry's judgment on the essentials of his reign and reputation as king gives us a richer and more complete understanding of his complex and conflicted character. Henry clearly distinguished himself as an overpowering figure in the legend and lore of late medieval European history largely because of his tenacity and leadership skills as a warrior. Most of his reign was spent in active campaigning in Normandy. The legitimacy of his claim to the French crown and the methods he used to obtain it remain open to criticism, but there is no denying that Henry was a brave solider and a charismatic leader. It is also fair to say that Henry's legacy was largely built on the English commemoration of the Battle of Agincourt, his eventual conquest of Normandy, and the legal acquisition of the crown of France for himself and his son, Henry VI.

Introduction

Lauded by English chroniclers, Henry V also earned the respect and admiration of some contemporary French authors who commented upon his untimely death. The miserable failures of the French ruling elite who were repeatedly humiliated by him stood in sharp contrast to Henry's courage, discipline, and military success. He was no doubt a learned man, a proficient and effective ruler, and an astute propagandist for his reign. But he was above all a ruthless and victorious field commander in a brutal, complex, and costly war of conquest. By the standards of his own day and age, Henry V was undoubtedly a highly successful warrior king.

ONE

Authority in Crisis

The Valois and Lancastrian Dynasties

Christendom in Crisis

From the outset of his career as king and warrior, Henry V labored in the face what appeared to be insurmountable obstacles to establish the legitimacy of his monarchy in England and the credibility of his cause for war in France. His public struggles to authenticate his claims to theocratic authority in both realms came at a time when the traditional centers of authority appeared to be on the verge of disintegration. Social, religious, and political tumult followed the catastrophe of the Black Death; war, death, famine, and rebellion seemed to push European Christendom to the brink of the Apocalypse.[1] Aside from the demographic collapse of the urban and rural communities of Western Europe, a tsunami of crises of authority threatened to topple the pillars of medieval society: the Roman Catholic Church and the dynastic, monarchic state. The Hundred Years War (1337–1453) was fought against the backdrop of deep and bitter division within the Roman Church that intersected with the political calamities that beset the English and French monarchies in the latter part of the fourteenth century.

The bloodletting of the long Anglo-French war was itself antithetical to the Apostolic Creed of "one, holy, catholic" Church and its ethos of spiritual unity among Latin Christians. The lengthy armed conflict between England and France also corresponded with one of the lowest points in Church history: the era of the Avignon Papacy (1309–78) and the Great Schism (1378–1417).[2] The move of the papal court from Rome to Avignon came after a violent clash over clerical taxation between the French king Philip IV (r. 1285–1314) and his Francophobe nemesis, Pope Boniface VIII (r. 1294–1303). As rival aristocratic political factions battled for control of Rome after the death of Boniface, his French successor Clement V (r. 1305–14) took up residence in the south of France (1309). There the papacy remained for most of the fourteenth century.

Despite its efficiency in conducting the business of the Church, the Avignon Papacy was tarnished for posterity by the Italian humanist scholar Francesco Petrarch (1304–74), when he nicknamed it the "Babylonian Captivity of the Church."[3] In truth, the symbolism of an exiled papal court was more damaging to the reputation of the papacy than the activity of the men who held papal office in southern France. The real scandal came later, when a disputed papal election in 1378 produced two new popes who excommunicated each other while presiding over two rival "churches" headquartered in Rome and Avignon. This Great Schism worsened when a group of clerics and theologians convened a Church council in Pisa (1409) and elected a third, Pisan pope Alexander V (r. 1409–10).[4]

During the Schism, England recognized the Roman claimant to the papacy, while unsurprisingly, the French allied themselves with the Avignon pope. The Pisan pope had virtually no support. Forming itself into an electoral college of five "nations," the Council of Constance (1414–18) elected a new Roman pope, Martin V (r. 1417–31), restored the papacy to Rome, recognized the integrity of the Roman line of popes, and thereby ended the Schism.[5] The English clerics representing Henry V at Constance had strongly endorsed the election of the Roman pope who ended the Schism. This alliance would prove to be a disappointment to Henry since Martin V refused to recognize Henry's claim to the crown of France, even after the English king had negotiated a treaty with the French which granted him that right.[6]

The Valois Dynasty and the Hundred Years War

The monarchy of France suffered a grave crisis of authority that began when a centuries-old dynasty came to an abrupt end in the fourteenth century. The Hundred Years War was at its inception a French political crisis writ large, triggered by the death of the last Capetian monarch, Charles IV (r. 1322–28), who had no male heir. The mother of the English king Edward III (r. 1327–77), Isabella (1295–1358), also happened to be Charles IV's sister, thereby allowing her son to be next in line for the crown of France.[7] The French intelligentsia later concocted a legal prohibition that prevented Edward from making good on this dynastic claim.[8] The rediscovery of the Salic Law—dating from the time of the first Catholic Frankish king, Clovis (r. 509–11)—formed the basis of a pseudo-legal propaganda campaign that would bar Edward's succession to the French throne through his mother. Since women did not wield political power, they certainly could not transmit it.[9]

Ignoring the rights of Edward III, the French promoted the succession of Charles IV's paternal cousin Philip Valois. Ironically, the marriage of the previous English king, Edward II (r. 1307–27), to Isabella was part of peace treaty (1303) ratified by Edward I (r. 1272–1307) and Philip IV (r. 1285–1314) that formally ended a long and violent struggle between the two kingdoms.[10] No one could have imagined that a union with peaceful diplomatic intent would wreak havoc on the French kingdom, setting the stage for the beginning of an armed conflict that would span more than a century.

Whether or not this 116-year conflict should be treated as one continuous war or as a set of political and military engagements spread across the fourteenth and fifteenth centuries, the Hundred Years War had two consistent causes for war: the assertion of English sovereignty over territories that the English monarchy held in France and the claim of dynastic succession to the French crown by English kings. These claims had their origins in the peculiar relationship between the French and English monarchies that began in 1152, with the wedding of the ambitious Plantagenet king, Henry II (r. 1154–89), to the indomitable Eleanor of Aquitaine (1122–1204).[11] This was her second marriage, and it came immediately after she had annulled her fifteen-year, sonless union with the monkish French king, Louis VII (r. 1131–80), on grounds of consanguinity. When the twenty-eight-year-old Eleanor married the nineteen-year-old Henry, she brought with her the vast duchy of Aquitaine, now detached from the French kingdom of her ex-husband and put under the authority of her new spouse, the English monarch. The resulting Angevin Empire—deriving its name from Henry's father Geoffrey, Count of Anjou (1113–51)—produced by this marriage united the realm of England with a large swath of territory that amounted to roughly half of modern France.[12] In fact, Henry II technically ruled more of what is now France than the French king himself.

During his long reign, Henry II fought mightily to keep these far-flung French territories within his grasp, violently suppressing rebellions instigated by the king of France Philip II (r. 1179–1223) that even involved Eleanor and his sons Henry the Younger and Richard. After the untimely death of his older brother Henry the Younger, Richard I (r. 1189–99) made his peace with his father and was crowned king of England. But Richard spent most of his reign outside of his kingdom, earning a legendary reputation as the quintessential crusader king, the Lionheart who was valiantly locked in mortal combat with his equally famous Muslim rival Saladin (1137–93), during the Third Crusade.

Richard's long absence from England caused a political calamity that imperiled English control of his ancestral lands in France. His former friend and now bitter rival, the French king Philip II with whom Richard had crusaded during the siege of Acre (1189–91), began the systematic conquest of Angevin territories to expand the reach and solidify the power of the resurgent French monarchy.[13] When he returned home from the Crusade, Richard was forced to wage war against the rebellious fortresses in his French domains, once again provoked by his nemesis Philip II. During the siege of the Castle of Chalûs-Chabrol, Richard was struck in the shoulder, near his neck by a crossbow bolt.[14] Since he was not wearing armor or chainmail, the deeply lodged arrowpoint from a lucky shot proved fatal. Thanks to the poor medical care he received, twelve days later the forty-one-year-old warrior king died of gangrene with his aged mother Eleanor of Aquitaine at his side.[15] His untimely death marked the beginning of the decline of Plantagenet power in France.

Richard's successor, the ruthless and autocratic King John (r. 1199–1216), was no match for the French monarchy that was determined to pry his Angevin patrimony from his grip. John's tumultuous reign was characterized by conflicts with the pope, who placed his realm under an interdict, and the king's poisonous relations with his barons, who forced him to accede to the provisions they imposed upon him in the Magna Carta (1215).[16] John's humiliating military failures in France underscored his reputation as perhaps one of the worst English monarchs of the Middle Ages. The Battle of Bouvines (July 27, 1214) dealt him a crushing defeat at the hands of Philip II and the resulting peace provided proof that John had squandered much of his Plantagenet inheritance in France.[17]

John's son and successor Henry III (r. 1216–72) was eventually forced to accept a treaty that acknowledged the English loss for good of Normandy, Maine, Anjou, and Poitou. The English king could hold Gascony and parts of Aquitaine as a vassal of the French crusader king Louis IX (r. 1226–70), provided that he did the proper homage. The Treaty of Paris (1259) produced an uneasy peace which more or less held until the conflict erupted once more when there was legal dispute over Edward I's homage to the French king Philip IV for the lands he held in Aquitaine. Edward crossed the Channel in 1297, to challenge the French king militarily, but lacking the support of his magnates and his supposed European allies, his saber rattling on the continent turned into a fiasco.[18] Edward agreed to another peace treaty in Paris (1303) that maintained the status quo; it would be capped off by the marriage of the Plantagenet prince Edward to the Capetian princess Isabella (1308).

When the male line of the Capetian dynasty died out in 1328 (the house that had ruled France since 987), the peculiar relationship between the Plantagenets and the French monarchy was once again brought into sharp focus, as a new political threat presented itself to the French. The patchwork of duchies and counties that had begun to congeal into a unified realm under the ruthless Philip IV now faced a grave crisis of succession and the centrifugal force of a restless French nobility that fought mightily to reassert its independence from the French monarchy. At the same time, the French aristocracy worked to prevent the crowning of an English king as ruler of France.

The coronation of Philip VI (r. 1328–50) brushed aside English claims to succession and established a new Valois dynasty, which at first Edward seemed to acknowledge. But Edward refused to recognize the new French king's full sovereignty over him as his vassal for his ancestral lands in western France; Philip confiscated these lands for Edward's lack of fidelity as his vassal. This political back and forth generated enough bad blood between the two countries to put them on a war footing.[19] Edward III and his advisers decided officially to register his claim to the crown of France as he began preparations for a broad and expensive alliance of European allies to make good on that claim.[20] He invaded France with a large army and continuously terrorized the French populace with his infamous son, Edward the Black Prince of Wales (1330–76).

What began as a war of extortion to return formerly English territory in France soon evolved into a bona fide fight for the French crown after Edward III's stunning victory at the Battle of Crécy (August 26, 1346).[21] Though vastly outnumbered, the English king, thanks to the work of his archers and their longbows, won a lopsided and legendary victory that would become part of a trifecta of English battles, long glorified by his countrymen: Crécy (1346), Poitiers (1356), and Agincourt (1415). The myth of English invincibility in open, set-piece battles would cast a long shadow over the French for the better part of the Hundred Years War. The chronicler Jean le Bel (c. 1290–1370), a native of Liège and an immigrant to England, remarked that in the 1320s, English soldiers were held in especially low regard on the continent. But after the victories of Edward III, the English were the most respected warriors in Europe.[22]

Despite his success on the battlefield, achieving a lasting victory over the French seemed to be beyond the reach of Edward III. His wars became burdensome and costly to his people. And only a few years after his glorious victory at Crécy, both France and England were devastated by the bubonic plague epidemic that killed more than half of the population of each country. Edward's own fourteen-year-old daughter Joan was one of the casualties of this epidemiological disaster. When the war was resumed by the English, the king's son Edward the Black Prince achieved yet another memorable victory against overwhelming odds at Poitiers (September 19, 1356).[23] Adding insult to grievous injury, the Valois king himself, Jean II (r. 1350–64), was captured on the battlefield—along with several hundred leading French men-at-arms—and paraded through the streets of London.[24] Held hostage in England, he eventually died as his full ransom went unpaid.

Just two years after this humiliating defeat, the disgusted French peasantry banded together and participated in a violent two-week rebellion in northern France that came to be known as the Jacquerie (May 1358).[25] This revolt was fueled by the peasants' loss of confidence in the ability of the monarchy or aristocracy to protect them from the depredations they suffered at the hands of English soldiers and the free companies of unemployed mercenaries who fought for them. The inchoate and leaderless mass of peasants was successfully suppressed by a violent aristocratic counterattack and France would not see such mob violence again until the Revolution of 1789.

Yet even with their impressive victories in the field and the political upheaval that afflicted the Valois dynasty in the aftermath of Poitiers, the sheer size of the French kingdom (it had roughly three times the population of England) made the permanent occupation of France by English forces exceptionally difficult.[26] When the Treaty of Brétigny was ratified (1359–60), it seemed as if this bloody conflict had finally come to a close, with the English declaring outright victory in France, while renouncing their claim to the throne of France in return for sovereignty over the lost territory of English Gascony. But this peace would soon prove illusory.

The Valois king, Charles V (r. 1364–80), eventually outsmarted the English and worked with great success to deprive them of their territorial gains from the first phase of the Hundred Years War.[27] Known as *le Sage*, or "the wise" king, Charles V had a well-founded reputation as a patron of the peaceful arts, amassing a large academic library in his palace in Paris and surrounding himself with renowned poets and scholars. He also provoked a revolt in Gascony that reopened a war of attrition against the English occupiers. Despite its share of atrocities committed by Edward the Black Prince, including the infamous sack of the city of Limoges (1370), this phase of the war eventually went the way of the French.[28] The size of the French kingdom and the lack of manpower to conquer and control a territory that could only be reached by sea worked against the best laid plans of the English monarchy. England was also buffeted by a number of natural disasters that made continued war and occupation exorbitantly expensive and practically impossible: another plague epidemic (1361), a massive hurricane (1362), and a great famine associated with more than a decade of adverse climate change (1369).[29]

By the time that Charles the Wise died, the English had lost nearly all of the territorial gains that came from the Treaty of Brétigny. Still, Charles V had not won any great military victories in the field, and the English did not completely abandon their foothold in France. A truce in 1389 was formally extended by the Truce of Paris (1396), ending this round of hostilities with peace between Richard II (r. 1377–99) and the new French king Charles VI (r. 1380–1422). This was the longest official truce during the entire Hundred Years War, lasting from 1396 to 1415. It was supposedly strengthened by the marriage of Charles' seven-year-old daughter Isabella Valois (1389–1409) to the recently widowed, twenty-nine-year-old English king.[30]

The Lancastrian Dynasty: Rebellion, Regicide, and Redemption

The untimely death of the Black Prince at the age of forty-five (1376), followed by the death of Edward III (1377), ended an age of heroic warrior kings and princes in England and opened a new chapter of political disaster for the realm. The Black Prince's Gascon-born son Richard became one of the youngest kings in English history, crowned when he was all of ten years old. The antithesis of his father the famed warrior, Richard's reign would mark the beginning of a tortuous phase of English history that featured violent rebellion among the peasantry, the end of the main line of Richard's Plantagenet dynasty, and establishment of the new Lancastrian monarchy when his cousin Henry Bolingbroke was crowned Henry IV (r. 1399–1413).

A defining moment for Richard's reign was the so-called Peasant Rebellion of 1381, led in part by the enigmatic Wat Tyler.[31] The king was only fourteen years old when his realm was shaken by one of the greatest threats ever to face the English monarchy. An orgy of looting, burning, and murder accompanied the rebels' demands for sweeping social and political reforms before Tyler was himself killed during a public parley with the young king and his advisers at Smithfield. After a series of rebel defeats and the trial and execution of notable leaders, the revolt was crushed.

This uprising no doubt had a corrosive effect on the authority of Richard II and contributed to his regal rigidity and distance from his subjects as his reign matured. His modern biographer Nigel Saul also notes that the Great Revolt was part of a larger pattern of popular assertiveness by the masses throughout Europe: "Representative assemblies and estates were making unprecedented bids for power; everywhere the social order seemed under strain. Rulers reacted to these challenges in broadly the same manner: by formalizing old hierarchies and emphasizing the people's obligation of obedience."[32] Despite his cultivation of courtly rituals emphasizing his regal splendor and his incarnation of the divine will, Richard II's reign came to an abrupt end when he was overthrown and forced to abdicate by the cousin whom he had exiled and whose duchy and estates he had confiscated, Henry Bolingbroke, Duke of Lancaster. After Richard's deposition, Bolingbroke had himself crowned Henry IV (October 13, 1399). A year later Richard died in a dungeon at Pontefract Castle, under suspicious circumstances that pointed to murder.[33]

Henry IV (r. 1399–1413). The overthrow and death of Richard II left a black mark on Henry's new Lancastrian dynasty. Allegations of usurpation and regicide would shape the early reign of his son and successor, Henry V. As his reign progressed, the elder Henry was beset by a series of rebellions and his health declined precipitously. He died at the age of forty-five (Ian Dagnall Computing / Alamy Stock Photo).

Even before his accession to the throne, the young Henry V lived in the long shadow cast by his father's usurpation of the English crown and the alleged regicide of his tragic predecessor. As will be discussed in subsequent chapters, this stigma weighed heavily on both Henry IV (r. 1399–1413) and his son, whose disfigured face—the younger Henry was gravely wounded fighting rebels with his father in 1403—bore testimony to the

Richard II (r. 1377–99). The son of the legendary warrior Edward, the Black Prince of Wales, Richard lacked his father's military skills and his reign ended in disaster. His cousin Henry Bolingbroke, Duke of Lancaster, became his rival and nemesis. Richard eventually exiled Henry for life, but he returned to England at the head of an army, overthrowing and imprisoning Richard, who died under suspicious circumstances (INTERFOTO / Alamy Stock Photo).

perils of being the son of a usurper. Henry IV's monarchy was fraught with peril from the moment of his coronation to his death. As Sumption observes: "The sacral kingship of the previous reign, supported by an essentially autocratic ideology and by rituals borrowed from the French court was dead. The new reign was to be dominated by constant warfare on the northern march, nationalist movements in Wales and Ireland and persistent conspiracies and rebellions in England."[34]

This volatility of the Lancastrian claim on the crown and the paranoia over rebellion and treason took a palpable form early in Henry V's own reign. On the eve of his invasion of Normandy to enforce his right to the French crown, Henry supposedly uncovered the Southampton Plot (July 31, 1415).[35] If it had succeeded, the new king and his brothers (Thomas, John, and Humphrey) would have been assassinated and Henry would have been replaced by the twenty-four-year-old Edmund Mortimer (1391–1425), great-grandson of Edward III and the presumptive heir of Richard II. Mortimer himself was not an active participant in this scheme and in fact revealed it to Henry; he accompanied the king on his Norman campaign and remained his loyal vassal.[36] On the face of it, this plot appeared to be the first serious challenge to the authority of the young king, discovered only a week before he would set sail for France. Henry's critics have argued that he already had a tenuous claim to the French crown, based as it was on the revival of the rights of his long-dead great-grandfather Edward III.[37] The discovery of a potential coup d'état could destroy whatever authority he asserted in both England and France.

Scholars have debated the truthfulness of the official Lancastrian record of a planned coup. In his controversial analysis, Pugh insists there was no plot to kill Henry and his brothers, that this indictment was made up to punish powerful peers for other offenses.[38] Allmand is skeptical, but is open to the possibility that Richard Earl of Cambridge was behind some sort of mysterious plot against the king.[39] Curry agrees that while the details are murky, the plot should be taken seriously as some sort of threat to Henry, or at least it might have been a sign of opposition to the king's invasion plans.[40] However, Strohm calls the plot a "threadbare fabrication, a plagiarization from scraps of actual 1400–05 conspiracies that happened to be lying around."[41]

The discovery of this deadly conspiracy, according to Strohm, was part of a larger propaganda effort by Henry V and his court to establish the justice of his cause by having him pass an initial perilous test or trial before his departure for France. An anonymous English cleric who accompanied Henry during his first Norman invasion wrote a glowing account of his

Northern France at the time of Henry's campaigns (Map by Susan C. Thibodeau).

campaign after the Battle of Agincourt. In the *Gesta Henrici Quinti*, or *The Deeds of Henry V*, this cleric solemnly declares that God allowed the king to be tested before his great expedition: "God, still wishing to make trial of the constancy of His elect, allowed him again to be tested and smitten by yet another hammer-blow causing great perturbation."[42] The author of the *Gesta* then blames the plot on demonic possession of the hearts of the conspirators and their greed for French bribe money. Strohm argues that the presentation of the plot in the *Gesta* forces us to conclude: "Penetrating treasonous schemes, God awards the crown to the just king."[43]

There could very well have been some ill-formed conspiracy against Henry, the details of which we may never know. But it is also quite likely that Henry maximized the perceived threat for propaganda purposes, as reflected by the account in the *Gesta*. Whatever the real or imagined danger to the king, the conspirators were promptly tried and beheaded. Henry's modern critics have seen his swift and brutal justice against the alleged "conspirators" as a sign of his continued anxiety about potential challenges to his authority or open rebellion during his extended absence from his realm. As Curry notes: "the Southampton Plot reveals his obsessive and cruel nature, made worse by the fact that he was constantly riddled with uncertainties."[44] The following week, Henry V's armada arrived in France, beginning the bloody, five-week siege that led to the capture of the port city of Harfleur. Only a few months later, Henry and his beleaguered troops won their great victory at Agincourt. This miraculous, lopsided victory convinced Henry V that his cause was just; his English monarchy and his claim to the French crown had been validated by God.

The Mad King and the Warrior King:
Charles VI and Henry V

Whatever stability Charles V had provided his realm was eventually shaken when the "wise" French king was succeeded by his eleven-year-old son, Charles VI (r. 1380–1422), also known as "the mad."[45] As a youth, Charles VI possessed many of the qualities necessary for a successful reign. He was handsome, jovial, athletic, and spirited, and his happy marriage to Isabeau of Bavaria (when he was sixteen and she fourteen) augured well for the future of the Valois dynasty.[46] When his regency ended and he fully assumed the monarchy (1388), Charles ruled effectively and earned the nickname "the beloved."

But after apparently contracting typhus and being gravely ill for several months, the French king suddenly seems to have lost his mind. Traveling near Le Mans with an armed escort (1392), he became delusional and killed four of his knights, while nearly killing his younger brother, Louis, Duke of Orléans (1372–1407). Charles' disturbing mental illness (he appears to have become schizophrenic) created political chaos throughout his realm, during a tortuous reign that lasted another three decades.[47] The mad king had frequent bouts of incoherence and withdrawal from public affairs: sleepless, unshaved, covered in feces, and unwilling to eat or speak. He sometimes howled violently or ate his meals off the floor of his palace; at other times, he believed that he was made of glass, and that if anyone touched him, he would shatter. Charles VI's mental breakdowns could last anywhere from several days to several months.

Despite the political turmoil that ensued from his mental illness, because of their belief in the sacrosanct nature of the royal blood, the French aristocracy never once seriously considered forcing Charles VI to abdicate. In her recent study of the political themes in the works of Valois court poet Christine de Pisan (1364–1430), Tracy Adams offers a convincing assessment of the mad king's long and turbulent reign: "The conviction that the king was divinely ordained, coupled with the fiction that he was in control when he appeared lucid, maintained through a series of royal ordinances that treated his mental illness as temporary 'absences,' prevented his deposition and the installation of a permanent regent."[48]

In the struggle to fill the political vacuum created by the king's inability to govern, longstanding political rivalries among the French princes of the blood exploded into assassinations and mob rule in Paris. A civil war eventually erupted for control of the royal court, with scores of murders committed in the capital that displayed levels of brutality against political opponents that shocked an age that was accustomed to violence. Once the crown jewel and the largest city of northern Europe—the home of Gothic architecture, the famed University of Paris, and a host of important religious foundations—the capital city of the French kingdom had lost about half of its population in the first two decades of the fourteenth century. The political violence surrounding the deranged king and his family turned Paris into an armed and besieged refugee camp, where public authority often seemed to have collapsed.

As rival factions fought for control of the government, food became scarce and the basic commodities of everyday life became astronomically expensive. To make matters worse, a smallpox epidemic ravaged the capital in the summer of 1418, killing perhaps as much as one quarter of the population.[49] According to the anonymous author known as the Bourgeois of Paris, more than likely a cleric who wrote an eyewitness account of life in the city during the civil war and the Anglo-Burgundian occupation (c. 1405–31), things got even worse when the city fell into English hands. The weather became unbearable, with brutally cold winters and wet springs, which compounded the misery of the starving population. Describing the horrific conditions of 1420–21, he declared: "You could hear sad weeping and wailing all over Paris, sad lamentations and little children crying 'I am dying of hunger!' … Day and night, men, women, and little children could be heard exclaiming, 'Oh! I am dying of this cold!' or another 'of hunger.'"[50]

This civil war of Armagnacs (supporters of Joan of Arc's eventual king,

Charles VII) and Burgundians (eventual supporters of English claims to the French crown) provided a pathway for Henry V's audacious claims to the French throne.[51] In some measure, the internal violence that afflicted France and had caused the implosion of the French monarchy did as much damage to the French war effort against the English as did Henry's artillery bombardments and starvation of fortified cities. Those who claimed to be acting on behalf of King Charles VI (the Armagnac party when Henry first invaded Normandy) were helpless in the face of the English determination to conquer Normandy, city by city. As Sumption argues, Henry's early campaign in northern France was so dispiriting to the average French citizen that resistance seemed futile: "And to what end should they resist? To preserve the nominal authority of a mad king and factional government which was incapable of governing the realm or defending them against invasion?"[52]

The murder of *Jean sans peur*, or John the Fearless (1371–1419), was a stunning example of the bloodletting and violence that had plagued the French aristocracy during the catastrophic reign of Charles VI.[53] It was also a pivotal moment that laid the groundwork for Henry's successful conclusion of his war for the crown of France. John the Fearless's murder was part of a long vendetta that began with the assassination of Charles VI's younger and only brother, Louis, Duke of Orléans (1372–1407), on the streets of Paris. The libertine Louis, who seemed to be a bit too close to the king's wife, Isabeau of Bavaria, had kept the deranged Charles VI within his grip and was alleged to have drained the royal coffers to support his and the queen's lavish lifestyle. Ambushed by a group of paid assassins, Louis's head was split in half by a halberd as he was knocked from his horse, and his brains were splattered all over the pavement.[54]

The Duke of Burgundy, John the Fearless (so named because of his courageous fight against rebels in Liège), was the first cousin of the king and soon took responsibility for the brutal assassination of his rival.[55] He even went so far as to get formal support from a theologian at the University of Paris, Jean Petit (c. 1360–1411), to defend his act of "tyranncide." The Burgundian duke's theological propagandists peddled the claim that Louis practiced sorcery (hence the king's madness), had tried to poison the king, and was set to murder Charles VI and his entire family.[56]

John the Fearless was initially popular among the Parisian masses, since he made sincere and often empty promises to purge the corrupt officials in the Valois court, to reform the business of government, and to reduce or abolish unpopular taxes. Amazingly, the mad king Charles VI initially absolved him of the murder of his brother and allowed him to flourish as the supposed defender of the French realm against the aggression of the English invaders. This pardon was later revoked, but soon thereafter a formal truce was negotiated between John the Fearless and the children of the murdered Duke of Orléans: the Peace of Chartres (1409).[57] In the long run, however, the Duke of Burgundy failed to live up to his bold reputation, and the lingering animosity and suspicion over his intentions led to him being expressly prohibited from helping the French forces that fought against Henry V at the Battle Agincourt in 1415. His brother, Anthony, Duke of Brabant, was one of the casualties of that famed battle.

When Henry V returned to France to complete his conquest of Normandy, John the Fearless's inability to defend the provincial capital city of Rouen (1418–19) from Henry's savage assault unmasked him as a ruthless politician who lacked the finances and military might necessary to defeat the English invaders. And more importantly, despite his rise to power as the de facto ruler of France for extended periods of time, the original sin of John the Fearless, the murder of the king's brother Louis, opened a dark chapter of bloodshed and civil war between Louis' followers, the Armagnacs, and their sworn enemies the Burgundians. John himself would become a victim of his own violent modus operandi.

The bitter blood feud between the followers of the murdered Duke of Orléans and John the Fearless had to be put on hold after Henry V's renewed war in Normandy. When it became clear to the warring parties in France that the young English monarch would boldly capitalize on their enduring conflict, they entered into an uneasy alliance against the common English invader. Much to Henry's dismay, representatives of the Armagnacs and Burgundians enacted a truce and began a formal process of détente and negotiation. But Charles VI's son, the Dauphin, or crown prince Charles, made a catastrophic miscalculation when he supported a well-planned and vengeful plot to kill John the Fearless at a parley on a bridge in Montereau (September 10, 1419).[58] He and his fellow conspirators seemed to have naively believed that all resistance to his own dynastic succession would collapse with John dead. In fact, the Dauphin's participation in this bloody murder would quickly undermine his authority and breathe new life into Henry's war of conquest.

While there are conflicting accounts of what happened when the two sides met, there is little doubt that the Dauphin was a lead conspirator in the meticulously planned assassination of his political nemesis.[59] Arriving in Montereau at the invitation of the Dauphin's court, John the Fearless had been lured there on the pretext that he would formalize some sort of political agreement with the Armagnacs. After entering a specially constructed tent at the midway point of a bridge over the Seine River, the Duke of Burgundy removed his cap and knelt in front of the Dauphin Charles, who then helped him rise. As John the Fearless stood, a Breton warrior named Tanneguy du Châtel shouted the order to kill, and the tent was flooded with armed men who supported the Dauphin. Tanneguy viciously struck the duke in the back with an axe. This was soon followed by several sword blows to the face and belly. The Burgundian troops who stood outside heard the clamor and sought to rescue their duke but were repelled by Dauphinist artillery and bowmen. The following morning, John's mutilated body was recovered and hastily buried in the graveyard of the church of Notre Dame in Montereau. Thanks to Henry V's capture of Montereau in July of 1420, John's body was exhumed by his son and given a proper burial in a Carthusian monastery in Dijon.

The Duke of Burgundy's murder was seen as a cowardly act of treachery that would lead to Charles' condemnation and disinheritance from the Valois monarchy when the Treaty of Troyes was ratified in 1420. While wary of the English rule of France, in whatever form that might take, John the Fearless's distraught son Philip III (1396–1467) became the mortal enemy of the Dauphin and the Armagnacs. The murder of his father pushed him into the orbit of Henry V, and in the short term, the Anglo-Burgundian alliance would tip the scales of the war in favor of the English. The tragedy of this reckless act was not lost on the Dauphin's descendants. In 1521, the French King Francis I (r. 1515–47) made a visit to the Burgundian capital, where a Carthusian monk showed him the fractured skull of John the Fearless. The monk is supposed to have said, "by that hole, the English entered France."[60]

Henry V's string of destructive sieges and bloody victories in France culminated with the Treaty of Troyes.[61] The treaty established an Anglo-Norman kingdom that would be ruled by Henry V and his heirs. Charles VI's seventeen-year-old son, the Dauphin Charles, was disinherited and exiled from France for his participation in the brutal murder of John the Fearless.[62] Charles VI formally adopted Henry V as his son; betrothed his eighteen-year-old daughter Catherine Valois to the thirty-three-year-old English king; named Henry as his regent while he remained alive; and conferred the French crown on Henry V and his legitimate male successors at his death. This settlement marked the legal extinction of the Valois dynasty and promised to preserve a peace that came, figuratively speaking, on the heels of Henry's "war to end all wars." The new dual monarchy would allow the French to maintain their own laws and customs, so long as they swore loyalty to Henry V and his descendants. The

English and the French would finally be at peace (of course, the exiled Dauphin refused to recognize this settlement).

But only two years later, both the young Henry V and the old Charles VI lay dead (1422), and Henry's political legacy in France was in serious jeopardy. If Henry V had lived just a few months longer he would have personally realized his dream of a joint Anglo-Norman kingdom. Instead, his infant son Henry VI—the youngest monarch in English history—became the king of England and France, when he was all of nine months old. Within the decade, a teenaged peasant girl from a Dauphinist enclave in Lorraine would claim that voices and visions from the saints commanded her to nullify this legal settlement and to ignore the young king Henry VI's claim to the French monarchy. Joan of Arc's (1412–31) supposedly divine mandate to restore the exiled and disinherited Dauphin Charles to his rightful place on the throne threatened to destroy everything that Henry V had labored to achieve.

By supporting and taking up arms for the Dauphin, Joan attached herself to an accomplice to a treacherous political assassination and paid with her life for loyalty to Charles Valois. After her failed siege of Compiègne (May 1430) against the Burgundian allies of the English, Joan was captured and held by Philip III, Duke of Burgundy. It is no surprise that he transferred Joan to English custody, knowing full well that she would be tried and executed. After a brutal period of imprisonment and a lengthy ecclesiastical trial, the nineteen-year-old Joan was found guilty of heresy and apostasy and publicly burned alive in Rouen (May 30, 1431).[63] But before she was executed and physically erased from history, she had accomplished what had once seemed inconceivable. The virgin warrior had led men in battle and "miraculously" lifted the English siege of the strategically important city of Orléans; revived a dispirited army and helped turn the tide of the war in favor of the French; and triumphantly helped crown a disinherited prince, Charles VII, as the rightful king of France. In a short but astounding military career, Joan of Arc upended Henry V's political legacy in France.

Two

The Usurper's Son

Prince Hal

From Prince Hal to King Henry V

Henry V's authority as king was largely established by his arduous but highly successful military campaigns in France. He worked tirelessly to revive and strengthen the depleted monarchy of his father, while simultaneously waging a difficult and costly war in Normandy. By all accounts, Henry possessed the intellect and skills required to meet these challenges. A physically fit and courageous soldier, he was also an excellent administrator with a sharp mind and a keen eye for the details of government, military planning, and international diplomacy. His preparation and execution of the Agincourt campaign demonstrated the logistical talents of a superb staff officer, while his tactical skills and bravery on the front line made him an outstanding field commander. Above all, Henry was so driven to uphold his reputation as a great king and warrior and to impose his will on the Norman cities that continued to resist him, that he literally wore himself out campaigning in France. He died of dysentery at the age thirty-five (August 31, 1422), leaving behind a grieving realm, a young French widow, and a nine-month-old son who became the youngest monarch in English history.

Despite his aristocratic birth, the glory of his reign, and the abundance of diplomatic and narrative primary sources documenting his life, Henry remains an enigmatic and controversial figure, subject to a good deal of speculation and a variety of interpretations regarding his basic character, personality, and vision as a ruler. Strohm illustrates how the copious contemporary literature that chronicles the usurpation and reign of Henry IV and his son Henry V is always disfigured by a political agenda; the "texts which promise access to their lives paradoxically screen them from view. No matter how benignly intended, these texts supplant the life, effectively installing them in its place."[1] This is nowhere truer than in the dramatic works of Shakespeare. His plays—*Henry IV*, 1 and 2, and *Henry V*—not only bequeathed the heroic image of the warrior king triumphing at Agincourt, but also the reckless adolescent who pursued a life of pleasure and frivolity until his *volte face*, when he found himself seated upon the English throne. By that measure, Henry V invaded France as much for the atonement of his own sins as for those of his father.

The modern academic community continues to debate the veracity of the Shakespearean tale of the riotous Prince Hal, who immediately after his coronation became the pious and chaste Henry V. Sumption and Curry conclude that there are too many contemporary references to Henry's wild youth in the otherwise reputable chronicle literature for us to dismiss these allegations altogether.[2] Matusiak speculates that Henry may have engaged in such behavior as a consequence of his bitter alienation from his father.[3] They were at odds over foreign policy in France, and for a time Henry was exiled from his father's council after he attempted to persuade the gravely ill Henry IV to abdicate.

According to the St. Albans monastic chronicler Thomas Walsingham (1376–1422), when young Henry became king, the supposedly reckless adolescent was instantly transformed into an exemplary Christian monarch through the grace of his coronation ceremony. Walsingham begins his account of Henry's reign with his public crowning at Westminster Abbey, describing this experience as a bifurcation of the new king's life, much like the conversion of a saint in medieval hagiographic literature:

> [A]s soon as he was invested with the emblems of royalty, he suddenly became a different man. His care was now for self-restraint and goodness and gravity, and there was no kind of virtue which he put on one side and did not desire to practice himself. His conduct and behavior were an example to all men, clergy and laity alike, and those to whom it was granted to follow in his footsteps accounted themselves happy.[4]

Despite its religious contours, Henry's sudden conversion to Christian piety and *gravitas* when he was anointed with the oil of kingship was also more than likely part of a well-conceived public relations campaign. This "miraculous" conversion might have been promoted by Lancastrian propagandists to legitimize the new dynasty in a spectacular way. Henry V's transformation at his coronation thus provides a catharsis for the trauma of his father's reign. As Strohm proposes: "With the sacramental coronation as the pivot, Henry's character change becomes an index of the spiritual recovery of his dynasty as a whole—and thus the more sudden and dramatic his change the better."[5] However Henry spent his late adolescent years, the English and French chronicles covering his reign paint a similar portrait of him as king.[6] *This* Henry is remembered as both a fair and just ruler and a fierce and effective warrior. In describing and lamenting his sudden, unexpected death, Walsingham says of Henry: "He did not leave his like on earth among Christian kings or princes, so that not only the people of England and France but all Christendom mourned his death as he deserved."[7]

Family Life and the Education of a Prince

The anonymous early fifteenth-century French chronicler of the royal Abbey of St. Denis—now commonly believed to be Michel Pintoin (c. 1350–1421)—wrote an official history of the monarchy of Charles VI and spoke favorably of Henry. Commenting on the young English king's death, he claimed that he was the model of royal comportment, both "feared and respected." He described Henry as being "handsome, authoritative, devout, wise, just, a man of few words, bold in action and regal in manner."[8] The French cleric and famous astrologer Jean Fusoris (c. 1365–1436) met Henry when he came to England on a diplomatic mission in 1415. Fusoris had a close friendship with one of Henry's favorite clerics, the bishop of Norwich Richard Courtney (who died of dysentery during Henry's Harfleur campaign). Fusoris was later tried for treason by a French court, accused of being an English spy after Henry's invasion of France. During these proceedings he stated that Henry had a "very princely demeanor, but it also seemed to him that he was better suited to be a man of the Church than a soldier."[9]

Other contemporary accounts note Henry's physical appearance and his habit of speaking bluntly and directly. He was of average height, had brown eyes, a long neck, and great physical strength, especially noted by his speed on foot when hunting deer.[10] As king, he assiduously avoided the company of women and forbade the presence of prostitutes in both his royal residence and military camps, with draconian penalties for those women who dared to defy him. Henry was laconic in his speech, attentive in his listening and direct and precise in conversation.[11] After he became king, no one ever recalled that he was a good storyteller or a man who enjoyed a good laugh. One memorable comment he made during his siege of Meaux (1421–22) might be taken as a macabre joke that could speak to his overall character. The French cleric and chronicler of the reign of Charles VI, Jean Juvénal des Ursins (1388–1473), recorded this anecdote. When the inhabitants of the city complained to Henry that he was devastating the countryside by setting everything on fire as he progressed towards the city, he somewhat flippantly remarked: "War without fire has no value; no more than sausages without mustard."[12]

For all his grandeur as a legendary warrior king, there are surprisingly few contemporary artistic depictions Henry V. Unfortunately, the original head and hands of the effigy that sits atop his tomb in Westminster Abbey were stolen in 1546. Replacements were added in 1971, the hands being modeled after Laurence Olivier's, who played the king in his 1944 film production of *Henry V*.[13] In sharp contrast, the reign of his ill-fated predecessor Richard II was documented with an abundance of monarchic images; more likenesses of him survive than any other English king before Henry VIII.[14] One of the most famous portraits of Henry V is a profile oil painting in the National Portrait Gallery, often featured as cover art for books about the king.[15] The work of an unknown artist of an undetermined date, ranging from the sixteenth or early seventeenth century, it is possibly a copy of an earlier painting. Rigid and stylized, it depicts the king in profile view, with a regal pose of authority. The National Portrait Gallery painting bears a very striking resemblance to an earlier portrait preserved in the Royal Collection, dating from the early sixteenth century.[16] Both paintings might also have been modeled after now-lost medallions of some sort depicting the king. Some of Henry's modern biographers have speculated that the profile view was designed to hide the disfigurement of the king's face from an adolescent war wound. This might also explain why when he became king, he rebuked commanders who looked him in the face while they spoke.[17]

The sixteen-year-old prince was gravely wounded at the Battle of Shrewsbury (July 21, 1403). An arrow struck Henry's face as he fought with his father Henry IV against the rebellious armies of the renegade Henry Hotspur Percy (1364–1403), the son of the powerful Henry, Earl of Northumberland.[18] The Percies had been leading northern allies of Henry IV in his coup against Richard II. But the bankrupt king was long in arrears in payment for the loyal and invaluable military service they had provided him. Henry IV had also sought to weaken the grip of the Percies on northern England by promoting the rival Nevilles to new positions of power. Not surprisingly, such callous treatment of formerly indispensable allies of the vulnerable Lancastrian king led to open rebellion. In July of 1403, Hotspur announced his intention to remove Henry IV from the throne, publicly declaring what he knew to be false: that Richard II was still alive. His real intention was to crown the eleven-year-old presumptive heir of Richard II, Edmund Mortimer.[19]

As the vicious combat at Shrewsbury unfolded, Henry IV was nearly killed, but his enemies were crushed, and at the end of the battle the rebel prince Henry Hotspur Percy lay dead.[20] Despite the severity of young Henry's wound—an arrow was lodged in a bone on the right side of his nose, penetrating about six inches into his face—some chroniclers made the hyperbolic claim that he stayed on the battlefield and led a counterattack.[21] By all accounts, this grave injury could have been fatal; a slight deviation in the trajectory of the arrow could have instantly killed him. Young Henry was taken to Kenilworth castle (about fifty to sixty miles from Shrewsbury), where the surgeons who first treated him failed to remove the arrowhead. The wooden shaft broke free, leaving the tip of the arrow buried deep in his face. It was more than likely a bodkin, or long, needle-like hardened point.[22]

Henry V (r. 1413–22). The few surviving portrait paintings of Henry feature him in profile view. Some historians suggest that this was done to hide the permanent facial disfigurement that he bore from a war wound. He was struck in the face by an arrow when he was sixteen, fighting against rebels with his father at the Battle of Shrewsbury (1403). The innovative surgical procedure used to extract the deeply lodged arrowhead may have also caused permanent neurological damage (World History Archive / Alamy Stock Photo).

Fortunately, within days the young prince received expert medical care from London machinist and royal surgeon, John Bradmore (d. 1412). Bradmore invented a set of metal tongs with a screw placed between them that ran their entire length. He used this device to enlarge the wound and extract the deeply lodged arrowhead from Henry's face. In his well-known Latin treatise on surgery, the *Philomena*, Bradmore provides a detailed description of his remarkable procedure, including a drawing of the tongs that he forged.[23] The modern consensus is that Bradmore offers a far more reliable and accurate description of

Henry's injury than the politically motivated chroniclers of his day.[24] We have no real evidence for Henry's state of mind during this long convalescence, nor any description of the disfigurement or neurological damage that remained from the wound and Bradmore's surgery. According to Bradmore, after about three weeks of the application of medicinal ointments, Henry's wound was fully healed.[25]

That Henry survived this whole ordeal is well worth pondering. The inventive surgical technique to which he was subjected carried great risks. It is a wonder that he fully recovered from it; he could have bled to death or easily developed a fatal infection. The legendary crusader king of England, Richard the Lionheart (r. 1189–99), was not so fortunate, since he died of a comparable injury. During the siege of the rebellious Castle of Chalûs-Chabrol in his French domains, a crossbow bolt struck him in the shoulder near the neck.[26] Thanks to the poor medical care he received, twelve days later the forty-one-year-old warrior king died of gangrene in the arms of his aged mother, Eleanor of Aquitaine.[27]

This traumatic war wound was undoubtedly a defining moment for the formation of Henry's character and it might have had a lasting neurological and psychological impact. But as Timothy Arner observes, for such a significant event in the king's short life, it has only recently been given meaningful attention by scholars of Henry's reign. This is not only due to some degree of neglect among modern academics but is also attributable to the efforts of Lancastrian chroniclers to minimize or "mask" the king's disfigurement for political purposes: "For the nation's wounds to heal and for Henry V to separate himself from his father's rule, Henry's scar would need to be erased by chroniclers and Lancastrian apologists."[28] In sharp contrast, as Henry IV's reign progressed, he was visibly afflicted with a number of debilitating illnesses, including painful skin lesions that served as an index of the enduring question of the legitimacy of his reign. Mortimer appreciates the gravity of Henry V's nearly fatal injury and argues that this harrowing first experience under arms formed the substance of his education: "The scar on Henry's face was a legacy from the Battle of Shrewsbury.... That was arguably Henry's true education—armed campaigning and military leadership."[29] Vale also believes that Henry's near-death experience played a critical role in shaping his character. Beyond the immediate severity of the injury and the physical trauma Henry endured, "that closeness to mortality may have made him more than normally aware, for his time, of his state of health."[30] His initial experience in mortal combat undoubtedly informed Henry's thinking when he crossed the Channel to wage war against the French.

41

Henry revised his last will and testament each of the three times he departed from England for campaigns in France. When he drafted his first will in the summer of 1415, it had been a full twelve years since he had fought in a pitched battle. Death in combat or from the many other physical afflictions that accompanied military campaigning was apparently never far from the king's mind.[31] Henry's successful treatment by Bradmore also undoubtedly explains why he was the first English king to enlist a corps of surgeons when he made his elaborate plans for the invasion of France in the summer of 1415.[32] One of them, Thomas Morstede (1380–1450), was not only Henry's personal battlefield surgeon but also founded the English College of Medicine (1423). He had studied the work of Bradmore and is believed to be responsible for the Middle English translation of his treatise on surgery, the *Philomena*.[33]

Despite his impeccable aristocratic pedigree and his access to the educational and socioeconomic resources of an English nobleman, Henry's early life was far from idyllic and he came of age at a time of grave danger for his family and the English monarchy.[34] Born at Monmouth Castle (September 16, 1386), hence his modern name "Henry of Monmouth," he was the first-born son of Henry Bolingbroke (1367–1413) and Mary de Bohun (c. 1368–95).[35] Mary was his father's second cousin and was probably around twelve years old when she married Bolingbroke. She was about sixteen and his father about eighteen when she gave birth to the future king Henry V, the first of her six surviving children. By all accounts, it was a happy marriage, but at the age of twenty-eight, Mary died soon after the birth of her last child, Philippa. Henry was about eight years old at the time. His father was so grief-stricken that he mourned her death for a full year. Ironically, Mary died the same week as Richard II's beloved twenty-eight-year-old wife, Anne of Bohemia.

The loss of his mother, with whom he spent considerable time as a child, must have been devastating to young Henry as well. He was emotionally and physically distant from his grieving father, and their relationship would become increasingly conflicted. Henry also had a peculiar relationship with Henry IV's second wife, Joanna of Navarre (c. 1370–1437), Duchess of Brittany and then Queen of England.[36] Henry Bolingbroke first met her when he lived in exile after Richard II's banishment (1399).[37] Henry IV and Joanna were publicly wed in Winchester Cathedral in 1403, and soon thereafter she was crowned queen in London. Chris Given-Wilson ultimately judges the marriage as a diplomatic failure, but a success on a personal level. Henry and Joanna were the same age, shared many common interests, and had genuine affection for each other.[38] The elder Henry's love for his wives stands in sharp contrast to the younger Henry's relationship with his own spouse, Catherine Valois (1401–37). Their marriage was an obvious political success but perhaps nothing more. When Henry V was dying in France, he did not ask to have his wife present at his deathbed, even though she was only a short distance away.

The younger Henry and Joanna were on cordial terms, and he even entrusted her with the regency during his Norman campaign of 1415. But their relationship would end badly. It began to unravel when Henry captured one of her sons, Arthur de Richemont (1393–1458), who was wounded at the Battle of Agincourt.[39] Dug out from a pile of corpses, the twenty-two year old was covered in blood but recognized by his coat of arms and brought before Henry V. According to the contemporary chronicler Guillaume Gruel (c. 1410–74/82), who entered Richemont's service around 1420, Henry "rejoiced in his capture more than any other."[40] Taken as a prisoner to England, Richemont was part of Henry's triumphant victory parade in London (November 23, 1415) and remained an English captive for about five years. According to Gruel, Joanna had not seen her son since he was ten, and tragically, he did not recognize her when she arranged a meeting with him.[41]

After returning to his homeland, Arthur supported Henry V's claim to the throne when the Treaty of Troyes was ratified (1420). The treaty formally recognized Henry V's right of succession to the crown of France when Charles VI died; it would then pass to his future son by his new bride, Catherine Valois, or any of his legitimate male relatives. But when Henry V and Charles VI both died only two years later, Arthur switched his allegiance to the Valois Dauphin (1424) and was made Constable of France through the influence of the Dauphin Charles' mother-in-law, Yolande of Aragon (1425). Richemont eventually had some sort of falling out with a few of the Dauphin's favorites and was permanently banished from the Valois court. But in yet another strange twist of fate, he fought with Joan of Arc against the English in the summer of 1429, not long after she helped lift the siege of Orléans.[42]

When Joanna interceded for her captured son's release, her relationship with Henry began to sour. The circumstances of her official fall from his graces remain murky. Joanna was incarcerated on the unproved allegations of a Franciscan friar who claimed that she was practicing necromancy and sorcery and therefore posed a grave threat to the king. She was then arrested and imprisoned in Leeds Castle (1419) for three years. The accusations of witchcraft and sorcery, involving some fatuous plot against his life, were never proven. In fact, Joanna was neither tried nor convicted of anything. The whole sordid affair appears to have served as a cover for Henry's exploitation of her vast financial resources during his cash-strapped war in France. Shortly before he died, he expressed regret for his bizarre and shameful treatment of his stepmother and cleared his conscience by freeing her and restoring her lands and incomes (1422).[43] Joanna lived another fifteen years and was eventually buried next to her second husband, Henry IV, in Canterbury Cathedral.

We get glimpses of Henry's early childhood in scattered contemporary sources, but we are especially well informed about his education. When their mother died, Henry and his younger brother Thomas lived within the household of their grandfather, John of Gaunt. Henry's maternal grandmother, Joan Bohun, Countess of Hereford (1347–1419), took him under her care and Henry showed great love for her until her passing.[44] Henry's formal academic studies began around the time of his mother's death, and he learned the essentials of Latin grammar and rhetoric, while also being introduced to the literary and musical arts.[45] Like his father, Henry was a musician (he played the harp) and was especially fond of music. As I noted in the introduction, he may have even composed a Gloria and a Sanctus for the mass.[46] Aside from the dialect of English that he spoke, he also learned to speak and write in both Latin and French. From an early age, Henry received training in the art of war, learning to ride and wield a sword, while developing a great passion for hunting. He was schooled in the strategic and tactical theories proposed by the widely read fourth-century Roman author Vegetius, whose *Epitoma rei militaris,* or the *Epitome of Military Matters* became a field manual for late medieval military commanders. In the summer of 1415, Henry's mastery of this text was demonstrated in his brutal siege of Harfleur.[47] By the time he was in his early teens, Henry excelled as had his father in both the peaceful and martial arts and vividly embodied the educational ideals of a late medieval prince.

From Hostage to Heir to the Throne

A critical moment of young Henry's life came when he was about twelve years old. In 1398, his father Henry Bolingbroke was forced into a ten-year exile by Richard II (r. 1377–99).[48] Bolingbroke had a very public dispute with his former ally Thomas Mowbray, Duke of Norfolk (1366–99), arguing before the king and Parliament that Mowbray was guilty of treason. Bolingbroke alleged that the duke defamed Richard in a private conversation. After Mowbray's vigorous self-defense and after lodging an accusation of slander against his rival, Richard ordered Mowbray and Bolingbroke to settle their dispute publicly in a trial by combat before the king in Coventry. But before any blows could be struck, Richard halted the duel and then exiled Mowbray for life and Bolingbroke for a decade (later reduced to six years).

When Bolingbroke's father, the wealthy and powerful magnate John of Gaunt, died (February 3, 1399), Richard confiscated the estates of his Duchy of Lancaster. Bolingbroke became a permanent outcast and his exile was extended for life. This reckless decision would eventually lead to the king's ruin. A rebellion in Ireland occurred soon thereafter, and Richard brought Bolingbroke's young son Henry with him when he campaigned against the rebels. Young Henry was now placed in the precarious position of being in the entourage of his father's nemesis. Richard II also had no heir and had sent conflicting messages on the order of succession, while remaining fearful of treachery on the part of Bolingbroke.[49]

The English realm that Richard II governed before his downfall still felt the reverberations of the tragic events that set the stage for the usurper's coronation. The burden of the early phases of the Hundred Years War in England, coupled with the social and economic disruption caused by the Black Death, helped foment a violent uprising that very nearly destroyed the monarchy of the adolescent king Richard II. In assessing the Great Revolt of 1381, it is difficult to posit a simple cause and effect scenario, where one specific event led to open rebellion against the king. The waves of bubonic plague, along with increased taxation for an unpopular government, without a substantial increase of wages in the midst of a labor shortage, fueled social unrest that would also manifest itself in political and religious forms. As Laura Ashe argues, the traditional label of "Peasant Rebellion" is probably a misnomer, since this revolt had support across all levels of English society and was driven by the texts and speeches of ambitious and well-educated individuals. The sociopolitical interests of the merchant class and the peasants seemed to reach a critical mass when Parliament enacted a harsh, fixed poll tax (1380).[50]

The uprising of 1381 fundamentally challenged the established feudal order, with its divinely sanctioned structures of nobility and clergy dominating and controlling the lives of the vast majority of the population, the peasantry.[51] An orgy of violence terrorized the ruling elite for the span of several months, but soon after the decapitation of its leadership, the rebellion abruptly ended. When one of the peasant ringleaders named Wat Tyler was granted a parley with the king at Smithfield, he had overturned the established social order by thrusting himself into higher echelons of the ruling caste. A peasant challenge to the legitimate authority of a dynastic king was more than the elite power structures could tolerate, and Tyler paid with his life for helping to lead this short-lived revolution.

There are conflicting accounts of how Tyler met his end as he rode into the presence of Richard II. He reportedly showed the king great disrespect, a scuffle ensued, and he was cut down. The parley might have even been a subterfuge for the assassination of Tyler, which was accomplished with relative ease. Richard himself rode into the midst of the frantic mob that accompanied Tyler and convinced them that he would make good on his pledges for the sweeping political and legal reforms that they demanded. It was not long, however, before the heads of rebel leaders would begin to roll and order would be restored through swift and ruthless justice.

The rebellion of 1381 was a defining moment for Henry Bolingbroke, and every interaction with his cousin Richard II should be viewed against this backdrop. Fourteen-year-old Henry took refuge in the Tower of London along with the king as violent mobs roamed the streets of London looking for aristocratic victims for their purge. Richard and his entourage departed to plot a strategy to defeat the rebels; young Henry had to fend for himself, along with a handful of adults who accompanied him. Henry then came within inches of his life when the mob burst into the Tower. If it were not for the last-minute intervention of one of the tower guards, who convinced the angry rebels that Henry was harmless, he would have shared the same fate as the archbishop of Canterbury Simon Sudbury (c. 1316–81), who was savagely beheaded by the mob.

Given that his father John of Gaunt happened to be one of the wealthiest and most hated men in England at that moment, it is a wonder that Henry Bolingbroke survived this brush with death. Mortimer speculates that this incident played a future role in Henry IV's treatment of Richard, arguing that it might be part of a larger narrative "of outright hostility to one another," culminating with Henry's coup against his cousin the king.[52] Throughout his biography of Henry IV, Mortimer offers convincing evidence that the bitter rivalry that developed between the two men was fueled by Richard's deep insecurities and his jealously over his cousin's idyllic embodiment of the best elements of chivalry.

The rebellion was crushed, but Richard II paid a high price for his botched rule. Richard's absolutist and narcissistic tendencies certainly expedited his downfall. But as Saul notes, the fact that he had transitioned his government from the "war state" of the illustrious warrior king, his grandfather Edward III, to a "peacetime state" that seemed to mirror the Valois court of Charles V fundamentally undermined his ability to secure the support of his people. The Gascon-born Richard was already viewed as being more "French" than "English" by some of his contemporaries. Certainly his conception of monarchy reflected French sacramentalism as opposed to the Plantagenet tradition of chivalric kingship, with displays of martial prowess.[53] Richard's new taxes and demands for servile obedience were not connected to any meaningful program of nationalism or foreign policy. According to Saul, under Richard's predecessors, "War had had the beneficial effect of stimulating loyalty to the king. Once its unifying quality was removed, it was not clear how a similar sense of loyalty could be created."[54] Despite its chronic financial distress, the new Lancastrian dynasty restored the traditional "war footing" of previous English kings with an aggressive foreign policy in France whose cornerstone was the continued threat of renewed hostilities with the French king. This "unifying quality" of warfare in France was exploited to the full early in the reign Henry V.

Richard II remained ignorant of his lack of strategic vision, aloofness, isolation, and alienation from his own subjects. And he continued to be bitter about the rule of the Lords Appellant (1387–88), powerful magnates who had impeached five of Richard's favorites in Parliament, for corruption and abetting tyranny; some of them were brutally executed for treason.[55] One of those Appellants had been Henry Bolingbroke. Richard was also the antithesis of his father, the famed war hero Edward the Black Prince (1330–76). And unlike his rival Bolingbroke, the champion jouster, Richard showed no interest in the military arts as a young man and could not present himself as a warrior king when such a leader was demanded at a time of national crisis. His murderous rage at those who criticized him and his absolutist tendencies reflected his deep insecurities and paranoia about any potential threats to his power. Bolingbroke's presence at court had been a constant and painful reminder of Richard's deficiencies. Because of his dramatic embodiment of the chivalric ideals of medieval kingship, Bolingbroke could be seen as a credible alternative to Richard's tyrannical persona. What Bertram Wolffe says in his biography of the failed Lancastrian king Henry VI is equally applicable to Richard: "A fifteenth-century English king both reigned and ruled.... On the personality of the king depended the tone and quality of the life of the nation."[56]

Richard had delusions of grandeur and was detached from the reality that his nation needed a king who could both "reign and rule." This created an opportunity for Bolingbroke to act boldly and decisively. With his father dead, his estates unjustly confiscated, his exile made permanent, and Richard openly behaving like a tyrant, Bolingbroke raised his standard and rallied his supporters in an armed revolt against his cousin. It is not entirely clear if the majority of the rebels believed they were engaged in anything more than the restoration of Bolingbroke to his rightful place as duke, followed by a reform of Richard's corrupt government. Contemporary accounts indicate that Henry swore some sort of oath not to take the throne by force, but that if Richard II abdicated, he would stand ready as the legitimate successor of the king. Before long, Richard II was abandoned to his fate by a number of defections and he soon became Henry's prisoner.

Forced to abdicate, Richard was also condemned by a Parliament that had been convened for the purpose of removing him from power.[57] Even though it had not been legally summoned by a reigning king as required by law, this Parliament hastened and applauded Richard's downfall. It joyfully accepted Bolingbroke's claim to the throne by right of succession, and equally important, *not* by right of conquest. When Henry dramatically seated himself on the throne before Parliament, the crowd burst into thunderous applause. As Mortimer observes: "If this was 'usurpation'— as it is usually described—it was the most popular usurpation in English history."[58]

This stunning reversal of fortune was complete when Henry IV (r. 1399–1413) was crowned king, and the deposed Richard lay dead in a dungeon in Pontefract Castle. Precisely how Richard met his end has been debated for centuries. The pro-Henrician chronicler Thomas Walsingham reports the official Lancastrian line: Richard was so depressed by the recent turn of events that he refused to eat and then died.[59] Richard more than likely was starved to death at the order of Henry IV, after a failed rebellion against the new Lancastrian king took place in early January of 1400. Richard could not be allowed to live and continue to be the rallying point for future uprisings against Henry. By mid–February of 1400, he had died and his body was publicly displayed in London so that everyone could see his face and recognize that he *really was* dead.[60] Regardless of how Richard met his end, Henry IV bore the ultimate responsibility for his demise.

Shakespeare reduced the sum total of the new king's reign to "usurpation." But Henry IV did not claim the crown by right of conquest and insisted that his succession was legal and just. The establishment of the new Lancastrian regime forced England to confront an exceptionally complex constitutional problem, involving two separate legal issues that eventually elided into one: By what right could a duly anointed king be removed from office? By what right could Henry Bolingbroke claim to be next in line for the kingship?

Saul believes that Pope Innocent IV's deposition of the Holy Roman Emperor, Frederick II, at the Council of Lyons (1245), served as a model for the removal of the English king.[61] The pope produced a long list of crimes that provided the legal basis for this bold ruling against Fredrick. Similarly, a catalog of Richard's crimes—thirty-three in all—was presented to Parliament when Henry's claim to the throne was acknowledged.[62] The description of Richard's deposition recorded by the contemporary English chronicler Adam Usk (c. 1352–1430) clearly mirrors the pope's deposition of the emperor. Usk says that this subject was debated by "doctors, bishops and others," including Usk himself:

> [T]hey decided that perjuries, sacrileges, sodomitical acts, dispossession of his subjects, the reduction of his people to servitude, lack of reason, incapacity to rule, to all of which King Richard was notoriously prone, were sufficient reasons—according to the chapter "Ad Apostolice" taken from "Re Iudicata" in the Sextus, and the other things noted there—for deposing him.[63]

As the Vicar of Christ and lord of Latin Christendom, Innocent IV claimed sovereign authority over any Christian subject, from peasant to king, upon which his ability to remove the Holy Roman Emperor was predicated. But critics of Bolingbroke could argue that a secular political body such as Parliament had no comparable authority over a duly anointed king.[64] England was centuries away from the constitutional monarchy of the Glorious Revolution (1688–89) that forced the abdication of James II and placed William and Mary on the throne through the invitation of Parliament.

Henry believed that his claim to succession was perfectly legal, since he had been designated heir to the English throne. If he outlived his father John of Gaunt, who was named successor by the dying Edward III (1376), he could legitimately claim the crown.[65] Still, whatever promises had been made to the Lancastrians resided in a secret document dictated by a dying king and known to only a handful of people. And Richard had probably destroyed the original text. This was hardly solid ground upon which to begin a new dynasty. So after intense consultation with leading clerics and legal scholars, Henry based his legal claim to the crown on his descent from Henry III (r. 1216–72).[66] When Henry IV formally accepted the crown before Parliament, this specific claim of descent was entered into the official record of the proceedings (in the English language).[67]

The Parliamentary records of Richard's abdication and Henry IV's acclamation were widely distributed by the new Lancastrian regime. According to David R. Carlson, this written record "was the Lancastrian victors' official account of what happened. Created for propaganda, it was treated like propaganda: put into the widest possible circulation, in various forms."[68] But despite the valiant effort of Henry IV to create a legal paper trail supporting his coronation as king of England, he could not disguise the residual ugliness of Richard's removal from power and his unnatural death. Richard was no doubt a bad king who misunderstood the subjects he ruled and the nature of their political institutions. He rode roughshod over the traditional rights and liberties of Parliament and came as close as any medieval English monarch could to establishing a divine right kingship. But did these political "sins" warrant coercive removal from duly anointed kingship, inhospitable incarceration, and eventual murder? As Pugh comments, Richard II "was condemned unheard," and contrary to Shakespeare's dramatic presentation, "no speech was made in his defense."[69]

Compiling a list of grievances with which to impeach Richard II and acclaiming Henry IV king through a Parliamentary decree could never mask the violence done to the institution of dynastic monarchy and to the legitimately crowned king himself. Ashe argues that Henry IV had unwittingly created a martyr out of Richard II, who was now remembered by the kingly ideal that he himself had constructed: "In appropriating Richard's cause, the rebels against Henry IV used him as a figure of true kingship, evacuated of the individuality which had caused his downfall—represented him, in fact, as Richard had always represented himself."[70]

Bolingbroke's overthrow of Richard and his alleged murder of the king would, for multiple reasons, weigh heavily on both the older and younger Henry at the beginning of each of their reigns. Some modern historians speculate that Henry V might have had some emotional attachment to Richard, who apparently treated him with kindness and had even knighted him. He could therefore have developed some sympathy for the doomed king's plight, even though he had been a de facto hostage in his court while his father lived in exile.

The monastic chronicler Thomas Walsingham paints a portrait of deep affection and respect between the younger Henry and Richard, thereby bolstering the Lancastrian claim to legitimate succession. Walsingham was a staunch supporter of Henry V, and his account of the reburial of Richard offers material evidence of Henry's proper veneration of the deposed king, as if Richard were his own biological father and predecessor on the throne. Walsingham notes that the transfer of Richard's body to Westminster "was not without great expense of money by the present king, who confessed that he owed as much veneration to Richard as to his own father of the flesh."[71] Beyond the supposed sentimentality of this complex relationship stands an astute political move by Henry V and his Lancastrian propagandists. The memory of this filial bond with Richard reestablishes the continuity of the monarchy after the usurpation of the crown and murder of the king by his father. Henry IV may have been his biological parent, but as Strohm argues, Richard would become his dynastic father.[72]

Still, Henry V's former friend, comrade in arms and then Lollard nemesis, Sir John Oldcastle, declared at his treason trial (November 1417) that no one could pass judgment on him "while his liege Lord, King Richard, was still alive in the kingdom of Scotland."[73] The Lollard sect to which Oldcastle belonged followed the teachings of the radical Oxford theologian John Wycliffe (c. 1320–84), who found a receptive audience in the post-plague unrest that gripped England.[74] Wycliffe's juxtaposition of the poverty of Christ with the worldliness and wealth of the Church crossed the line into heterodoxy. In the aftermath of the Great Rebellion of 1381, Wycliffism was effectively associated with sedition and rebellion against legitimate authority by clerical propagandists who defended the ecclesiastical status quo.

The English government of Henry IV had resorted to the threat of coercion and violence with the nonconformist Lollards. While their number was relatively small, they were condemned as heretics and outlaws by an act of Parliament in the reign of Henry IV, and his son and successor unhesitatingly continued this policy of persecution and execution for treason. Henry IV's coronation was soon followed by the first public burning of a heretic in England, the priest William Sautre at Smithfield (1401).[75] Later in the same year, a parliamentary statute, *De heretico comburendo* ("on the burning of heretics") validated this new, horrifying punishment for religious dissidents. Young Henry himself attended the public burning of the heretical layman John Badby (1410), whom he tried to convert back to orthodox faith as his death sentence was being carried out. He was pulled from the fire and given one last chance to recant. Henry's effort was to no avail.[76] In 1417, Oldcastle's defiance led to an immediate death sentence, whereupon he was drawn, hanged, and burnt. His blunt response to Oldcastle's charge of treason was a painful reminder to Henry that his reburial of Richard had not fully expunged the memory of usurpation, nor did it completely put to rest the rumors that he was still alive.

Whatever the nature of young Henry's bond with the murdered king, his rapport with his own father became increasingly difficult and eventually acrimonious. As Henry IV's reign evolved and his health began a precipitous decline, tensions mounted between father and son, reaching a breaking point when they were at daggers drawn over English foreign policy in France. Henry IV formally allied with the Armagnacs, while young Henry strongly favored and cultivated an alliance with their sworn Burgundian enemies. The king prevailed over his son, much to the younger

Henry's embarrassment (he had maintained a close diplomatic relationship with the ruthless Duke of Burgundy, John the Fearless). Henry adamantly believed that his father had totally misjudged the political situation of France and had chosen the wrong side in the civil war that had nearly ruined the French monarchy. In the short run, Henry IV seemed to have chosen the "right side" in the French civil war. But in the long run, the Burgundians would become the staunch allies of the English during critical moments of Henry V's campaign in Normandy.

Young Henry had taken on an increasingly powerful position in Henry IV's council, repeatedly asserting himself as his father's health deteriorated. While reflecting on his father's debilitating health conditions—he suffered from a painful skin disease, among other things—Henry also floated the idea of his father abdicating and putting him on the throne instead.[77] The horrendous physical afflictions which accompanied Henry IV's demise were also taken as signs of divine disfavor with his monarchy. Even the sympathetic contemporary chronicler Adam Usk (c. 1352–1430) could not deny the misery of his condition when he died in his mid-forties: "the infection which for five years had cruelly tormented Henry IV with festering of the flesh, dehydration of the eyes, and rupture of the internal organs, caused him to end his days."[78]

Not surprisingly, Henry IV steadfastly refused to step aside and young Henry could be seen as proposing his own usurpation of the crown. He had a falling out with his father, was exiled from the royal court, and deprived of a command of English troops sent to France to aid the Armagnacs. Henry's younger brother and rival, Thomas of Lancaster, Duke of Clarence (1387–1421), led that expeditionary force with great results. When he arrived with his troops and learned that the Armagnacs had double-crossed the English by mending their differences with the Burgundians, he declared war on the former and began a plunder raid to restore England's power in its traditional domains in France.

The success of Thomas' campaign, with the revival and stabilization of English authority in Gascony and its long-term impact, is frequently overlooked by modern scholars. This expedition also established the framework for Henry V's future campaigns in Normandy, since with Gascony secure, he could focus his energies on northern France. As Given-Wilson notes, Thomas' "expedition shocked and shamed the French. This was the first English campaign in France for a quarter century, and the sight of Clarence's army marching virtually unchallenged from Normandy to Bordeaux ... revived the reputation of English arms abroad and struck terror into the French."[79] Thomas later fought valiantly and effectively when commanded by Henry V in his conquest of Normandy. But his reckless abandon as a soldier would eventually cost him his life in the Battle of Baugé (March 22, 1421), a disastrous defeat of the English by a combined French and Scottish force.

Henry's exile from his father's council and his being pushed onto the sidelines of foreign policy and campaigning in France were undoubtedly a heavy blow to his honor and dignity. Some of Henry IV's councilors seized upon the eldest son's vulnerability and accused him of the embezzlement of funds during his stewardship of the English outpost of Calais. There were even hints that he planned a coup against his father. This campaign of defamation produced a sharp and lengthy response in the form of a manifesto issued by young Henry in Coventry (June 1412), whose principal audience was more than likely his father.[80] He denounced the evildoers who plotted enmity between himself and his father, who were alleging that young Henry was even planning to overthrow him.

When he was granted an audience with the gravely ill Henry IV at Westminster Hall (September 1413) just months before he died at the age of forty-five, he asked his father to punish the evildoers. Henry IV's seemingly tepid response, with a reference to adjudication of the matter by Parliament, left him wanting. According to an account written a century later, but based on the testimony of an English earl who was in London when it took place, a dramatic scene then unfolded.[81] Young Henry offered his father a dagger and asked him to kill him with it if he were displeased with him. The dying king thereupon burst into tears, tossed away the dagger and forgave his son of any wrongdoing. A month later, young Henry was fully cleared of any accusations of mismanagement of funds in Calais.

Despite the drama of this reconciliation and the legal exoneration of young Henry, alienation and bitterness between father and son from the final days of Henry IV's reign cast a pall over the early reign of Henry V. They would always share the common bond of the Lancastrian dynasty being predicated on usurpation and tainted with the blood of a murdered king. A generation after the death of Henry IV, the Burgundian chronicler Enguerrand de Monstrelet (c. 1400–53) recounted what was probably an apocryphal legend of Henry IV's final words to his son that encapsulated this Lancastrian curse. As Henry IV hovered between life and death, there came a point where the prince assumed that his father was dead, and thereupon took possession of his crown. When the supposedly dead king came back to life, he asked for his crown, and the younger Henry was summoned to his father's bed. The dying king admitted that neither he nor his son had any right to the crown.[82] Prince Henry declared to his father that he would nonetheless hold it as his father had, by the sword. As Given-Wilson notes, despite its being a "too good to be true" legend, it was immortalized by Shakespeare and in fact embodied "an enduring moral truth of Henry's reign": the stigma of usurpation and regicide would continue to define his kingship among his domestic opponents and foreign enemies.[83]

THREE

The Sins of the Father

Expiation and Restoration

A Funeral Fit for a King

From the time of his accession to the English throne to his early campaigns of conquest in northern France, Henry V struggled to overcome the dishonor of Lancastrian usurpation of the English crown and the mistreatment and murder of a reigning monarch. By contrast, the French had long tolerated their schizophrenic king, Charles VI. No serious thought had ever been given by the French magnates to the deposition and replacement of their deranged ruler. Even when they were at war with each other, neither the Armagnacs nor Burgundians sought to overthrow the king: they wanted to control him and dominate his court. The indelible character of the French king's sacramental coronation—comparable to priestly ordination—shielded him from judgment by any political body or association, even if he were incapacitated with mental illness for extended periods of time. Needless to say, the French were appalled and outraged that the English would so quickly adapt themselves to the deposition and murder of a legitimate ruler.[1]

Henry V moved quickly with a bold and very public gesture of reconciliation to make amends with the tragic king that his father had deposed. After he died, Richard II had been given a largely unceremonious burial and his body remained at the Dominican friary of King's Langley for the entirety of Henry IV's reign (over thirteen years). Henry IV would not allow Richard to be buried next to his first, beloved wife Anne of Bohemia in the ornate tomb he had constructed in Westminster Abbey, robbing him of his enduring regal dignity.[2] But soon after his coronation, Henry V had Richard's body exhumed and put in its proper, final resting place, at a time when rumors of Richard's continued existence had reached a fever pitch. No expense was spared for a magnificent ceremony that Henry V himself attended. Strohm documents massive expenditures of money for, among other things, a carriage for Richard's body, a coffin, torches, candle wax, and alms for the poor.[3]

As contemporaries noted, Henry V seemed to have spent a good deal more money on the reburial of Richard II in his lavish tomb than the burial of his own father; he also endowed chantries to celebrate masses for the repose of Richard's soul.[4] Saul notes that there still was a deep feeling among Henry V's contemporaries that Lancastrian "usurpation had unbalanced the world," and that the younger Henry's translation of Richard II's remains to his chosen resting place was fueled by deep religious and political anxieties. In short, Henry desired "to atone for his father's usurpation," while also needing "to silence the rumours that Richard was still alive."[5] There were also strong and sophisticated political motivations at work in the translation of Richard's remains to Westminster Abbey. This public display of filial piety and the regal fanfare of a proper funeral were, according to Strohm, "conducive to the orderly transfer of Richard's sanctified aura to his own kingship.... As sponsor of Richard's reburial, Henry V was able to display himself in a role of rightful successor that was unavailable to his own usurping father."[6]

The Enduring Scandal of Usurpation

Henry V would also find another form of atonement for usurpation and Richard's death in the conquest of northern France. The toxic aftermath of his falling out with his father and his exile from court also still weighed heavily on him as he assumed his new role as king. He undoubtedly understood that rallying his nation behind a war would do more to legitimize his reign and draw his subjects into closer bonds of loyalty with their new king than the proper interment of an overthrown monarch. But Henry would have to deliver meaningful victories of lasting consequence if this ideology of regenerative violence were to work.

Henry's capture of the critically important port city of Harfleur, after a long and difficult siege, and his stunning victory at Agincourt created a general euphoria in England, while finally providing legitimacy to the Lancastrian dynasty that he so desperately craved. The king's triumphant entry into London after Agincourt (November 23, 1415), with its pageantry and gaudy theatricality, gave the appearance of Henry being a Christ-figure entering Jerusalem. His chancellor, Thomas Beaufort (1377–1426), articulated with concision the official propaganda that would be deployed by the English king for continued campaigning in France. In a letter that he penned to the king, Beaufort declared: "The winter of sloth and idleness, timidity and folly has passed away and the spring flowers of youth and martial vigor are here…. What wise man, I ask, looking back on this campaign, will not stand amazed and attribute it to the power of God himself?"[7] Henry was also amply rewarded by a compliant Parliament when the Commons voted to award him unprecedented subsidies for the continuation of the war in France.[8]

Henry's early triumph in France also stood in marked contrast to his father's largely ineffectual initial forays into international diplomacy. As Henry IV struggled to find his footing at the beginning of his reign, he was besieged with serious uprisings on the borders of his kingdom (Scotland and Wales) and rebellions centered upon imposters posing as Richard II returning from exile. Under these circumstances, it was difficult for him to have a well-thought-out plan when it came to England's tortuous relationship with France. Henry IV's clumsiness with the fine points of diplomacy also threatened to renew a war with France at any moment, before he was fully prepared for the fight. Such a conflict could not be funded since his government was essentially broke. The overthrow of Richard II not only created a crisis of confidence and authority in the new Lancastrian regime within the English realm, it also undermined the ability to maintain the tenuous peace that had held between France and England since 1396.[9]

For the first few years of his reign, the French ruling aristocracy refused to recognize Henry IV as legitimate king, continuing to refer to him by his ducal title. The threat of war with France was compounded by the usurpation and the unfulfilled demand that Richard II's widowed (second) wife, the ten-year-old French princess Isabella Valois (1396–1409), be returned to the French court with her dowry as soon as possible.[10] Although Richard II had treated her with kindness, love, and compassion, Isabella was only a child of seven when she became the English king's wife, and she had spent three miserable years in a foreign country married to a man who was more than twenty years her senior. Henry IV stalled the negotiations for several months, proposing a marriage with his own son Henry. The French monarchy would have none of it. In 1401, the widowed queen returned to France, but the bankrupt Henry IV refused to return her dowry.[11]

Henry V always seems to have had a clear head when it came to the French, understanding at the start of his reign that he needed to move quickly to exploit the paralysis of the Valois court. The trauma of the reign of the schizophrenic Charles VI spawned the murderous culture of French politics that surrounded his monarchy. His chronic inability to lead France evolved into a political crisis that metastasized into a full-blown civil war between the Armagnacs and Burgundians. Charles's immediate successor was his eighteen-year-old son, Louis of Guyenne (1397–1415), who was barely able to govern on behalf of his father, let alone take an army into the field against the English. Henry would need to mobilize his nation quickly and make a daring move if he were to take full advantage of the historic opportunities that had been placed before him.

Even as he meticulously prepared his coming invasion of France (set for early August 1415), Henry V still publicly parleyed and postured with an embassy from the French court that had come to negotiate with the king one last time to prevent the war that Henry had already decided was inevitable (June 1415). For several months, delegations from England and France had crossed the Channel with proposals and counter-proposals that would keep the peace and prevent future bloodshed. Despite his public pursuit of diplomacy, Henry V had resolved to go to war, especially since the political polarity in France and the chaos in the Valois court gave him a window of opportunity that would soon close. In fact, in February of 1415, the warring Armagnacs and Burgundians had agreed to an uneasy truce, fearing that the English would launch a full-scale invasion. Massive preparations for war began in the fall of 1414, and by the spring of 1415, the vast fleet of ships and the army of knights, archers, and laborers who would build and maintain the infrastructure of the English expeditionary force began to take shape.

The Dauphin, Louis of Guyenne, had recently outmaneuvered his nemesis, the Duke of Burgundy, John the Fearless, who already had extensive contact with Henry V and was attempting to forge some sort of alliance. An embassy from Charles VI's court was sent to England for one more attempt to prevent an invasion and to counter the interference of John the Fearless. The early fifteenth-century English cleric and chronicler John Streeche reports that Louis personally offended Henry's manhood and honor by offering to send him a gift of tennis balls with which to play instead of threatening war against the Valois king.[12] This provocation is dramatically presented in the opening scenes of Shakespeare's play, with the delivery of a full box of balls to the king. Henry's angry response to the Dauphin's gift (*Henry V*, 1.2.281–88) is legendary:

> And tell the pleasant Prince this mock of his
> Hath turned his balls to gunstones, and his soul
> Shall stand sore charged for the wasteful vengeance
> That shall fly from them—for many a thousand widows
> Shall this his mock mock out their dear husbands,
> Mock mothers from their sons, mock castles down;

Three. The Sins of the Father

Ay, some are yet ungotten and unborn
That shall have cause to curse the Dauphin's scorn.[13]

Historians continue to be divided over the truthfulness of this humiliating gesture. If Louis wanted to avert a war, why would he offer such an egregious insult to Henry? Barker sees this incident as pure English propaganda, arguing that the young Dauphin was not directly involved in these negotiations. As far as the offer of tennis balls, she declares: "This simply did not happen."[14] Sumption also refers to this story as "a fable."[15] On the other hand, Curry has no doubt of this tradition's authenticity. In one of her studies of the Battle of Agincourt she declares: "The story of the dauphin sending a gift of tennis balls to Henry in the spring of 1414 or 15 is almost certainly true and was intended as an insult."[16] But in her short biography of Henry, she believes that such an exchange actually took place in Paris, when the French ambassadors made a cutting remark to an English delegation. In whatever form the "tennis ball incident" transpired, Curry is quick to note that "it reflects Henry's poor international reputation in the early stages of his reign. The French did not take him seriously."[17] Mortimer notes that the incident is mentioned in a number of contemporary English sources and that there might be a kernel of truth to it. Some incident might have taken place in Paris, among the French and English ambassadors, where an offhand remark was made that "may have been of minor interest, of no consequence—but which nevertheless deeply injured [Henry's] pride."[18] After the surrender of Harfleur, Henry famously challenged the Dauphin Louis to a single trial by combat to end the war and determine to whom the crown of France should ultimately go. The fact that Henry offered such a challenge to his rival lends some credence to the story of the taunt with tennis balls. The Dauphin offered no response.[19]

In June of 1415, a French delegation arrived in Winchester and met with the English king at Wolvesey Castle.[20] Henry had more or less resolved on an invasion, perhaps with an eye to winning the major territorial concessions to which no previous embassy had agreed. His *casus belli*—supported with a plethora of ancient documents and legal rulings, cloaked with biblical language—was his right of succession to the French crown. But it is also possible that at this stage of his preparations for war, his claim was a pretext for vast territorial conquest and plunder. The French soon learned that Henry's exorbitant territorial demands, involving direct English sovereignty over the better part of their country, was an impossible bar to reach. Henry might have cynically made such unrealistic demands precisely for the purpose of having them rejected, thereby having a solid case for war.[21]

After several tense meetings over the course of a several days, Henry presided over one of his famous staged public gatherings, impeccably arrayed in a long robe of gold cloth, seated on his throne (but not wearing his crown) and flanked by ecclesiastical and knightly dignitaries. The king had entrusted archbishop of Canterbury, Henry Chichele (1364–1443), with the task of informing the French of his resolution to reject their proposals and to invade France and rightfully take by force what was his. Chichele spoke in Latin and then gave copies of his speech to the French embassy.[22]

The Burgundian chronicler Enguerrand de Monstrelet (c. 1400–53) narrates a series of back-and-forth meetings that demonstrate the intransigence of Henry when it came to his bold claim to the French throne. When it was clear that the diplomatic niceties had become pointless, archbishop of Bourges Guillaume Boisratier (r. 1409–21), the senior diplomat among the French, rebuked Henry for threatening so much bloodshed among Christians. The French, he said, made their generous offers not out of fear of the English but out of their love for peace. Boisratier declared that Henry would either be captured or killed if he invaded France.[23]

According to a much later and questionable chronicle tradition, Boisratier eventually lost his patience with Henry and asked for permission to address him in French. Henry agreed and as the young king sat at a distance on his throne, the French cleric tore open the old wounds of the Lancastrian dynasty afresh. He declared: "My lord, our sovereign lord [Charles VI] is the true King of France and you have no right to any of these things that you claim…. Our sovereign lord could never safely make a treaty with you anyway, for you are no King even in England but merely one claimant jostling for position with the true heirs of the late King Richard."[24]

That the French archbishop subjected Henry to this humiliating public diatribe, with allusions now to *two usurpations* by the Lancastrians, seems a bit far-fetched. But whatever really happened, Henry ended the negotiations after the French final offer, dismissed the delegation, and soon left for London. The die had been cast and Henry would have to prove the legitimacy of his claim to the crowns of both England and France on the battlefield. In early July, Henry officially declared war on France, arguing that he had been compelled to act against "rebels" who denied him "justice" (his claim to the crown). The anonymous cleric who accompanied Henry on his Agincourt campaign also notes in the *Gesta Henrici Quinti*, or *The Deeds of Henry V*, that the king formally notified the Holy Roman Emperor-elect, Sigismund of Luxembourg, and the clerics assembled at the Council of Constance of his intention to wage war for his just rights.[25] Despite the numerous risks involved with a full-fledged invasion of Normandy, Henry wanted the world to know of his intent, and might have wanted as large an audience as possible for his forthcoming trial by combat. He must have believed that he would be victorious.

The sins of the father, so cuttingly highlighted by Archbishop Boisratier, undoubtedly fueled the son's passion for an invasion of France where he could subject himself to the *Judicium Dei*, or the Judgment of God, on the battlefield. His lopsided victory at Agincourt would soon humiliate his French detractors and become a template for the validation of his reign and the legitimacy of the Lancastrian dynasty. It would also dramatically revive the mythos of English invincibility in the Hundred Years War. The invasion of France by Henry, predicated on his claim to his rightful inheritance and the justice of his cause, might have originated as a political ploy to extort some sort of vast territorial concessions and a marriage alliance from the Valois court. While it appears that Henry truly believed that his cause was just when he met with the French embassy on the eve of his invasion, after Agincourt he was unshakeable in his conviction that he was entitled to the French crown, even as he kept open the possibility of renouncing it for full English sovereignty over large swaths of territory in the west and south of France.[26]

The meticulous planning of his expeditions and the deprivations that he was personally willing to suffer and impose on his men in his successive campaigns demonstrate that Henry would endure any hardship and spend any amount of money to implement his grand plans. (His incessant warfare in effect bankrupted the English government.) He was also disposed to shedding rivers of blood and inflicting untold sufferings and death on increasingly larger numbers of the civilian population of France. Henry's ruthlessness on and off the battlefield was often justified, in his own words, by a divine sanction. When the famed Dominican preacher St. Vincent of Ferrer (1350–1419) chastised him in a sermon for the violence he did to the French during his siege of Rouen, he famously retorted: "I am the scourge of God, sent to punish the people of God for their synns."[27] The suffering of the French was their just punishment for the denial of his right to the throne and the sinfulness and treachery of the French ruling class. His victory at Agincourt was so stunning and complete that even the French interpreted their loss along similar lines: it was God's just punishment for the moral depravity and sinful pride of the French aristocracy.

Atonement and Reformation

Henry V's relationship with the Church also posed great challenges to his authority early in his reign. The new king not only inherited the political stigma of usurpation and regicide, but also the heavy baggage of his father's execution of an archbishop after a botched rebellion in the north of England. In May of 1405, the old Percy alliance against Henry IV had been revived and now included his formerly exiled nemesis, Thomas Mowbray. One unlikely participant in the uprising was the pious and scholarly archbishop of York, Thomas Scrope (c. 1350–1405).[28] Scrope had little experience in power politics and more than likely saw himself as a mediator between Henry IV and the newly revived rebel coalition. His public rhetoric in the form of a blistering sermon denouncing the corruption of the Lancastrian government fueled the passion of the rebels and inspired a call to arms and mass mobilization of even more rebels. He had crossed the line into treasonous conduct.[29]

But the rebellion collapsed almost as soon as it had begun. When Scrope and Mowbray left York at the head of a large army, they encountered the Lancastrian force of the Earl of Westmoreland, sent to quell the uprising. They were tricked into a parley with the earl, who implied that the grievances of the northern rebels would be studied for an appropriate remedy. After giving the order to dismiss their rebellious troops, Scrope and Mowbray were arrested. The king's justice was swift and brutal. The rebel leaders were summarily sentenced to death by Henry IV and beheaded shortly thereafter. The protests of the other English primate, archbishop of Canterbury Thomas Arundel (1353–1414), came to nothing. Henry deceived him into thinking he would consider his request when in fact he had Scrope executed before Arundel was even aware of the sentence being carried out.

Scrope's death, for "the laws and good government of England," as one contemporary source has him declare as his last words, blackened the Lancastrian monarchy in a manner that was reminiscent of the most famous clerical martyrdom of medieval England, the murder of archbishop of Canterbury St. Thomas Becket (1172), supposedly at the behest of Henry II (r. 1154–89).[30] Becket, who refused to hand clerics over to the king's secular courts for criminal prosecution, paid with his life for the core principle of the papal reformers of the eleventh and twelfth century: the separation of priestly authority and secular power. In commenting on Henry IV's handling of the Scrope affair, Given-Wilson observes: "His [Scrope's] afterlife as a miracle-worker began almost immediately, and some believed that soon after this Henry contracted leprosy. Never before had an English king dared to execute a bishop, let alone an archbishop."[31] While Henry IV had, in the short run, thwarted any further attempts at rebellion in the north, the execution of Scrope had a toxic afterlife: "The result was a propaganda coup for Henry's opponents—already a regicide, this was a king who executed archbishops."[32] Scrope's execution also coincided with a very painful manifestation of an increasingly debilitating skin disease that would afflict Henry until he died. His critics undoubtedly saw this as divine retribution for the unprecedented killing of a high-ranking prelate, in addition to the murder of a king.

In his quest to assert his legitimate authority as a new king, Henry V was burdened with allegations of Lancastrian regicide and the martyrdom of a high-ranking English prelate. Henry was responsible for a number of pious benefactions that could be viewed as costly expiation rituals for these "crimes." Certainly the proper burial of Richard II counts as one. So too do the handsome sums of money that Henry spent in religious benefaction: the foundation or maintenance of chantries and the endowment of austere religious houses.[33] At the top of that list was the Brigittine Abbey of Syon, founded in February of 1415, at the very time that he was preparing for his invasion of Normandy to claim the French crown.[34] Henry even saw an express linkage between his foundation of Syon and his Agincourt campaign. As Nancy Bradley Warren notes, when he drafted his first will before leaving England (July 1415), he appealed to the patronage of St. Bridget (Birgitta) by name, bequeathing a hefty sum of money to the nuns of Syon for the construction of their convent.[35]

The Brigittine Order was founded by St. Bridget of Sweden (1303–73), a widowed mother of eight who devoted herself to a life of prayer and service to others after her husband's untimely death. She eventually established a new order of female and male religious, the Order of the Most Holy Savior—better known as the Brigittines—and spent most of her life in Rome, where she died just five years before the start of the Great Schism (1378–1417). Bridget was also a mystic and visionary who reported that she began to receive religious apparitions at the age of ten.

The English seized upon some of her adult revelations in the early fifteenth century and interpreted them as promoting the justice of the English claim to the French crown. Two such revelations became part of the official English propaganda campaign to justify the tenacity of the English claim to the throne of France, going back to the reign of Edward III (r. 1327–77), whose mother Isabella (1295–1358) was the daughter of the Capetian king of France, Philip IV (r. 1285–1314). These prophecies, recorded in the fourth book (chapters 104 and 105) of her celestial visions, the *Liber Caelestis*, were vigorously promoted by the English as a divinely sanctioned "peace through marriage" plan that supported the Lancastrian claim to the crown of France.[36] In a prophecy dated 1345, titled "A Proposal for Peace between England and France," St. Bridget records Christ's declaration: "If these two kings of France and England wish to have peace, I shall give lasting peace to them. However, given that one of the kings has a just claim, I would have peace brought about by means of a marriage. In this way the kingdom can attain a legitimate successor."[37] St. Bridget was thus deployed with great effect in English propaganda in the final stages of Henry V's invasion preparation. She became, along with St. George, an "archetypically English saint."[38]

Henry V's costly Brigittine foundation was both intercessory and expiatory. And it honored a pledge made by his father Henry IV that was never fulfilled. The Roman pope of the Great Schism, Gregory XII (r. 1406–15), accepted the king's version of the events that led to the rebellious Archbishop Scrope's execution. Henry was officially exonerated for this act in a papal bull, but as a consequence of this ruling, he had supposedly promised to endow three monasteries to expiate the archbishop's blood, a task left to his successor and son.[39] Henry V was only able to complete two of these foundations: the Brigittine monastery of Syon and the Carthusian monastery of Bethlehem at Sheen. The third endowment, of a Celestine monastery of Benedictine monks—so named after the founder of the order, the ascetical Pope Celestine V (r. 1294)—was barely established before Henry's first Norman campaign. According to David Knowles, it foundered over financial questions and then was suppressed in the summer of 1415, since it was a French monastic community that could not be sustained in the generally hostile environment towards France that now gripped England.[40]

The original location of the Abbey of Syon (probably due west of the royal manor of Sheen, on the left bank of the Thames) can also be judged as expiatory since it was situated in a place closely affiliated with Richard II and his beloved first wife, Anne of Bohemia. It was there that she died of the plague in 1394. After Anne's unexpected death, a grief-stricken Richard had the manor leveled. Henry had it rebuilt and founded a Carthusian monastery there; the abandoned Celestine monastic foundation also would have been situated in close proximity.[41] During the reign of Henry VI, the nuns of Syon successfully petitioned the king (c. 1431) to move the monastery to a new location farther downstream, on the opposite side of the Thames River. They claimed that the original site was too small and too damp.[42] It became one of the wealthiest monastic foundations in England before its assets were confiscated during the reign of Henry VIII.

Vale describes Henry's pious benefactions, especially the establishment of new monasteries, as the formation of a "'gigantic power-house of prayer' for the Lancastrian dynasty, creating a sort of 'spiritual royal household.'"[43] There is considerable evidence in Henry V's wills and his endowment of chantries that he sincerely viewed these pious donations as having tremendous *intercessory* value in supporting his reign and achieving victory in his war in France. But as Warren perceptively argues, the *expiatory* benefit was equally important in the mind of Henry. In choosing the original site of Syon Abbey, "Henry V symbolically forged a connection with Richard II, eliding his father Henry IV's usurpation of the throne."[44] But despite his lavish obsequies and his costly public campaign of atonement, no one would ever forget the original sin of his father.

Henry V's impact on the Anglo-Norman Church went well beyond pious devotions and expiatory rituals. At a bureaucratic and institutional level, he in effect ran a proto-Anglican Church, a century before the Reformation radically configured the ecclesial structures of England. His express approval was required for all major ecclesiastical appointments in his English and Lancastrian Norman realms. He effectively restrained the power of the higher clergy, going so far as to prevent his loyal servant and uncle (formerly Lord Chancellor) Henry Beaufort, bishop of Lincoln and Winchester, from receiving a cardinal's hat from Pope Martin V. Beaufort had wrongly assumed he could accept his elevation to the college of cardinals without getting Henry's permission.[45] But Henry did not want a papal envoy interfering in the business of the English government and quietly stopped the appointment. Beaufort eventually obtained his red hat four years after Henry died.

Henry took great interest in the quality of religious life in the many monastic foundations that had played such an essential role in the religious culture of England throughout the Middle Ages. The monastic chronicler Thomas Walsingham notes that Henry was alarmed by the reports he received of the decline in discipline in some of these monasteries. He ordered a meeting of Benedictine monks at Westminster, not long before he died. At this gathering of several hundred monks, the king urged the Benedictines to return to strict observance of their rule, while calling on them to undertake serious reform:

> [T]he king himself spoke to them about the religious life lived by the monks in olden days which had led to his predecessors and others showing their devotion by founding and endowing monasteries, and about the failure of men of his own day to show a similar devotion. He put before them certain matters which they were to put right and he earnestly pleaded with them to return to their former way of life and to pray without ceasing for himself and the well-being of his kingdom and of the church.[46]

The scandal of the Great Schism, with the specter of two and then three rival popes claiming control over the Church, also played its part in solidifying his control over the English Church. In the troubled reign of Richard II and at the height of the papal Schism, Parliament passed the Statute of Praemunire (1393) to prevent appeals to the papal curia against the ruling of an English court.[47] The legal authority of the papacy in England was now subject to the king's veto power; if appeals to the papacy were determined to be in violation of English law, they were null and void. By the end of his reign, Henry V's rigid control of the English and Norman Church presaged some of the components of his successor Henry VIII's ecclesiology. Henry VIII would invoke Praemunire to break with Rome and invest himself with the administrative functions of the papacy in his realm, when Parliament passed the Act of Supremacy (1534).

Preceded by the Avignon Papacy, which eroded the reputation of the papacy, the Great Schism created an outright crisis of authority that festered in various forms until the sixteenth-century Reformation. The legitimate authority of ecclesiastical powers—beginning with the head of the Church itself, when there were three popes essentially governing three rival "churches"—created a perfect opportunity for an ambitious man like Henry V to take advantage of the new realities of church-state relationships. The Hundred Years War, in its various phases, helped to exacerbate this problem, with conflicting national allegiances to different popes who had excommunicated each other. The popes also divided the clerical establishment of prelates and abbots, as well as the Christian intelligentsia of theologians, canonists, and spiritual writers.

Henry's war in Normandy caused its own crisis of authority for the ecclesiastical hierarchy of the French Church. The capture of cities that were episcopal sees, or the capture of territories that housed large religious foundations, drew the immediate attention of the king as he deposed, exiled, and replaced clerics who refused to swear fealty to him for the temporalities of those choice clerical offices. It is fair to say that despite Henry V's attention to the details of maintaining loyal clerics or deposing Dauphinists in his Norman realm, his policy must have put a serious strain on the morale of the Norman clergy and caused lingering tension between those who were rewarded for their loyalty and those who were dispossessed. The same could be said for the bloody chaos in the French Church during the Armagnac and Burgundian civil war that preceded Henry's conquests.

Henry's coronation was no guarantee of a successful reign, nor did it automatically vest him with the authority of a legitimate ruler. But despite the cloud of legitimacy that hovered over Henry's accession, he was considered by the majority of his subjects to be the rightful king of England. He could summon Parliaments, issue writs, adjudicate legal disputes that fell within his prerogative, and levy and command troops for his many military campaigns. He had also spent many years, despite his strained relationship with his father, preparing to be king. After his coronation, he tirelessly pursued the restoration of the English monarchy and the revival of English nationalism. His victory at Agincourt and his conquest of Normandy would provide evidence to his subjects that God favored both his monarchy and his military campaigns.

FOUR

Contracting with God
for Holy War

Penance and Oblations

The anonymous "Agincourt Carol," composed shortly after the battle that it commemorates, rejoices in Henry's victory over the French with sacral language and a lively melody that elevates him to a special place reserved for God's holiest warriors. When we study Henry's conception of holy war, one line in particular is worth pondering:

> *Then went him forth our King comely;*
> *In Agincourt field he fought manly;*
> *Through grace of God most marvelously*
> *He hath both field and victory;*
> Deo gracias, Anglia redde pro victoria[1]
> [Give thanks, England, to God for victory]

The "Agincourt Carol" notes that Henry fought with the "grace of God." Therefore, his success did not simply derive from his courage, which the carol celebrates, and his tactical genius, which modern military historians admire. Henry's asceticism and personal piety, and the discipline that he enforced on his men were all part of a contractual agreement with God to effect a good outcome in his clash of arms with his enemies. Arrayed for battle in the rain-soaked fields of Agincourt, Henry faced the possibility of either glorious victory or the shame of defeat and even his own death. In the *Gesta Henrici Quinti*, or *The Deeds of Henry V*, the anonymous English cleric who was with Henry that day declares that the king made his soldiers confess their sins before their encounter with the enemy.[2] As the *Gesta* recalls: "And then every man who had not previously cleansed his conscience by confession, put on the armour of penitence; and there was no shortage then save only one of priests."[3] The *Liber Metricus de Henrico Quinto*, or *The Metrical Life of Henry the Fifth* (c. 1418), of the contemporary English monastic chronicler Thomas Elmham confirms this event.[4] Elmham also notes that Henry's men "all made true confession to God. There was a shortage of priests, so many confessed to each other."[5] On the day of the battle, the author of the *Gesta* also remembers that Henry only stepped onto the battlefield "after offering praises to God and hearing Masses."[6] If the dispirited forces that Henry rallied were to have any chance of victory, they would also have to engage in rituals of penance and forms of military asceticism that he himself practiced and promoted with great vigor.

Henry's personal conduct as a holy warrior obviously paid great dividends at Agincourt and the battle became a paradigmatic moment for his kingship, his war in France and the identity of his nation. More than any other event of his reign, it would create his enduring legend as God's warrior king. And this great victory would be attributed to divine intervention, built in part on the military equivalent of the Catholic theology of good works. As king and warrior, Henry was actively engaged in forms of piety whereby one could solicit God's blessings and tip the scales of history through one's zealous asceticism and religious devotion.

There is no doubt that in his bearing, discipline, daily religious rituals, and benefaction of religious institutions Henry lived up to his reputation as the model of Christian kingship described by Thomas Walsingham (1376–1422), when he eulogized him after his untimely death.[7] But it is equally true that the king's "personal" piety—which was often conspicuously displayed or recounted by his literary agents—was part of a much broader enterprise: Henry's conscious attempt to expiate the "sins of his father" and to put to rest the slander of Lancastrian usurpation, regicide, and sacrilege. The killing of an anointed king and his hasty burial still scarred the national memory at the outset of his own reign. The execution of the archbishop of York Thomas Scrope (c. 1350–1405) by Henry IV for his role in a failed, treasonous rebellion remained an open wound in the consciousness of the ecclesiastical and political elite. Scrope's execution even required the solicitation of a papal pardon by Henry's father. When this was granted by the Roman pope of the Great Schism, Gregory XII (r. 1406–15), the elder Henry promised that he would establish religious foundations for the repose of Scrope's soul.[8] Despite the deeply troubling events that preceded them, Henry V's elaborate rituals of atonement were quite conventional for someone of his social rank. Henry exhumed the body of Richard II at great expense and provided him with a proper and costly burial. He also endowed Brigittine monasteries and established chantries to create a spiritual bank account for the souls of departed predecessors as well as his own.[9]

Shakespeare's *Henry V* vividly captures this ethos of expiation and validation, while also showcasing the contractual theology of warfare that Henry personified. In Shakespeare's presentation, the miraculous victory at Agincourt validates Henry's monarchy in England and the justice of his cause in France. But before he wins this figurative trial by ordeal, Shakespeare has the king deep in prayer on the eve of battle, beseeching God to look with favor upon his prayers and monuments of expiation for the crime of Richard's death (*Henry V*, 4.1.281–93). These oblations and petitions are, in effect, a sacred bartering ritual with God, a reminder of Henry's richly endowed religious foundations that corresponded with his departure for France in 1415:

> O not today, think not upon the fault
> My father made in compassing the crown.
> I Richard's body have interred new,
> And on it have bestowed more contrite tears
> Than from it issued forced drops of blood.
> Five hundred poor have I in yearly pay
> Who twice a day their withered hands hold up
> Toward heaven to pardon blood. And I have built
> Two chantries, where the sad and solemn priests
> Sing still for Richard's soul. More will I do.
> Though all that I can do is nothing worth,
> Since that my penitence comes after ill.
> Imploring pardon.[10]

Liturgical Quid Pro Quo

The pious oblations described by Shakespeare are consistent with the historical record of Henry's religious activities. They are all well documented in a wide range of contemporary sources, offering unmistakable examples of the intercessory and expiatory motives that fueled the king's pious benefactions. After his coronation, Henry was on the whole rigid and predictable in his performance of his devotions and rituals. His mechanistic forms of piety—founding monasteries, endowing chantries, stockpiling intercessory prayers—reflect the widespread spiritual mercantilism of fourteenth- and fifteenth-century England that gave priority to mindful recollection of death and the creation of a treasury of grace for the afterlife. Mindfulness about one's mortality had deep roots in the early Christian faith. As the ancient saying admonished medieval Christians, *memento mori*: "remember you will die." Aside from the harsh circumstances of everyday life, successive waves of the bubonic plague epidemic ensured that death was never that far from anyone's mind in the early fifteenth century.

Because of this deeply rooted culture of "remembering death," by Henry's time intercessory prayer for oneself or for departed loved ones had reached a fever pitch. At the center of this enterprise was the chantry priest, whose primary and often sole function was to "chant masses" for the dead. He often had no other real pastoral care, hence the term "sinecure" to describe his religious life (from the Latin phrase *sine cura animarum*, or a post "without the care of souls" attached). The chantry priest symbolized one of the basic tenets of medieval Christian faith: that life in this world was lived in anticipation and contemplation of the afterlife, where damnation, purgatory or heaven awaited the deceased. The practice of clerics celebrating untold masses for the dead, from potentates to peasants, was therefore woven into the fabric of the liturgical life of the medieval Latin Church.

This intercessory function of the clergy, for the spiritual health of the king and his countrymen, was also reflected in Henry's attempt to reform the Benedictine monks of his realm shortly before he died. The monastic chronicler Thomas Walsingham notes that Henry called hundreds of monks to a meeting at Westminster Abbey in 1422. The king urged them to return to the strict observance of their rule, precisely for the benefit of their intercessory prayers. Walsingham says that Henry "put before them certain matters which they were to put right and he earnestly pleaded with them to return to their former way of life and to pray without ceasing for himself and the well-being of his kingdom and of the church."[11] In reflecting on the king's piety, monastic historian David Knowles observes: "Henry's reliance upon the intercessory prayer of the monks and his lively sense of the *quid pro quo* implicit in benefactions to religious is wholly in keeping with other utterances of his."[12]

Of all the forms of prayer that existed in the late medieval Church, including the canonical hours of cathedral clergy or the divine office of monks, the mass was the centerpiece of the celebration of the mystery of Christian salvation.[13] On any given day, the cathedrals, monasteries, and parish churches of Henry V's realm were teeming with vested clerics offering the holy sacrifice of the altar for both the living and the dead. For the dead, this sacrificial rite helped expedite their passage from purgatory to heaven. In the cathedrals and abbeys of England, multiple altars would simultaneously be used on a daily basis. This stock form of liturgical piety— the mass production of intercessory rituals of expiation and salvation— remained a constant in England until Henry V's successor Henry VIII

(r. 1509–47) extinguished the flames of purgatory. In his break with Rome, the Tudor king suppressed the monastic foundations of England through acts of Parliament (Acts for the Dissolution of Monasteries in 1536 and 1539), thereby ending this long and lucrative tradition of intercessory prayer, filling the king's coffers with vast sums of money.

While placing Henry V squarely within this bustling liturgical activity of late medieval England, Vale also argues that his piety was distinguished by the cultivation of a private devotional life, evidenced by his fine collection of religious books, his numerous charitable works, and his exercise of a "disciplined conscience."[14] In assessing the depth of Henry's religious devotion, Vale takes his cue from the anonymous author who accompanied Henry on his Agincourt campaign. In the *Gesta*, or *The Deeds of Henry V*, the English cleric declares that from the start of his reign, "so fervently had he been devoted to the hearing of divine praises and to his own private prayers that, once he had begun them, there was not anyone, even from amongst his nobles and magnates, who was able, by conversation however brief, at any time to interrupt them."[15]

By this account, Henry's multiple acts of benefaction were the outward expression of a deep, inward piety. In documenting his establishment of austere religious foundations, charitable works of almsgiving, and reform programs for the Church, Vale goes so far as to declare that Henry should be compared to the sainted king of France, Louis IX (r. 1226–70). He believes that in "some respects," Henry can be seen as an English equivalent to Louis IX: "the intensity of their personal devotion, their fervent promotion and lavish endowment of the more ascetic religious orders, and their espousal of a higher cause than conflict between Christians suggest certain affinities between the two men."[16]

While the overall sincerity of Henry's religious convictions might have been authentic, his public performance of his role as Christian king cannot be detached from his carefully calculated public relations campaign to revitalize and support the Lancastrian claim to the crown and to draw the nation closer into bonds of obedience, loyalty, and devotion to the new king. Relying on the anonymous Lancastrian propagandist who wrote the *Gesta* and taking what he says about Henry's piety at face value risks ignoring the political dimensions of his religious displays and their promotion by his acolytes. In her meticulous analysis of Henry's royal chapel, McHardy insists that "the king's liturgical observance and spiritual support shaded into propaganda, because the private Christian was inseparable from the public ruler."[17] In commenting on the superb quality of Henry's liturgical composers and the highly skilled singers of his chapel, McHardy sees the propaganda value of this high level of performance, calling his chapel "a mobile advertisement of his righteousness, magnificence and his exquisite and adventurous taste."[18]

With Henry, there was always more than meets the eye; his religion was political and his politics were religious. The principal audience of the *Gesta* was undoubtedly the clerical intelligentsia in England as well as the clerical and political elite that participated in the great ecumenical Council of Constance (1414–18). Its author therefore did his utmost to emphasize the piety of the English king, his personal righteousness, and the justice of his war in France by highlighting his consistent and ostentatious displays of religiosity. Giving Richard II a proper burial, establishing costly religious foundations, and waging war as an exemplary Christian knight were all part of a master plan that required the intellect, tenacity, and stamina that the new monarch possessed in abundance. And his objectives were as much political as they were religious. Henry was engaged in very concrete and public forms of devotion or "good works" that built up his reputation among his contemporaries and future generations in his realm.[19]

As was the case with the majority of the members of the warrior class of his day, Henry's was largely a religion of "doing" good works through pious benefaction, not primarily of contemplative reflection on a belief system such as the piety promoted by the *Devotio Moderna*, or the Brothers and Sisters of the Common Life.[20] Henry's religious activity focused on "doing enough, and more" to keep his equilibrium with God and to build up a treasury of merit that could be tapped in times of great danger and duress.[21] The *Gesta* tells us that Henry heard three different masses on the day of the Battle of Agincourt; here the mass is perceived as a spiritual talisman or insurance policy in the face of death by combat.[22] The author of the *Gesta* sat atop a horse with the king's baggage while the battle was raging. He reports that Henry had made provision for the clergy to be with the baggage, forming a "clerical militia," as they offered prayers for his protection and success:

> And then we who have been assigned to the clerical militia and were watching fell upon our faces in prayer before the great mercy-seat of God, crying out aloud in bitterness of spirit that God might even remember us and the crown of England and, by the grace of his supreme bounty, deliver us from the iron furnace and the terrible death which menaced us. Nor was God unmindful of the multitude of prayers and supplications being made in England, by which, as it is devoutly believed, our men soon regained their strength and, valiantly resisting, pushed back the enemy until they had recovered the ground that had been lost.[23]

In Henry's mind, the mass production of good works, pious benefactions, and sustained intercessory prayer would build a protective aura around the religious philanthropist who risks injury or death every time he walks onto the battlefield.

While he was campaigning in the field, Henry also made sure that he had access to a "traveling church," where confessions could be heard and masses celebrated on a daily basis for himself and his men. McHardy has done a detailed analysis of Henry's clerical entourage while he waged war in Normandy, identifying roughly fifty clerics who accompanied him in his first expedition. While their number may seem small in relation to the thousands of soldiers and laborers who provided the vital military infrastructure for his war in France, McHardy notes that these men "were deeply valued by the king"; they also provided "liturgical drama and spiritual succor to the royal household."[24] Because the English delegation had played a critical role in the election of the Roman Pope Martin V (r. 1417–31) at the Council of Constance, the new pope was only too happy to oblige Henry with his request for special clerical and liturgical privileges in times of war. Martin V granted him the right to use portable altars, to celebrate mass at times that were not allowed by canon law (e.g., before daylight or in places that were under interdict), and to translate relics from one church to another.[25]

Memento Mori

By the time he invaded France in the summer of 1415, Henry had trained for war most of his life and was keenly aware of the serious risk to life and limb on the medieval battlefield. There is little doubt that Henry's near-death experience at the Battle of Shrewsbury (July 21, 1403), when he was only sixteen years old, was a defining moment of his life; it probably was never very far from his mind. In that perilous moment, an arrow struck him in the face, giving him an injury that could have easily killed him. The pain Henry endured when he was wounded and the traumatic procedure he had to undergo to remove the arrow lodged deep in his face might have forced him to contemplate his mortality in ways that put him well beyond his years.

The scar on his face and the possibility of lasting neurological damage were a personal *memento mori* with which Henry lived every day of his life. He scrupulously revised his last will and testament on each of the three occasions that he left England to fight in France. Despite his confidence in his military abilities and his ironclad belief in the justice of his war, Henry knew that he was a mortal man who could be killed outright or could succumb to a host of diseases that accompanied any medieval army on campaign. As it turned out, such fears were not unfounded, since he died of dysentery while campaigning in France, just seven years after his victory at Agincourt.[26]

Henry was twenty-nine—only a year older than his mother, Mary de Bohun, when she died after childbirth—when he composed the first version of his last will and testament. It remains one of the best sources for understanding his overall religious outlook. Drawn up shortly before he embarked on his first campaign to Normandy (July 1415), Henry revised his will two more times when he crossed the Channel at the head of an English army. The last version (June 1421), along with the codicils Henry dictated on his deathbed in France (August 1422), superseded his first will.[27] But on the whole, the provisions for religious benefaction for the repose of his soul are consistent across all versions of the text. In the 1415 will, he calls himself "Henry, by the grace of God, King of England and France, and Lord of Ireland," and proceeds to set forth the arrangements for his funeral and the execution of his estate. [28]

In these simple documents, Henry reflects on his own mortality and his soul's passage into eternity. His understanding of Christian faith and piety at its most basic level is therefore brought into full view. Given that he had already had a near-death experience in his first deployment in a pitched battle, there is nothing *pro forma* about the original text, nor can we doubt the sincerity of his belief that he could build a spiritual treasury from which to draw in the afterlife if he endowed enough chantries for his soul and bequeathed enough money for the maintenance of the religious houses that he had founded.

Composed in Latin but amended in English and signed with his own hand, Henry's will is rightly characterized by Vale as a rare window into the mind of a powerful man who spoke few, if any, autobiographical words:

> The declared wishes of a testator may reveal much about them. Especially at times in history when people rarely speak to us in their own voices, the words recorded in their wills and testaments, it has been said "deserve the closest scrutiny." In the later Middle Ages, disclosure of their last wishes can enable us to come closer to the beliefs, intentions and preoccupations of individuals than any other source.[29]

Henry's will is striking for its clarity and specificity. He clearly places his money, so to speak, on betting that the mass production of intercessory prayers will provide the greatest aid to his immortal soul. For modern observers, the quantity of masses Henry endowed is astounding: in all, twenty thousand masses were to be sung for him when he died.[30] In addition, each monk of Westminster Abbey was to celebrate three daily masses for the king, in perpetuity, as he lay entombed among the relics of King Edward the Confessor's chapel. Henry also left a sizeable sum of money to the two monastic foundations he had established on the eve of his Agincourt campaign: the Brigittine foundation of Syon Abbey and the Carthusian monastery of Bethlehem at Sheen.[31]

Henry not only transacted religious business for the afterlife, but also regularly availed himself of the grace of the sacraments in this life, especially the Eucharist. The king was known among his contemporaries for his active participation in the sacramental life of the Church. He was well remembered for devoutly receiving communion on a regular basis at a time when "seeing" the elevated host at mass or seeing it displayed in a monstrance was widely accepted as a substitute for physical reception of the Body of Christ. In that sense, his Eucharistic devotion could be considered noteworthy.

The thirteenth-century practice of elevating the host at the moment of consecration and its reservation in a tabernacle had led to the objectification of the Eucharist as a sacred object of devotion among the laity. As Caroline Walker Bynum notes, elevation at the moment of consecration was understood by the laity as a "second sacrament." Even though the Fourth Lateran Council (1215) had produced a dogmatic definition of the real presence of Christ in the consecrated bread and wine (transubstantiation), it only required communion once per year for the laity. For the great majority of men and women in Western Christendom, "seeing" the host became an acceptable form of "receiving" it.[32] By the end of the thirteenth century, the Eucharist had been reduced to a sacred *object*, the sacred relic *par excellence* of Christ's body and blood, to be reverenced and adored from a distance by faithful Christians.[33]

There is no doubt that Henry had great reverence for the consecrated host, but he also went well beyond viewing it from a distance as a sacred relic of Christ, by his regular reception of communion, and his ingestion of the salvific grace of Christ's real presence. Interestingly, on the day of the Battle of Agincourt Henry ordered his men to kneel with him and to kiss the ground and place a morsel of earth in their mouths, creating a communion service of sorts. As Barker observes, "This extraordinary ritual combined elements of both the Last Supper and its commemoration.... Physical death and spiritual salvation were thus presented in a single act."[34]

At end of the Middle Ages, the consecrated host was often reserved and carried in a pyx (a small metal case) to be administered to faithful Christians who might be dying or too ill to attend church. The pyx's contact with the transubstantiated body of Christ would also make the container itself a sacred vessel, even when empty. Henry showed great reverence for these liturgical artifacts for both religious and political reasons and he expressly forbade his men from absconding with any such objects while campaigning in France. He feared that he would incur the wrath of God if his men were guilty of sacrilege; he also did not come to France as a "conqueror" of foreign soil but as the true king of the people who rebelled against him. It would therefore be foolhardy to allow his men to despoil *his own* churches and religious foundations in Normandy.

In the ordinances that he issued for his army when he invaded Normandy, the king threatened the death penalty for anyone who desecrated a church or any holy object. According to the testimony of the English cleric who accompanied him in the *Gesta*, Henry summarily sentenced to death by hanging one of his archers who had stolen a pyx from a church in Normandy. Thinking it was made of gold, when it was actually made of copper gilt, the soldier had hidden it in his sleeve. Henry had the pyx with the host returned to the church from which it was stolen and hanged the culprit from a tree in full view of his men before he ordered them to march again.[35]

There is considerable irony in Henry imposing capital punishment on the pyx thief. As Mortimer points out, for all his supposed reverence for clerical rites and liturgical objects, Henry was so short of money before his first invasion of Normandy that he pawned religious relics, along with his crown jewels, to pay his troops. The royal chapels at Windsor Castle were emptied out of numerous precious liturgical vessels, including crosses, chalices, and censers. Amazingly, Henry even pawned sacred relics, including a supposed piece of the Holy Tunic and the True Cross. And Mortimer comments, with obvious irony: "Pawning relics to pay soldier's wages does not accord with the traditional image of Henry as a pious man."[36] Written almost a century before Mortimer—his source for the inventory of ecclesiastical artifacts that Henry pawned—the three-volume life of Henry V by J.H. Wylie and W.T. Waugh is equally critical:

> Not only were the cupboards and buffets ransacked but inventories were drawn up of the valuables in the chapel of the royal household at Windsor which might be parted with to raise the necessary funds, and the king, whose veneration for the externals of religion is so highly praised by the churchmen of his time, was preparing to pawn the most sacred Church fitments to carry out his plan of invasion.[37]

But since Henry believed that he was fighting a holy war as God's agent for justice, in his mind his methods of financing his war were just and fitting. While there was no guarantee of success in the field, the king's moral certitude and overall confidence in his claim to the French crown compensated for the potential loss of these sacred ecclesiastical treasures. His victory at Agincourt would validate his decision to pawn religious objects to pay the soldiers that helped him win this glorious victory on that fateful day.

FIVE

Holy War

The Scourge of God

A New Man: The Grace of Coronation and Conquest

In spite of his enduring reputation as a courageous and victorious warrior, some of Henry V's contemporaries observed that he seemed better suited, by temperament and bearing, for the religious rather than the military life. Like his father, Henry had a sharp and inquisitive mind and was a bookish sort who went to great lengths to cultivate the peaceful arts, amassing a fine collection of spiritual, literary, and academic works.[1] The Parisian cleric and astrologer of great renown Jean Fusoris (c. 1365–1436) met Henry when he was part of a French diplomatic mission to England in the summer of 1415. Fusoris concluded that the young king had a "very princely demeanor, but it also seemed to him that he was better suited to be a man of the Church than a soldier."[2] The pro–Lancastrian monastic chronicler Thomas Walsingham (1376–1422) emphasized the religious nature of Henry's rule, describing the warrior king's untimely death in France as a disaster for the people he governed. Walsingham eulogized him as the quintessential Christian king:

> He had a pious mind and his words were few and well-judged. Far-sighted in his planning and shrewd in his judgement, he showed modesty in his bearing and magnanimity in his actions. He worked unceasingly, frequently went on pilgrimage and was a generous almsgiver. He was a devout Christian and supported and honoured the ministers and servants of the church. He was also a distinguished and fortunate leader in war, who in all his battles, always came off the victor. His construction of new buildings and his foundation of monasteries were on a magnificent scale. He was a munificent giver of presents, and in all matters he hunted down and fought against the enemies of the faith and the church.[3]

Walsingham also characterizes Henry's public crowning as a dramatic conversion experience, mirroring the traditional plot line of a medieval hagiographic legend of a male sinner who becomes a saint at some precise moment of religious epiphany. The pleasure-seeking Prince Hal is suddenly transformed into the chaste and pious King Henry V. This trope of radical reconfiguration of one's personhood through the power of the sacraments is reflective of a medieval clerical model of ordination or consecration. A recipient of holy orders became, as it were, a "new man" and was invested with a spiritual presence that was absent before his elevation to clerical status (a comparable example is a papal election; the new pope would assume a new papal name to symbolize this profound change of identity).

Through the grace of his coronation, Henry would continue to be favored and fortified by God's grace on the battlefields of France. While the tales of his wild youth are probably exaggerated, there is more than likely some truth to them. There is, however, no doubt that the burden of governing England and the need to expiate the sins of his father played a significant role in Henry's personal transformation and the formation of his piety when he became king. This responsibility also helped shape the religious ideology that Henry forcefully articulated as a Christian monarch and warrior. While he might have felt some sense of remorse or guilt for his reportedly licentious behavior as an adolescent and for his bitter alienation from his dead father, Henry's "conversion" after his assumption of the monarchy also had a powerful political value that would be promoted relentlessly by the king and his propagandists.

Walsingham's encomium accurately and succinctly itemizes the pious activities of Henry's nine-year reign: modest personal behavior, pilgrimage, almsgiving, endowment of religious houses, divinely supported warfare, and the persecution of heretics. But most of this list, filled as it is with time-honored religious tropes, could also be applied to any number of medieval monarchs. So how did Henry distinguish himself as such an overpowering figure in the legend and lore of late medieval European history? That reputation was largely built on the commemoration of a battle that would be the touchstone for Henry's reign, while serving as the basis for the lasting image of the deeply religious, divinely favored warrior king. Few people in modernity would remember the grinding and unglamorous siege warfare in Normandy that consumed the last five years of Henry's reign and that eventually took his life. But thanks to Henry's Lancastrian propagandists and Shakespeare's iconic drama, few could forget Henry's "miraculous" victory over the numerically superior French forces that he faced at Agincourt.

Henry's stunning defeat of the French not only validated his authority as king of England, when he subjected himself to a trial by ordeal in the muddy fields of Agincourt, but also the legitimacy of his claim to the French crown. The English victory even inspired the composition of multiple poems and epigrams celebrating his triumph, reminding his countrymen of the miraculous quality of Henry's success at Agincourt. Regardless of its origin, in her analysis of the "Agincourt Carol," Barker offers a compelling assessment of the role it continued to play in shaping English public opinion about Henry and his war in France. There were undoubtedly many such ballads about the Hundred Years War that have been lost and forgotten, but this happened to be the only poem about Agincourt that was put into carol form. Barker notes that the songs of wandering minstrels, celebrating these great deeds of chivalry, "ensured that news of the king's victory reached the more remote rural communities, encouraged a feeling of national pride and unity and were a powerful recruiting agent for Henry's new campaign. Indeed, it might be argued that they preserved the place of Agincourt in the national consciousness for centuries to come."[4] It is possible that this carol originated with Henry's royal chapel, and given his own love of music and his musical skills as a harpist and composer, it is not difficult to imagine that he played some role in patronizing or encouraging its composition. This would obviously be in keeping with Henry's use of the literary and musical arts to promote his reputation as a righteous king and holy warrior.

Modeling Holy War

After his coronation, Henry seemed to believe that his own personal conduct would be a mitigating factor in the eventual success or failure of his military campaigns. But to achieve victory, the king would have to be a worthy vessel of the divine will and impose a strict moral code on the armies that he commanded. Holy war required holy warriors, in both character and action. Thus, Shakespeare's Henry goes from being a riotous, iniquitous youth to a holy knight who practices self-discipline and piety in a dramatic about-face. The judgment of God that he would face in France would require chastity, vigils, penance, and prayers.

After he became king, Henry cloaked himself with this religiosity in word and deed. His speech was always laconic and to the point and he avoided needless profanity. He attended mass regularly and outwardly behaved in a manner that set a high bar for the soldiers that he commanded, as he assiduously avoided the company of women. He issued strict ordinances for his men with respect to the pillaging or desecration of ecclesiastical property. In attempting to comprehend the essence of Henry's understanding of kingship, Mortimer offers the intriguing possibility that in Henry's mind, his very existence as ruler of England (and France) was by definition a holy war fought by a holy warrior. For Henry, "kingship was itself a crusade. All its facets were part of a spiritual journey in which he saw himself delivering a perfect rule."[5]

Henry's "conversion" at his coronation speaks to his public embrace of a Christian code of conduct that was supposedly absent during his adolescence. The chronicler known as Pseudo-Elmham famously paid tribute to Prince Hal's libidinous behavior in the *Vita et Gesta Henrici V*, or *The Life and Deeds of Henry V*.[6] In a memorable passage, with an obvious double entendre, the anonymous author declares that the prince was "an assiduous pursuer of fun, devoted to the organ instruments which relaxed the rein on his modesty; although under the military service of Mars, he seethed youthfully with the flames of Venus too, and tended to be open to other novelties as befitted the age of his untamed youth."[7]

The bifurcation of Henry's life that suddenly occurred with his coronation and then conversion from Prince Hal to King Henry V might well have been an overdone bit of Lancastrian propaganda to help reestablish the damaged dynasty of Henry IV. But there are enough references in scattered sources to indicate that Henry needed to make a very public and concerted effort to repair his own reputation with the people that he now governed. The most Christian king would engage in extravagant forms of religious benefaction while practicing a personal form of asceticism that was most commonly embraced by male saints in the annals of medieval hagiography. The new king would now remain chaste, from the moment of his coronation to his marriage of Catherine Valois. The *First English Life of Henry V* (1513) records a statement by his close friend Bishop Richard Courtney (d. 1415) to a French diplomat: Henry had not had sex from the day of his father's death to his marriage of Catherine Valois.[8] Of course, the implication is that Henry *was* sexually active before he became king, and that he had practiced a full seven years of abstinence.

If Henry's reputation as a party-loving womanizer is true, this radical transformation could serve a dual purpose. First, the sacramental grace of his coronation had made him a new man and showed that God's favor rested on the Lancastrian dynasty in the miraculous transformation of Henry's character. Second, Henry's new asceticism could become the equivalent of athletic training for holy war, in much the same way that Joan of Arc would demand conformity to her rigid moral codes of conduct among her men when they were campaigning. The truest sign of devotion to his righteous cause would be to foreswear sexual relations. We are not well informed about Henry's experience with women before he became king, but his aloof personality and his generally laconic disposition after his coronation are difficult to reconcile with his legendary status as serial womanizer. He undoubtedly was sexually active, but with whom, where, and how often is difficult to know. And unlike his father Henry IV, who fathered an illegitimate child, there is no record of Henry V having any children before the birth of his son and successor, Henry VI.[9]

From the surviving contemporary evidence, it appears that while he was actively campaigning, Henry lived a celibate life, and in his military ordinances, he banned "camp followers"—the medieval euphemism for prostitutes—from tagging along with his armies. For Henry V's and Joan of Arc's soldiers, this was a startling deviation from the normal affairs of medieval warfare. And amazingly, when the great ecumenical Council of Constance met in Germany (1414–18), aside from the bevy of merchants and tradesman of all sorts who invaded the city, there were around seven hundred prostitutes who conducted their business in stables or houses that they rented.[10] It appears that in the fifteenth century, "camp followers" could also easily become "council followers."

Henry's war ordinances offer a fascinating look into his mindset as he waged his holy war in Normandy, providing good evidence for his top priorities in maintaining strict discipline among his troops. Curry provides an authoritative analysis of the manuscript tradition of these texts and their historical contexts. She demonstrates that the textual tradition of the ordinances is quite complicated, and the precise dating of various redactions, in both Middle English and Latin, including hybrid versions of Henry's decrees remains a challenge.[11] There is no doubt that Henry issued ordinances in the opening of his first campaign in Normandy (1415). The anonymous English cleric who accompanied him and thereafter composed the *Gesta* records that the king issued ordinances prohibiting, "under pain of death," the despoliation of ecclesiastical property, or the harming of a "woman or a priest or servant of the church," unless they offered armed resistance to his soldiers.[12] Curry concludes that Henry's ordinances were revised and reissued again in 1417 and 1419. The prohibition against desecration of churches and the injury of clerics or women remained a constant.[13]

There are unique clauses in some versions of the ordinances, imposing draconian penalties on prostitutes who might enter Henry's military camp or his captured Norman cities. Prostitutes who would dare to be within three miles of his army risked devastating injuries as punishment for their crime. For the first offense, such women would be expelled from the camp and told not to return. For the second, they would have their left arm broken:

> Prostitutes not to be allowed to stay with our host, especially at sieges of towns, castles, or fortresses, but to be located at least one league removed from the army. This is also to be observed in towns, castles, fortresses taken by us and our captains, or surrendered to us. Such women are not to stay within towns, castles, or fortresses or maintain any house, large or small, on penalty of breaking of their left arm if after one warning they are found at large or hidden in the prohibited place.[14]

We can understand why Henry did not want his men, on the march in enemy territory, to be distracted by prostitutes, or sullied by their trade. But the barbarism of this order, specifying the horrific physical mutilation of second offenders, might be indicative of Henry's continued struggle with the sordid rumors of his own past. Aside from the reference to this brutal decree in his ordinances, there are no known cases of its enforcement in the chronicle literature. We might conclude that the severity of the punishment and the reputation of Henry's ruthless resolve in times of war had the desired effect of scaring off any would-be prostitutes from approaching or infiltrating his camp. Joan of Arc had an equally dramatic reputation for driving prostitutes from her ranks while campaigning. The French monastic chronicler of the Royal Abbey of Saint-Denis, Jean Chartier (1385–1464), notes that even though Joan forbade concubines from being present in her camp, some of them did enter, which caused her to beat them back with her sword. Eventually it broke and could not be repaired, and then her power as a military leader was forever lost.[15]

In assessing the savagery of his punishment for prostitutes, some of Henry's modern critics have applied a psychoanalytic approach to this ordinance, interpreting it as a sign of the king's sexual dysfunction. Mortimer describes the young king campaigning in France as being "single, celibate, facially disfigured, somewhat aloof and obsessed with religion, justice and war."[16] Henry was adamant that he would marry a Valois princess, Catherine, whom he had never met or even seen. Unlike the two marriages of his father, this would be a political union that showed few, if any signs of love or affection (when he was on his deathbed in August of 1422, he did not even bother to have his wife at his side). Mortimer describes Henry's isolation from and indifference towards women as one of his chief character flaws. Before his marriage to Catherine Valois, "he did not sleep with women, and he seems to have spent little time in their company. He did not tolerate prostitutes in the royal household (unlike some of his forebears)."[17] While modern scholars are free to speculate about Henry's psychological disposition and its relationship with past sexual experiences, it is just as likely that this savage ordinance constituted a form of political and religious theater. It could serve as an effective piece of propaganda that would magnify the righteousness of the king and promote the holy aura of his army, as Henry waged a political crusade for the crown of France.

Waging Holy War

Henry's surprisingly difficult and brutal conquest of Harfleur (August–September 1415) marked the opening of his first military campaign in France. It is also one of the best examples of Henry's new type of holy war, where the secular and the sacred are combined in the construction of a biblical code of siege warfare derived from the Book of Deuteronomy (20:10–18). According to Curry, Henry was the first king in Western Europe to establish and enforce a Deuteronomical template for the siege of a city. On the authority of this text, Henry and his clerical propagandists claimed that he could kill all the male combatants, enslave the women and children, and confiscate the goods and property of a captured city that had unjustly rebelled and refused to surrender. During the siege of Harfleur, Henry threatened annihilation of the city if it did not open its gates.[18] The king also engaged in religious PSYOPS as he stood before the walls of the city. As McHardy documents in her close study of Henry's clerical entourage while he was campaigning, several weeks into the siege, the king ordered a clerical procession in front of the city: "the bishop of Bangor and the members of the chapel royal, fully robed, were employed as a psychological battering ram before the town walls."[19]

Henry's campaign against the Norman port city of Harfleur demonstrates that the king's siege was done "by the book." Actually, Henry followed *two books*: the fourth-century Roman Vegetius's *Epitoma rei militaris*, or the *Epitome of Military Matters*, and the biblical book of Deuteronomy. Thanks to Vegetius's counsel, Henry's men had burnt and leveled the suburbs of the city and then wheeled their cannon and other siege weapons within range of the city walls proper.[20] The thousands of gunstones that pounded the walls day and night were physically and psychologically devastating. The destruction was so great that the English would find it difficult to defend Harfleur from a French counterattack once they occupied the defeated city.

Harfleur was eventually smashed into submission by the relentless bombardment of English artillery, and the loss of life on both sides was

great (many of the English soldiers were stricken with dysentery). The pro–
Lancastrian monastic chronicler Thomas Walsingham, a great admirer of
Henry V, spares us no details about the horrors inflicted by indiscriminate
bombing of the city, which led to its eventual capitulation:

> [T]he French lords who were in command at Harfleur ... could not endure
> the repeated battering of the walls and their houses inside the town, and the
> other perils which they had suffered from our king's guns (for the stones that
> flew through the air from these guns with the huge force of their blow smashed
> everything that got in their way as they landed, not only killing the bodies
> which they flattened, but also scattering around whole, bleeding limbs, and the
> weapons of the besieged yielded one by one to their blows, and not only were
> the combatants laid flat but also the beautiful buildings of the town).[21]

After the French garrison surrendered, the English king showed "mercy"
by expelling the surviving civilian population; their homes and possessions
were then confiscated by the English.

Henry had appropriately forewarned the inhabitants of Harfleur of the
consequences of continued resistance.[22] When he sent a herald to offer his
ultimatum, he had invoked Deuteronomy as the template for the negotiations. He had already made this type of reference in a letter that he sent to
Charles VI, roughly a month before his invasion of France.[23] Now the warn-
ing was much more ominous and threatening. If they did not immediately
open their gates to Henry, the citizens of Harfleur would suffer the terrible
fate of rebellious cities, prescribed in Deuteronomy 20:10–16:

> When you draw near a city to attack it, offer it terms of peace.
> If it agrees to your terms of peace and lets you in, all the people to be found
> in it shall serve you in forced labor. But if it refuses to make peace with you and
> instead joins battle with you, lay siege to it, and when the LORD, your God,
> delivers it into your power, put every male in it to the sword; but the women and
> children and livestock and anything else in the city—all its spoil—you may take
> as plunder for yourselves, and you may enjoy this spoil of your enemies, which
> the LORD, your God, has given you. That is how you shall deal with any city at a
> considerable distance from you, which does not belong to these nations here.
> But in the cities of these peoples that the LORD, your God, is giving you as a
> heritage, you shall not leave a single soul alive.[24]

The anonymous English cleric who authored the eye-witness account
of the *Gesta* goes to considerable length to justify Henry's siege and details
the logic of his methods, based on this Deuteronomical code of warfare:

> [O]ur king, who sought not war but peace, in order to arm with the shield of
> innocence the just cause of the great enterprise upon which he had embarked,
> offered, in accordance with the twentieth chapter of the Deuteronomic law,

peace to the besieged if, freely and without coercion, they would open the gates to him and, as was their duty, restore that town, which was a noble and hereditary portion of his crown of England and of his duchy of Normandy. But when, spurning and making light of this offer, they strove to hold and defend the town against him, our king, summoned as it were unwillingly to do battle, called upon God as witness to his blameless quarrel, informing them of his penal edicts contained in the aforesaid law which it would be necessary to execute upon them as a rebellious people should they thus persist in their obstinacy to the end.[25]

Whether Henry took this biblical text as some sort of divine revelation for the conduct of his siege, or whether he cynically cloaked his savagery with a biblical mandate (both motives were probably combined), he unleashed the full fury of his army with devastating results when the city would not yield. The siege was much longer and more costly than he had anticipated, producing not only untold French casualties, but also a number of English deaths from an epidemic of dysentery that also invalided at least 1,330 soldiers who had to be shipped home.[26] Whatever his motives, Henry's holy war against Harfleur, with the use of a biblical passage to justify his conduct, set a grim precedent. As Curry declares, Henry "is the first Western European king known to have explicitly cited this biblical precedent for war, which allowed rulers to act harshly against places which they considered to be theirs by right and which resisted their authority."[27] After one open field battle at Agincourt, Henry's conquest of Normandy would be dominated by grueling sieges of strategically important cities. Harfleur served as the model. This was the first French city that capitulated to Henry, and when it came to exploiting this victory for the purpose of public relations, he made the most of it.

During the Hundred Years War, the most brutal form of warfare was the siege of a city.[28] After a difficult siege, a city's capitulation could be accompanied by some ritual of humiliation, such as the ones famously used by Henry. When Harfleur surrendered, Henry forced the French garrison captain Raoul de Gaucourt and some his soldiers to come out of the city with ropes tied around their necks. According to the English chronicler Adam Usk (c. 1352–1430), when the town was blasted into submission by Henry's artillery, "its inhabitants—stripped naked, and with halters and nooses around their necks—and all their goods, were surrendered to him."[29] This humiliation of a defeated enemy mirrors the treatment of the French forces who surrendered to Edward III after his great victory at Crécy in the summer of 1346. When the French king refused to send a relief force to Calais to repel the English siege, Edward demanded that the keys to the town be presented to him by six of the most prominent citizens with nooses around their necks.[30]

Such rituals of humiliation for prisoners were not simply a form of revenge or the punishment of opposing forces. According to Barker, they also had the larger symbolic and religious purpose of serving "as an example to any other town or garrison that dared to resist him…. He had enforced his just claims by the sword and had won Harfleur because his cause was righteous; the French had lost it because they had acted contrary to God's will and justice."[31]

When he returned to France after his great victory at Agincourt, Henry once again mercilessly besieged the cities of northern France, bombarding soldiers and civilians alike with his primitive but deadly artillery pieces. The thriving and prosperous city of Caen, whose population was probably close to forty thousand people, was the administrative center of lower Normandy and was vitally important to the English war effort. It took the brunt of Henry's forces on opposite ends of the city in a savage one-month siege that ended in disaster for its inhabitants (September 20, 1417).[32] When Henry's soldiers finally broke through the defenses of Caen, a horrifying massacre occurred. Henry had given the order to his men that no harm should come to women and clergy, but apparently not everyone obeyed his command. One of Henry's most vehement modern critics, Seward, offers this episode as clear evidence of Henry's criminality in the conquest of Normandy:

> [T]he victors then herded all the population they could find, civilian as well as military, regardless of sex, into the market place where, on Henry's orders, they massacred at least 2,000 of them. Blood ran in streams along the streets. The king ordered the killing to stop after coming across the body of a headless woman with a baby in her lap still sucking her breast. Instead he sent his men through the streets crying "Havoc!" to loot and rape.[33]

The indiscriminate killing of close to two thousand residents of Caen (men, women and children included), and the pillaging of their goods was a calculated act of terrorism.[34] Hoping to soften further resistance to his demands for the surrender of the fortifications of Normandy, the aftermath of the fall of Caen was reported far and wide.

Henry's long siege of the capital city of Normandy, Rouen (July 1418–January 1419), proved equally fatal for many of that city's inhabitants. Henry wanted to avoid the devastating consequences of his artillery, as he had witnessed at Harfleur, when his army surrounded this prized city. His primary weapon would be starvation. As the noose of famine tightened around the city, its military defenders expelled those who were now considered "useless mouths": the elderly, women, and children, and the sick. Henry showed no mercy to these wretched exiles. Trapped in a no-man's-land of ditches that had been dug by the English between the walls of the city (which formed a barrier of about five miles in circumference) and English troops, they slowly died of exposure and starvation during the harsh winter months. Eventually numbering several thousand, the English refused the exiles safe passage and the defenders of the city kept them locked out. The continued conflict among the French aristocracy, who fought for control of the court of the mad King Charles VI, led to a political paralysis that prevented the mobilization of a French relief force.

The English poet John Page claimed to have been an eyewitness to the siege and wrote a long, Middle English poem praising Henry's heroism but also bemoaning the pitiable fate of the civilians who suffered so terribly on account of his actions.[35] Henry's obduracy in the face of such misery even elicited sympathy from Page, who describes women clutching their dead babies, babies trying to suckle from their dead mothers, and children whose parents had died begging for bread.[36] Page quotes the king as saying that he was not responsible for their misery, that he did not put them there.[37] Henry sincerely believed that "his city" was in a state of rebellion and had insulted and offended his "majesty"; it now received its just punishment.

Henry's modern critics point to a pattern of disingenuous rhetoric with such claims, criticizing him for never taking personal responsibility for the horrors he inflicted on innocents. Henry would often self-righteously shift the blame to his political and military opponents. If they had simply obeyed his commands and surrendered their cities, they would have been spared untold suffering. In other instances, Henry would appeal to his religious ideology of holy war. When the celebrated Dominican preacher St. Vincent of Ferrer (1350–1419) chastised Henry for spilling so much Christian blood in France, he vigorously defended himself by declaring that he was "the scourge of God, sent to punish the people of God for their synns."[38]

Henry V also believed that he had the authority to declare and wage "holy war" against fellow Christians, in pursuit of what amounted to a political goal: deciding who would wear the crown of France. The theological framework for Latin Christian holy war, dramatically articulated by Pope Urban II (r. 1088–99) at the Council of Clermont (1095), called for the defense of Christians and their holy places in the east. This papal call to arms, the First Crusade, preached religiously sanctioned violence against the Muslim conquerors of what Christians identified as their Holy

Land. The Christian knights of Europe who would take a vow to fight for the recovery of the Holy Land would have as their battle cry, *Deus vult*, or "God wills it!"

The concept of divinely sanctioned warfare achieved a high degree of sophistication among the earliest historians of the Crusades, who repeatedly attributed the victories of Christian knights over their Muslim enemies directly to the miraculous intervention of God. Even the title of one of these crusading histories bears witness to this providential, theological paradigm. In discussing the chronicle of the monastic historian Guibert of Nogent (c. 1055–1124), Crusade historian Jonathan Riley-Smith notes: "So the special nature of the crusade, the reason why it was such an astounding demonstration of God's strength, was that it witnessed a conjunction of divine interventionary power and the good intentions of the participants. It really was, as the title of Guibert's book indicated, 'The tale of God working through the French' (*Gesta Dei per Francos*)."[39] On the other hand, Christian chroniclers of later, failed Crusades would attribute these losses to the sinfulness and vanity of the kingdoms that deployed crusading armies. Similar thoughts would be expressed by French and Burgundian chroniclers of the Hundred Years War, when their own armies were slaughtered in the field by the English.

From the bloody capture of Jerusalem by Frankish knights in the summer of 1099, to the era of Henry V and Joan of Arc, crusading and its religious ideology were woven into fabric of Latin Christendom. The ideal of the holy warrior fighting in service of Christ continued to count among its ranks many legendary figures, including the English warrior king Richard the Lionheart (r. 1189–99), who spent most of his reign outside of his realm, and the sainted crusader king of France, Louis IX (r. 1226–70).[40] Even Henry V's own father had enlisted and fought at some considerable expense and sacrifice in a Lithuanian crusade against supposed pagan holdouts after the conversion of their king to Christianity.[41]

Holy war by Christians against Christians was, however, in a wholly different category than a war against "infidel" Muslims. The demonization of an exotic religious "other" was much easier if he were a Muslim, and high-ranking clerical authorities had given their blessing to the killing of such enemies. But drawing the blood of a fellow Christian could be considered a mortal sin, unless he had strayed into heresy or renounced his faith. A precedent for holy war within the boundaries of European Christendom was established with the so-called Albigensian Crusade (1209–29). The bloody assault on the heretical communities in the south of France provided a model for the mobilization of Christian armies against fellow countrymen who had grievously deviated from the established norms of the Roman Church.[42] The crusade against the Cathars in Provence, declared with great vigor by Pope Innocent III (r. 1198–1216), demanded submission of the heretics or threatened them with outright slaughter.[43] The Cathar stronghold of Béziers witnessed just such a massacre in July of 1209. The city was overrun by "crusaders" and several thousand people were indiscriminately killed, even those who had taken sanctuary in the cathedral.[44] No mercy would be shown to heretics who offered armed resistance to the armies defending orthodoxy.

What Henry V represented was a new version of an old concept of Christian holy war. Even though he never used the term "crusade," according to Green, by the latter phases of the Hundred Years War, the battle between the English and the French "acquired some of the connotations of a crusade, and evolved from a dynastic struggle into one between chosen peoples."[45] Kaeuper methodically documents this transformation of the original crusading ideal into a concept of justified violence that suited the needs of an increasingly literate and sophisticated warrior aristocracy. The chivalric literature that flourished at the time of the Hundred Years War argued that fighting against other misguided Christians, who deprived an aggrieved party of their just rights, could be spiritually meritorious for the combatant.[46] The great warrior king Edward III saw his triumph at Crécy as a divine intervention and validation of the justice of his claim to the crown of France, providing a foundation for Henry V's interpretation of his stunning triumph at Agincourt.[47] Henry V played a critical role in promoting this concept of political holy war. He radically transformed the crusading ideal from its original intent—the liberation of holy places, the defense of Christian territory from infidels, the defense of orthodoxy against heretics—into a distinctly political ideology that appealed directly to God as judge and arbiter of his righteous cause.

Despite the religiosity of his public proclamations, Henry's cause for war was political, and yet he divined that his cause was noble, just, and somehow the enforcement of God's will. The Crusades and the various wars against heretics began with an express call to arms by an ecclesiastical authority, most often a pope, who promised spiritual benefits (such as indulgences to the holy warriors who took up arms for Christ). But Henry modeled a new sort of holy war, in effect declaring his cause "holy" on his own authority. And he subjected himself and his cause to the *Judicium Dei*, or the Judgment of God. Even though the Fourth Lateran Council (1215) had expressly prohibited clerical participation in a trial or ordeal by combat, a decisive victory on the battlefield was still widely viewed by the protagonists in the Hundred Years War as a divinely sanctioned duel.[48] With God as umpire and judge, the winner could claim that He had chosen his side in a dispute that could only be settled by violence and bloodshed. By this standard, Henry's victory at Agincourt offered incontrovertible evidence of God's judgment in his favor.

Six

Miraculous Victory

Agincourt

The Myth of Agincourt

Thanks in part to the immortal words that Shakespeare put on Henry V's lips—the venerable St. Crispin's Day speech in *Henry V*—the Battle of Agincourt has gone down in the annals of history as a defining moment of English nationalism. Alarmed by the size of the French army that faces them across the field, some of Henry's terrified soldiers wish aloud that they had more men at their disposal. The young English king rebukes them, exclaiming (4.3.23): "God's will, I pray thee wish not one man more."[1] Henry then offers an inspiring oration for his bedraggled and frightened army, rousing his men to courageous resolve, to hold their ground against a vastly superior French force. Invoking a brotherhood of arms that cuts across all social orders, Shakespeare's Henry rallies his troops with egalitarian calls for English unity in the face of death. He also appeals to the future glory and honor of the "happy few" and the "band of brothers" who will fight with him that day, while those now in England will long lament their absence (*Henry V*, 4.3.56–67):

> This story shall the good man teach his son,
> And Cripsin Crispian shall ne'er go by
> From this day to the ending of the world
> But we in it shall be remembered,
> We few, we happy few, we band of brothers.
> For he today that sheds his blood with me
> Shall be my brother; be he ne'er so vile,
> This day shall gentle his condition.
> And gentlemen in England now abed
> Shall think themselves accursed they were not here,
> And hold their manhoods cheap whiles any speaks
> That fought with us upon Saint Crispin's day.[2]

Henry V, Holy Warrior

Despite the fictional composition of the real king's "performance" in *Henry V*, and even though it is impossible to know what he actually said to his men before the battle, there are precedents in the contemporary chronicle literature that match well with Shakespeare's verse.[3] One such account is the *Gesta Henrici Quinti,* or the *Deeds of Henry V*, written by an anonymous English cleric who was present for the battle and circulated his brief chronicle of the Agincourt campaign within a few years of Henry's victory. In the *Gesta* we find the following exchange between a knight and the king:

> [A] certain knight, Sir Walter Hungerford, expressed a desire to the king's face that he might have had, added to the little company he already had with him, ten thousand of the best archers in England would have been only too glad to be there. "That is a foolish way to talk," the king said to him, "because, by the God in Heaven upon Whose grace I have relied and in Whom is my firm hope of victory, I would not, even if I could, have a single man more than I do. For these I have here with me are God's people, whom he deigns to let me have at this time."[4]

After the battle, when the tally of the French and English dead is read to Henry V, Shakespeare has the king order his men to march to the village, but he threatens death to any man who would dare boast of the victory and take the praise away from God. Fleuellen then asks the king if the English are allowed to tell how many died at the battle. Henry replies (4.8.117–18): "Yes, captain, but with this acknowledgement,/That God fought for us."[5] The widely read Burgundian chronicler Enguerrand de Monstrelet (c. 1400–53) confirms that this was indeed Henry's understanding of what had just transpired. He walked among the French corpses that littered the field with a group of his princes to survey the carnage he had inflicted with his troops. Monstrelet presents the following dialogue between the English king and a French herald:

> Whilst his men were busy stripping and robbing those who had been killed, he summoned the herald of the king of France, the king at arms called Mountjoye, along with several other heralds both French and English and said to them, "It is not we who have caused this killing but God Almighty, on account of the sins of the French, for so we believe."[6]

The English monastic chronicler Thomas Walsingham (1376–1422) provides similar testimony in his *Chronica Maiora,* or *Major Chronicle*: "King Henry ascribed all these successes to God, as was right, and gave boundless thanks to Him who had given him unexpected victory and crushed the fiercest of foes."[7]

The miracle of Agincourt, codified and celebrated for the ages in

94

Shakespeare's drama, was later seen as a tipping point in Henry's war of conquest in Normandy. This victory was so complete that in his play, Shakespeare immediately moves to the negotiations associated with the Treaty of Troyes (1420) and the betrothal of Henry and the Valois princess, Catherine. Despite the memorable depictions of the battle in modern film adaptations of *Henry V*, the brutal combat itself is absent from Shakespeare's play.[8] More importantly, the ugly and devastating sieges that consumed the last five years of his reign are totally ignored. For Shakespeare as it was for Henry himself, Agincourt was a religious and moral victory that served as the foundation for his later diplomatic and political triumphs. It provided spectacular proof that God "fought" for the English that day, that Henry's claim to the French crown was legitimate and his war was just. By this reckoning, the "hand of God" steered the course of human history and the Almighty chose the side that should triumph based on the merits or sins of the combatants.

From the pioneering theoretical reflections of John Keegan to the

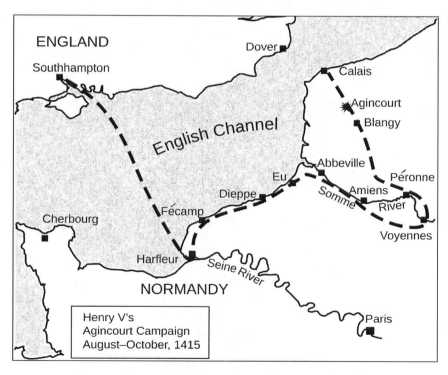

Henry V's Agincourt campaign (Map by Susan C. Thibodeau).

meticulous and exhaustive research of Anne Curry, Agincourt remains one of the most studied and commemorated medieval battles in modern academic literature. The recent 600th anniversary of this legendary clash of arms witnessed a renewed interest in Henry's victory, as evidenced by a number of publications on the battle, Henry's reign, and the Hundred Years War in its final phases.[9] But Henry and his propagandists essentially had "the first word" about what happened on that fateful day. And that "word" cast a long shadow that reached to the time of Shakespeare and even into the twenty-first century, as demonstrated by the title of the superb work of a leading historian of the battle, Juliet Barker: *Agincourt: Henry V and the Battle That Made England.*

In the weeks and months that followed Agincourt, its paradigmatic and legendary quality were vigorously promoted in a variety of forms: the religiously fueled speeches to Parliament of Henry's chancellor and bishop of Winchester, Henry Beaufort (c. 1375–1447); the triumphant celebration of Henry's victory when he entered London in November of 1415, with its ostentatious pageantry; the composition of the anonymous "Agincourt Carol," a spirited and well-crafted musical piece that helped popularize the glory of the warrior king among the mass of his subjects; and the Lancastrian propaganda of the *Gesta,* or *The Deeds of Henry the Fifth.*[10] Many other English chroniclers followed suit, composing detailed accounts of the Agincourt campaign that always showcased and celebrated Henry's courage and martial prowess. In short, the legend of Agincourt began with a propaganda blitz that originated in Henry's court and reverberated through English society for decades to come. But despite the glory of the English victory, when viewed within the full context of Henry's systematic and dogged conquest of Normandy, Agincourt is an outlier.

This epic battle was preceded by the surprisingly difficult siege of Harfleur, which devastated the city and took an extraordinarily high toll on Henry's soldiers as dysentery immobilized a large part of his fighting force. When the French challenged him to fight at Agincourt, Henry's hungry and exhausted army was making its way to the English garrison of Calais, from which it would make a return trip home to fight another day. But a large French military force shadowed Henry and his men on his long march to the Norman coastal port and eventually provoked him into an all-out battle. The stakes could not have been higher for the English at Agincourt. The Norman campaign had gotten off to a difficult start, beginning with a purported plot to assassinate Henry and his brothers in Southampton. After making a safe passage across the Channel, Henry's expeditionary force met with no real opposition until he arrived at the strategically important fortress of Harfleur. There Henry faced considerably more resistance than he had anticipated and his army was seriously depleted by an outbreak of dysentery, during an unexpectedly long siege.

After Harfleur, Henry was not eager for a military engagement with the French, and Agincourt was a battle that he more than likely wanted to avoid.[11] But when his passage to Calais was blocked by a French army that significantly outnumbered his, Henry was forced to do battle on October 25, 1415, at a place the English would name Agincourt (Azincourt, in French). Had the French prevailed, it would have been a crushing and humiliating end to Henry's war for the crown of France. An English loss might have even toppled Henry's own insecure monarchy that still struggled under the weight of allegations of usurpation and regicide. Worse still, the king could have been captured and held hostage in France or killed outright. Such high stakes made the victory even more "miraculous" for Henry. And thanks to Henry and his propagandists, no one would ever forget his moment of triumph at Agincourt.

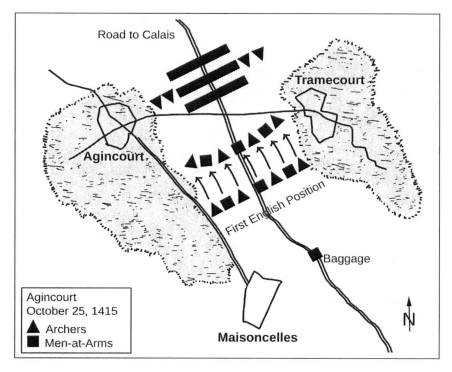

The Battle of Agincourt (Map by Susan C. Thibodeau).

Henry V, Holy Warrior

As the decades and centuries passed, few people would remember that when Henry returned to France in 1417, he began a grueling five-year campaign of siege warfare to make good on his claim to the French crown. Henry then resorted to his preferred weapons of siege warfare, with fire on the outskirts of cities; famine that starved populations into surrender; indiscriminate artillery bombardments that inflicted massive damage to vital infrastructures, not to mention the collateral damage of the loss of civilian life; and the exile of thousands of civilians from captured Norman strongholds and their colonization by Englishmen. But this unglamorous conquest of cities would soon be forgotten, while the memory of the courageous king and his feats of chivalry would be cultivated in favorable chronicles, carols, and stage dramas.

In the short run, however, Agincourt provided no political advantage to Henry in France, and he had to spend vast sums of money and endure miserable conditions with his men as he waged continuous war against the Valois monarchy until the French acceded to his demand of the crown. Even after the Treaty of Troyes (1420) legally recognized his right of succession, Henry was still compelled to continue his difficult and costly investment of rebellious cities, right up until his death in the summer of 1422. For reasons that were as obvious to Shakespeare as they are to us, Agincourt has a mythic quality and chivalric glamour that is absent from the dreary sieges of cities that were required to enforce Henry's claim to the French monarchy. Although it would be the only open field, pitched battle that the king fought in the entirety of his war in France (1415–22), in popular culture Henry's war would be reduced, as it was in Shakespeare's drama, to his glorious victory at Agincourt.

How did this anomalous battle—which most definitely was *not* decisive, from a political perspective—become the enduring memory of Henry's military career and how did it survive as an icon of English nationalism and patriotism in the popular culture of military history? The answer to such questions can be found in Henry's and his propagandists' brilliant public relations strategy that produced one of the most successful marketing campaigns in early modern European history. Fortunately, the study of the construction of this official "public memory" of events can be predicated on the exceptional work of a crowded field of Agincourt historians: Keegan, Barker, Rogers, Mortimer, and Curry. At present, the definitive books on the battle have been written. But there continues to be an opportunity for refined interpretation and analysis of the creation of the nationalist myth of the warrior king and his triumph over the French in the muddy fields of Agincourt. That myth was largely crafted by Henry himself. And as with everything that Henry did as king, it involved a conscious effort to fuse the political, military, and religious components of his biography into one compelling narrative that would prove that God's favor rested on the Lancastrian monarchy, while also validating his claim to the French crown and the justice of his war.

The Norman Invasion and the Siege of Harfleur

Henry had engaged in a flurry of supposed peace seeking, diplomatic activity throughout the summer of 1415, even as he made massive and methodical preparations for an invasion of France. Several thousand men, along with horses, artillery pieces, weapons, and victuals, would have to be transported across the Channel for Henry to have any hope of mounting a successful campaign.[12] The launch point of Southampton was humming with this activity when Henry supposedly uncovered a plot to murder him and his brothers and to create a new monarch. The modern debate continues over whether or not the discovery of such a conspiracy was a subterfuge for the removal of Henry's political rivals in England while he was absent. Regardless of it being a real or imagined threat to Henry and his family, the shock of the Southampton plot and the execution of its leaders could have been psychologically debilitating to the English war effort.[13]

After this brief disruption of Henry's planned invasion of Normandy, the Channel passage went according to schedule. The disembarkation of the English forces that landed in Normandy experienced no opposition. The campaign was off to a successful start. Then came the grueling siege of the strategically important port city of Harfleur, with its seemingly impregnable defenses that protected a population of about five thousand people. If it did not capitulate to Henry, he would have no base of operations from which to wage war in western and central Normandy. He would return home empty-handed after generating a surge of patriotism and xenophobic animosity towards the French. Henry had also raised vast sums of money through subsidies and loans, even pawning crown jewels and sacred relics from his chapel, while cloaking his Norman adventure with religious language about the justice of his cause and the piety of his intentions.[14] By his own standards and those of his countrymen, his much touted expedition would have been a humiliating failure if Henry did not capture Harfleur.

Though in the end successful, the siege of Harfleur proved to be tactically more difficult and logistically more costly than Henry had first imagined. A supposedly short siege turned into more than five full weeks and it could have easily evolved into a Phyrrhic victory. The anonymous English cleric who authored the *Gesta*, or *The Deeds of Henry V*, witnessed the siege first-hand and marveled at the cunning and resolve of those who defended Harfleur:

> [T]he enemy had craftily made ready on the walls, in considerable quantity, jars filled with burning powders, sulphur and quicklime, to throw in the eyes of our men if an assault should be made, and barrels of inflammable powders and oils and burning fats, to set fire to and burn our siege equipment when brought close up to the walls for an assault. Nor, in men's judgement, could a people under siege have resisted our attacks more sagaciously, or with greater security to themselves than they did.[15]

The impressive walls and fortifications of the city were put to good use by the French commander Raoul de Gaucourt, and his tenacity forced Henry to bombard Harfleur indiscriminately with his artillery until it was blasted into submission. Henry had seventy-eight gunners working in shifts, bombarding the city day and night.[16] The thousands of gunstones they hurled were devastating. The St. Albans monastic chronicler Thomas Walsingham (1376–1422), a great admirer of Henry, spares us no details about the horrors inflicted by the king's indiscriminate artillery fire at the city, which led to its eventual capitulation:

> [T]he French lords who were in command at Harfleur ... could not endure the repeated battering of the walls and their houses inside the town, and the other perils which they had suffered from our king's guns (for the stones that flew through the air from these guns with the huge force of their blow smashed everything that got in their way as they landed, not only killing the bodies which they flattened, but also scattering around whole, bleeding limbs, and the weapons of the besieged yielded one by one to their blows, and not only were the combatants laid flat but also the beautiful buildings of the town).[17]

After the French garrison surrendered, the English king showed "mercy" by expelling the surviving civilian population; their homes and possessions were then confiscated by the English. Henry also ordered the public burning of the city's charters and all documents associated with the ownership of private property.[18] Harfleur was now an English possession. The author of the *Gesta* was an eyewitness to the capitulation of the city and describes the pitiable scene of the exile of its inhabitants when Henry took possession of it:

> [Henry] sent them away from the town further inland into France wherever they wanted to go, and they numbered about two thousand; and, amid much lamentation, grief, and tears for the loss of their customary although unlawful habitation, he had them escorted under armed guard beyond the limits of

the army, lest they should be molested on the way by thieves amongst us who are given more to pillage than to pity and care nothing for the tears of the innocent as long as they can lay hands on their plunder. And thus, by the true judgement of God, they were proved sojourners where they had thought themselves inhabitants.[19]

In addition to the steadfast resistance of the inhabitants of Harfleur, the weather was unusually hot and the mounds of human and animal excrement produced by the siege wreaked havoc on the English fresh water supply, causing an outbreak of disease. Henry's woes were compounded when large numbers of his soldiers were stricken with dysentery—what the English called "the bloody flux"—and were incapable of fighting. Many of them had to be shipped back home (1,330 by Curry's count).[20] Henry's dear friend and bishop of Norwich, Richard Courtney, was one of the victims of this epidemic, dying a week before Harfleur officially surrendered.[21] There were more English casualties from disease at Harfleur than from combat in the entire Agincourt campaign.[22]

After Harfleur surrendered, Henry's depleted forces—he probably lost between 10–20 percent of his army—could not make an immediate return trip back across the Channel to the original embarkation point, Southampton.[23] The armada of ships that he hired (close to fifteen hundred in all) had long since returned to England. Henry would have to leave a sufficient number of men to occupy the wrecked Norman port, whose defense was now in question after the destruction wrought by Henry's artillery. When the English entered Harfleur they saw firsthand that critical infrastructure was in ruins and that the defensive walls of the city had experienced tremendous damage. This now created a logistical challenge for Henry who immediately put his men to work repairing the walls in anticipation of a French counterattack. Could the small garrison—three hundred men-at-arms and nine hundred archers, by Curry's count—that Henry left behind as he marched northeast repel the French?[24] Had the siege taken less time and had his own casualties been much lower, Henry might have next moved to another city (perhaps Honfleur or Rouen) to begin a new siege. But as Dan Spencer notes in his meticulous study of English artillery at Harfleur, Henry had used up most of the munitions he had transported with his fleet, and he now lacked the firepower to continue with might have been his original plan.[25] And beyond his logistical problems after the siege, no one really knows for sure what his original intentions were beyond the capture of Harfleur.

Henry's position was precarious, both in defending his conquered port and preserving his winnowed army. Between the loss of sick men and the need to garrison Harfleur, Rogers estimates that "only about half of his original field force remained fit and available for service."[26] When news of Henry's capture of Harfleur reached the Valois court in Rouen, where Charles VI and his son Louis of Guyenne were being kept up to date on the siege, French inertia was now transformed into action. French troops began to answer the king's call for the defense of the homeland against the brash English invader.

Despite the contrary counsel of his peers, who saw this as an exceptionally dangerous undertaking, Henry ordered an overland march to Calais.[27] As modern Agincourt historians are quick to note, this was a tremendous risk, but it was predicated on Henry's insistence that he was not a foreign conqueror. His march through Normandy would symbolize the justice of his cause and the legitimacy of his claim to the French crown. As Sumption comments, Henry was obsessed "with his image in France and to some extent in the rest of Europe.... He wanted to demonstrate to the French the impotence of their rulers and the inability of the Dauphin to protect them."[28] A direct overland route to Calais would have been about 120–40 miles, but the Fabian tactics of the French forces that shadowed Henry increased that distance to roughly 250–75 miles. Looking back on the rubble of Harfleur, the lost English lives, and the demobilization of large numbers of his soldiers, Henry must have realized that he would have to redouble his efforts to maintain the cohesion and morale of his army as he began the long trek that would take him safely home.

Henry's destination, Calais, was captured by Edward III after his spectacular victory at Crécy in the summer of 1346 (it remained in English hands until 1558).[29] This English colonial outpost would provide safety for Henry and allow his men to rest and recover before their return to England. But the English king would have to march his poorly fed, tired, and outnumbered forces through enemy territory and avoid sieges and pitched battles, while maintaining strict discipline and boosting the morale of his forces. The interval between the capitulation of Harfleur up to and including the engagement of the French at Agincourt was one of the most perilous times in Henry's reign, when everything could have gone wrong, ending both his French campaign and his English monarchy in the deadly fields of France.

The Battle of Agincourt

Thanks to the methodical and exhaustive research of a number of modern historians, we can reconstruct many of the details of the Agincourt campaign, beginning with Henry's departure from Harfleur to his victorious return to England. We can also outline with a considerable degree of precision the distinct phases of the Battle of Agincourt itself. In studying his Norman campaign of 1415, modern experts agree that Henry was a brilliant staff officer who had a keen grasp of the logistics of warfare. The young king was also a courageous field commander who could inspire his men to overcome hardships and adversities in what turned out to be an unexpectedly difficult and dangerous expedition. But Henry's order to kill the French prisoners at Agincourt continues to divide the modern academic community, eliciting strong responses from his critics, including moral condemnation and allegations of criminality. No history of Henry's triumphant victory can exclude an analysis of the circumstances of this controversial order and its implementation. Even Shakespeare recognized its historical importance and did not shrink from including it in his play.

In one of her more recent works, written to commemorate the 600th anniversary of Agincourt, Curry offers a succinct yet well documented chronology of Henry's activities, from the fall of Harfleur (September 22, 1415) to his arrival in Calais (October 29, 1415).[30] Sometime between October 6 and October 8, 1415, Henry left Harfleur for Calais. Contrary to what is commonly believed, the men who marched with Henry were still physically capable of fighting; those who were too weak or sick to continue with the campaign had already been sent back to England. It appears that Henry's original plan had been to take a reasonably direct route, with the intention of fording the Somme River in the same location used by Edward III before his legendary Battle of Crécy, in the summer of 1346. But a crossing at Blanchetaque proved impossible, since a French army of several thousand men was waiting for Henry on the other side of the river when he arrived.

The contemporary English monastic chronicler Thomas Elmham (c. 1418) notes that the French did everything in their power to impede Henry's progress to Calais:

> Everywhere the bridges and causeways were broken by the enemy. Their company continued to grow. There were scarcely supplies for eight days for the king. The French devastated the farms, the vineyards and food supplies. They were keen to harry the people by hunger so that they might ruin them completely by making them weak without even fighting.[31]

The English were forced to take a much longer route southward on the west bank of the river, in search of a new crossing point, as a large French force paralleled their movement. At the start of his march to Calais, Henry's army was moving at a rapid pace, about sixteen to seventeen miles per day. The disruptive activities of the growing French forces that continued to shadow Henry's every move slowed him down to a pace of about ten or eleven miles per day.[32] The tactics of the French must have also begun to take a psychological toll on the king and his anxious men.

Henry's initial evasion of the French provides compelling evidence that he wanted, if at all possible, to avoid a major conflict with the enemy before reaching the safe haven of Calais.[33] The risks posed by an open field battle were too great. Despite his courage, Henry was no reckless fool and he appears to have anticipated attempts on his life in France. His capture or death were distinct possibilities, and according to one contemporary French account of the Battle of Agincourt, based on the recollections of one of its most famous survivors, Henry was nearly killed and supposedly used body doubles while he fought. This testimony comes from Arthur de Richemont, in the chronicle of his servant Guillaume Gruel (c. 1410–74/82). Gruel says that during the battle, when Henry shielded his wounded younger brother, Humphrey, Duke of Gloucester (1390–1447), he "received such a blow to his crown that he fell to his knees. Two others who were dressed just like the king were killed."[34] Richemont was the twenty-two-year-old son of Henry V's stepmother, Joanna of Navarre. Dug out from a pile of bloody corpses at Agincourt, he was captured and sent to England where he would remain a hostage for the next five years. He eventually fought against the English again with Joan of Arc.[35]

Not long after Henry forded the Somme, between Bethencourt and Voyennes (October 19–20), he was challenged by three French heralds to do battle. When Henry arrived at the open field between Azinocurt and Tramecourt (October 24), a large French army was once again waiting for him. He had no choice but to engage the French since they blocked his passageway to Calais. However, it is difficult to know why the French had chosen that precise location and also how many men they had at their disposal. The location—roughly two miles long by one mile wide, flanked on either side by woods—is especially puzzling. Rogers sees this as fatal error on the part of the French commanders. Had they met Henry and his forces just a few hundred yards north of the battlefield, they more than likely would have defeated him: "Considering their vastly superior numbers and especially their overwhelming superiority in cavalry, the French clearly should have chosen a more open battlefield, where their horseman could easily have enveloped the English line."[36] After a night of heavy rain, Henry arrayed his troops for battle the following morning; after a two to three hour engagement, the English claimed victory. The exhausted English slept on the battlefield, and the next day, they began their forty-five-mile march to Calais.[37] Three days later, they arrived at their destination, and so far as we know, Henry never again set foot on the field of Agincourt.

For the reconstruction of the precise chronology of the battle itself, we can follow the narrative of Keegan, from his classic study of three major battles in British history (Agincourt, Waterloo, and the Somme).[38] He believes that twelve distinct "episodes" of the battle can easily be identified from "seven or eight chroniclers, who do not materially disagree over the sequence, character or significance of events."[39] Using Keegan's reconstruction, we can identify twelve separate phases of the engagement of Henry and his troops with the French, even if we can now question some details of presentation, including Keegan's placement of the attack on the English baggage:

1. Waiting
2. English advance
3. English archers strike
4. French cavalry charge
5. French infantry advance
6. Clash between English and French men-at-arms
7. Intervention by English archers
8. Flight of French survivors
9. Period of waiting and another, smaller French charge
10. French attack on the English baggage
11. Massacre of French prisoners by order of Henry
12. Departure from the battlefield by both sides; recognition of English victory

When the sun rose on Friday, October 25, 1415, Henry was seriously outnumbered by enemy forces, but he proved his mettle as a battlefield commander with his courage and superior leadership. The French, on the other hand, had a divided command that pitted rival interests against each other. They also fell victim to the hubris that often comes with a large numerical advantage. In his account of the battle, Allmand underscores the leadership deficit on the French side: "What was lacking was one man of natural authority and personal prestige to lead the large French army drawn from many parts of France. It was at this moment that France missed the presence and personal leadership of an inspiring king. The English, on the other hand, had both."[40] Aside from ineffectual leadership, Curry also notes that one of the main disadvantages of the French army leading up to the battle was the arrival of its troops at Agincourt "in dribs and drabs."[41] The French force that stood roughly seven hundred yards away from Henry on the morning of the battle was also hesitant to make a move against him, holding a defensive posture as they waited to reach a critical mass of troops before attacking.[42]

In addition to his courage in the thick of combat, Henry also deserves great credit for maintaining the discipline and morale of his men on the eve of the battle, as well as in the hours that they stood looking across the field at the vast French host. Even one of his most ardent modern critics is impressed with his leadership at such a critical moment: "one has to give Henry credit for holding his nerve and providing such controlled leadership, especially in the wake of his own ill health. Few other men could have done it, in such appalling circumstances."[43] Thomas Elmham recounts that when the English sought to make camp that night around the village of Maisoncelles, "their hearts were quaking with fear."[44] Henry demanded strict silence among his soldiers, while they struggled to cope with the difficult weather and the undoubted anxiety they felt about the coming engagement. Elmham notes that the weather was miserable and nerves were frayed among the English, while the French assured themselves of a speedy victory:

> That rainy night, the people there, without bread, overflowed with the offering of prayers and vigils to the Lord. The enemies, pondering that the English were spending the night in silence, thought therefore that the king was intending to flee. They rode quickly over the fields by several routes. They threw dice to determine which [of the English] they should each have.[45]

Whether or not this was Elmham's intention, the French rolling dice for the spoils of English prisoners is not only a sign of their arrogance, but also parallels the Gospel account of Jesus' crucifixion, when Roman soldiers tossed dice for the tunic he had worn before he was put to death (Jn 19:23–24).

On the day of the battle, Henry methodically organized his forces, taking account of the terrain that the French would have to cross to reach him, and positioning his archers for maximum effect. Henry ordered his archers to plant long wooden stakes that they had cut days before (the so-called "hedgehog") as a protective barrier against a French cavalry charge. If their mounted troops reached their ranks, the archers could drop back behind this barrier and the French horses would be impaled by their sharpened points.[46] Matthew Bennett argues that Henry's ingenious use of portable stakes reflected his advance knowledge (gathered from a few French prisoners) of the French strategy to disrupt and overwhelm them with a cavalry charge at the start of the battle.[47]

While building a portable protective wall to shield them, Henry deployed thousands of archers—precisely where they were all positioned is difficult to determine from the primary sources—as his men-at-arms stood their ground in the center of their ranks. According to Curry, the archers were one of the major English assets that determined the outcome of the battle. They outnumbered the English men-at-arms by a ratio of 5:1, totaling seventy-five hundred men to the fifteen hundred men-at-arms under Henry's command.[48] By contrast, roughly 60 percent of the French force was comprised of men-at-arms. Mass volleys of arrows shot from English longbows were devastating in their effect, becoming the medieval equivalent of automatic weapons fire in modern combat. The English monastic chronicler Thomas Walsingham refers to these volleys as a "cloud of arrows."[49] The English longbows had an effective range of about 300–50 yards, and would immediately disrupt the orderly movement of French troops. Fired at a flat trajectory, their arrows could be lethal at about seventy yards.[50] While modern scholars continue to debate the velocity of their arrows and the range at which they could pierce armor, there is no doubt that the repeated volleys of arrows wreaked havoc on the French and threw their ranks into chaos.

As the French awaited the arrival of even more soldiers with which to crush Henry, the English king was forced into action. The English probably stood their ground for two to three hours before Henry realized that the French would remain immobile. The nerves of his tired, famished, and fearful men might break if they did not engage the enemy in short order. Henry finally moved forward, ordering his archers to pull up their stakes and reposition themselves. The French were now within effective range of their longbows, roughly three hundred yards from the first French line. Rogers argues that the French should have ordered a cavalry charge at the first sign of movement in the English line. As the archers pulled up their stakes and began to reorganize their line, an immediate cavalry attack would have had a profound psychological impact.[51]

When Henry moved his men up, the English chronicler Thomas Elmham states that he rallied them with battle cries that invoked the name of Saint George and the Mother of God: "St. George, George saint and knight be with us! Holy Mary bestow your favour on the English in their right. At this very hour many righteous English people pray for us with their hearts. France, hasten to give up your fraud!"[52] On the other hand, Barker says that Henry might have also uttered something much more laconic: "Felas, lets go!"[53] This burst of activity goaded an initially reluctant and totally surprised French vanguard to cross the freshly plowed, wet fields to engage his men-at-arms in close fighting.

Their strategy and the difficult terrain of the battlefield played a critical role in the resounding defeat of the French. They appear to have relied on an overwhelming show of force to rout the English. The Italian chronicler Tito Livio Frulovisi highlights this French overconfidence in numbers. A native of Ferrara, he took up residence in England in the 1430s, entering the service of Henry's younger brother, Humphrey, Duke of Gloucester. In his *Vita Henrici Quinti*, or *The Life of Henry V* (c. 1438), Tito Livio observes:

> In very truth, the French placed so much confidence in the fact that they had
> very powerful and splendid horses as well as superior arms that, on coming to
> the battle, several of the great princes had left behind their lesser knights and
> servants, as well as several banners and military symbols, because they were cer
> tain of a most speedy victory.[54]

The French believed that the superiority of their numbers—anywhere from twelve thousand to thirty-six thousand men, depending upon which modern estimate we use—and the mass attack of their cavalry and then men-at-arms would crush the English in an initial and decisive encounter. While the French had a substantial contingent of crossbowmen, they do not seem to have had much of a role in the fighting. They were probably placed behind the first and second French line, with orders to move to the side when the second line advanced. The memory of the slaughter of the Genoese crossbowmen used by the French at Crécy (1346) more than likely prevented the deployment of the French missile troops on the front line at Agincourt.[55]

Relying on cavalry and men-at-arms proved to be a costly mistake. The rain-soaked, muddy ground made the French deployment exceptionally difficult and slow, as knights and horses were trapped in the suction of the thick mud that stood between them and the English. In his description of the Battle of Agincourt, the French chronicler Jean Juvénal des Ursins (1388–1473) emphasizes the disastrous consequences of riding and walking through the muddy fields for the French:

> [T]hey came to a field where the ground was very soft for it had been raining for
> a long time and they sank into the ground. The French were heavily armed and
> sank into the ground right to the thick of their legs, which caused them much
> travail for they could scarcely move their legs and pull them out of the ground.
> They began to march until arrowfire occurred from both sides. Then the lords
> on horseback, bravely and most valiantly wanted to attack the archers who
> began to aim against cavalry and their horses with great fervor. When the horses

felt themselves pierced by arrows, they could no longer be controlled by their riders in the advance.[56]

Most modern military historians agree that the skill and discipline of Henry's archers proved to be the tipping point of the battle. The French cavalry were supposed to overrun the archers at the start of the battle, but they were devastated by the rain of arrows that struck their horses, some of which were also impaled by the sharpened stakes. The French men-at-arms, encumbered by heavy armor (weighing between sixty to seventy pounds) and weapons, struggled to cross the muddy fields of Agincourt and were trapped by the repeated volleys of the longbowmen. According to Barker, a professionally trained archer could fire as many as twenty arrows per minute, and some of these arrows called "bodkins," with hardened and sharpened points, could penetrate armor at a range of 150 yards.[57] By contrast, despite his ability to shoot as far if not farther than a longbowman, a crossbowman could only fire two bolts per minute.

The vulnerable French knights who had initially crossed the field with confidence in their victory were stopped by a hail of arrows and slaughtered in close combat as the archers abandoned their bows and struck them with other handheld weapons. The French began to bunch up for protection from the arrows, but they were so tightly packed together that they could scarcely wield their own weapons as English archers savagely attacked them with improvised weapons. As the author of the *Gesta*, or *The Deeds of Henry the Fifth*, recalls, the English archers who had dropped their bows attacked the French flanks, "seizing axes, stakes and swords and spear-heads that were lying about, they struck down, hacked and stabbed the enemy."[58]

The relentless and deadly volleys of arrows ground the French advance to a halt, with fatal consequences. French troops were funneled into a death trap that stood between two wooded flanks of the English army as arrows rained down on them. As the French casualties mounted, their corpses began to pile up in heaps before the English. The anonymous English cleric who witnessed the battle offers a vivid description in the *Gesta* of the horrors endured by the French as they reached the English lines. The pile-up of French men-at-arms, some of whom might have suffocated to death, was so great that the English climbed atop and struck down the French beneath them:

> For when some of them [the French], killed when battle was first joined, fell at the front, so great was the undisciplined violence and pressure of the mass of men behind that the living fell on top of the dead, and others falling on top of the living were killed as well, with the result that, in each of the three places where the strong contingents guarding our standards were, such a great heap

grew of the slain and of those lying crushed in between that our men climbed up those heaps, which had risen above a man's height, and butchered their enemies down below with their swords, axes, and other weapons.[59]

Thomas Walsingham offers an equally dramatic account of the carnage at the front line, while glorifying Henry for his courage and feats of arms:

> King Henry himself, fulfilling the role of soldier as well as of king, was the first to charge the enemy. He inflicted and received cruel blows, giving his men in his own person brave examples of daring as he scattered the enemy ranks with his ready axe. And in the same way the knights, emulating the acts of the king, strained with all their might to lay low with the sword that forest of shouting Frenchmen which opposed them, until at last force made a way and the French did not so much fall back as fall dead to the ground.[60]

It is impossible to determine with any precision just how many Frenchmen perished at Agincourt (contemporary estimates range from four thousand to ten thousand casualties).[61] As with many medieval battles, the chronicle narratives engage in hyperbole and exaggeration when it comes to the numbers of combatants and fatalities, with wildly variant figures that are difficult to reconcile. Curry's detailed research leads her to conclude that a French body count of "1,500 and 2,000 is credible."[62] The battle did not end with a "rout," in the traditional sense, where panic ensued and thousands of French soldiers turned and fled, only to be cut down *en masse*. The French simply stopped fighting when they saw the futility of their continued assaults. Henry and his men claimed victory, as they surveyed the French dead and the remaining prisoners in their custody (some had been massacred). They also tallied their own dead, one of whom was Henry's cousin Edward, Duke of York (c. 1373–1415).

There is no arguing that Agincourt did more than any other event in Henry's life to create his legend and fill him with resolve to conquer Normandy and make good on his claim to the crown of France. But as Curry underscores in her study of the battle, the "greatest bone of contention" among modern historians has been the actual number of combatants on each side.[63] This matters a great deal for the perpetuation of the myth of Henry's "miraculous victory" against an overwhelming enemy force. The French humiliation that Shakespeare immortalizes with the dying words of Bourbon (4.5.3–5)—"All is confounded, all./ Reproach and everlasting shame/Sits mocking in our plumes"—loses some of its rhetorical power if the wildly inflated numbers of French forces (3:1 or even 10:1) is scaled down to a more even match.[64] Curry's painstaking research has allowed her to produce a table of the statistics for the battle provided by each of the medieval chronicles, including the supposed number of combatants on each side and the number of their dead.[65] Some of these accounts have in excess of one hundred thousand French taking on eight thousand Englishmen!

The modern community of professional military historians also displays a wide range of numbers for the battle, but with more reasonable variations than some of the medieval chronicles. Keegan posited a number of twenty-five thousand French to Henry's five thousand to six thousand English.[66] In her more recent work, Barker has a ratio similar to Keegan's, but she pushes the French number to thirty-six thousand to the English six thousand.[67] Rogers places the total number of French combatants at around twenty-four thousand, concluding that the French had a 10:1 advantage with men-at-arms and an overall advantage of 4:1.[68] On the other hand, Curry has upended this traditional view of overwhelming odds against the English by closing the gap to twelve thousand French to Henry's nine thousand English. In her calculation, Agincourt is still a great victory for Henry since he was outnumbered by roughly three thousand men. Mortimer is critical of Curry's numbers; her methodology for the English tabulation is sound, but he thinks her French number comes up short. He believes that the English were outnumbered 2:1, with fifteen thousand Frenchmen facing eight thousand one hundred Englishmen.[69]

Whether or not Curry's tallies will become canonical, because of her meticulous research, the hyperbole of the medieval chronicle sources and the modern romantic legend of the miracle of Agincourt is brought back to reality. Despite his successful propaganda campaign in the aftermath of his victory, these reduced figures make the battle much less "miraculous." And Curry offers an important caveat about the myth-making that continues to take place when the validity of her forensic work on numbers is called into question: "[Critics] prefer books on the battle that tell the story they want to hear. The David and Goliath image of Agincourt continues to be attractive, especially to English readers, and in an age where delight continues to be taken in English one-upmanship against the French. The Agincourt story remains for many a matter of faith rather than reason."[70]

In the aftermath of the battle, there was much soul searching on the part of the shocked French elite. If they seriously outnumbered Henry and his underfed soldiers, and if they provoked him to fight at a time and place of their own choosing, why did the French lose the Battle of Agincourt in such a spectacular fashion? The contemporary chronicles, especially those written by clerics, are filled with mournful religious tropes that highlight French vanity, degeneracy, and sinfulness, in contrast to the moral superiority of the English and divine intervention for their cause. The French chronicles also emphasize the universal grief, shock, dismay, and sadness felt by the French ruling elite when news of Henry's triumph reached them. Some of the Burgundian chronicles also praise the feats of arms and courage of the slaughtered French nobility, as if these things alone were worth the horrors they suffered.[71]

The reactions recorded among the French also included moral condemnations and bitter denunciations of treachery, cowardice, blasphemy, and luxurious living among rival political factions in France that undermined successful opposition to the English. In reflecting on the consensus among the French for the causes of their defeat, Sumption observes: "It was a judgment curiously similar to Henry's own."[72] The political rivalry between the Armagnacs and Burgundians no doubt played a role in Henry's success on the battlefield. The Burgundian party in Paris was said to have experienced some degree of *schadenfreude* when they learned of the debacle. Some of the greatest men in France were captured by Henry, including the dukes of Orléans and Bourbon, and the counts of Eu, Vendôme, and Richemont. As Barker observes, aside from Charles VI and the young Dauphin (who would be dead in only a few months), and the dukes of Berry and Anjou, "every Armagnac leader of any consequence had been killed or taken captive."[73] But when reflecting on the catastrophic loss of the French at Agincourt, few chroniclers on either side seem to have dwelled at any great length on the battle's outcome from the perspective of military strategy and tactics.[74] And for the English, the just and divinely endorsed Henry V had defeated his wicked and unjust opponents in a trial by combat.

Modern historians agree that several factors combined to give Henry such an impressive victory. Despite their numerical advantage over Henry's soldiers, the French troops were hampered by the lack of a fully integrated command structure and a unified and cohesive fighting force. The French Marshal Jean II le Meingre Boucicaut (c. 1366–1421) and the Constable Charles d'Albret (1368–1415) were nominally in command, but they obviously did not have the decisive control over their troops that Henry had over his. (Boucicaut was captured at Agincourt and died in captivity in England, while d'Albret was killed in the battle.) And equally, if not more importantly, Henry's men had been on the march with their charismatic king and courageous commander for months and he had enforced a strict code of military discipline on them. Neither the king of France, Charles VI, nor the Dauphin Louis of Guyenne were present for this great battle. And even if they had been, it is doubtful that the mad king and the inexperienced Dauphin would have been particularly helpful. They awaited news of the outcome of the battle in the Norman capital of Rouen.

The French also seemed to lack a coherent strategy to defeat Henry beyond their confidence in superior numbers. The same lack of strategic vision had been exhibited during Henry's siege of Harfleur. Between the obstinate resistance of the city's inhabitants and the epidemic of dysentery that afflicted his camp, Henry would have found it difficult to fend off a well-organized counterattack by the French. But no meaningful French relief force ever materialized. This same indecision manifested itself at Agincourt. The Valois court in Rouen struggled to come up with a clear plan with which to defeat Henry. And when a battle plan was finally drawn up, it was either poorly executed or proven to be ineffective.[75] In reflecting on the poor decision-making of the French commanders, some of whom were respected and experienced soldiers, Rogers concludes, "the decisions made by the French leaders even before the battle had begun go a long way toward explaining the outcome ... to array their forces in the way they did, on the ground they chose, was little short of idiotic."[76] The lack of effective command and meaningful orders, and the disarray of the French who were funneled into a death trap of arrows, mud, and corpses, gave Henry and his men the upper hand.

As the English chronicles are quick to observe, Henry himself was fully armored and wearing a helmet with a crown, standing shoulder-to-shoulder with his men in the thick of battle. The example of the courageous warrior king, engaged in the fierce fighting of the front line, undoubtedly inspired his men to hold the field against the formidable French host. In fact, the role Henry personally played at Agincourt cannot be overemphasized. In accounting for the French forces' surprising *disadvantage* as the battle commenced, Barker concludes that "despite its overwhelming superiority in both numbers and armament," the French army "lacked the thing that was absolutely essential. It had no commander. And it was about to face an enemy whose sole advantage was that it was supremely well led."[77] Mortimer is skeptical about the patriotic speeches attributed to Henry by the English chroniclers, which, even if he had delivered them, would have been heard by only a handful of men. But he agrees with Barker that Henry's very *presence* at the front line was critical to the success of his army: "Just to know he was there was an inspiration to many"; for his soldiers, "it was important to know he was sharing their danger, and in control of his army."[78]

Even if we reject the inflated troop numbers of the medieval chronicles and cast a critical eye on their death tolls, and even if we are mindful of the concerted propaganda campaign by Henry and his acolytes in the aftermath of the battle, we can still admire his personal courage and his stunning success as a field commander. Henry's war for the crown had just begun. While the battle provided no new territorial concession or advantageous political gain in France, it rallied the English nation around their new king in ways that had eluded both Richard II and Henry IV. And the day was inscribed in the English psyche as a momentous and heroic victory for the ages.

The Massacre of Prisoners

Neither the king of France nor the crown prince came to Agincourt to rally their troops in person. But when their French forces clashed with Henry's army, their presence was felt when the *oriflamme*—from the Latin words *aurea flamma*, describing the "golden flame" against a red background—was unfurled at Agincourt. This pennant was housed at the royal abbey of Saint-Denis, just north of Paris, the traditional burial place of the French monarchs. After the solemn celebration of the mass in the abbey church, Charles VI had the *oriflamme* put into the care of an elderly knight named Guillaume Martel (on September 10, 1415), with the order that it be displayed in the coming conflict with Henry.[79] Its precise origins in the eleventh century are obscure, but when the French brought the *oriflamme* to battle, it was a symbol of *guerre mortelle*, or a fight to the death. As long as the banner remained upright, there would be no quarter until it was lowered.[80] This deadly order applied to commoners and aristocratic men-at-arms alike who could expect death at the hands of the French instead of capture and ransom. The intended purpose of this ritual display was to terrorize enemy combatants and undermine their resolve to engage in a fierce fight with the French royal army.

Ironically, despite its supposedly potent symbolism, the *oriflamme* had only been used at two previous engagements in the Hundred Years War. Each of them turned out to be a catastrophic failure for the French: Crécy (1346), where Edward III routed the opposing army commanded by Philip VI (r. 1328–50); and Poitiers (1356), where the fully armed Jean II (r. 1350–64) was soundly defeated and captured in the clash of arms with Edward the Black Prince. Jean II would remain a hostage of the English and eventually die in captivity. The bearer of the *oriflamme* at Poitiers was none other than the celebrated theoretician of chivalry Geoffroi of Charny (1300–56), author of the well-known *Livre de chevalerie*, or the *Book of Chivalry*.[81] Charny was killed in the battle. At Agincourt, the display of the *oriflamme* effected no better outcome than with its previous uses. Its bearer Guillaume Martel was killed, and of course, the English claimed the field.

The *oriflamme* was lost in the battle; trampled into the mud, it was never recovered.[82]

The presence of the *oriflamme* at Agincourt was a clear message to the French troops defending their king, and the English troops on the opposite side of the field, that the consequences of a lost battle would spell disaster for the English. Given the small number of men-at-arms and the abundance of common soldiers (archers) on the field, if the French routed the English, the loss of life would be cataclysmic.[83] And as the testimony of Arthur de Richemont indicates (describing the king's use of body-doubles who were killed in the battle), Henry himself was fully aware that he would be a target of capture or assassination on the battlefield. His heraldry and crowned helmet would make him easy to recognize. But as was the case at Crécy and Poitiers, the fabled banner once again compounded the ignominy of the defeat of the French at Agincourt.

There is no doubt that the English took prisoners that day, many of whom were killed after they surrendered. But the contemporary chronicles provide conflicting details about the timing of their surrender, the numbers involved, and the precise circumstances of their execution. What is not in dispute is that a number of French soldiers, many of them wounded, surrendered to the English when the battle was winding down. At some point before the battle *officially* ended, several prisoners (how many is unknown) were killed in cold blood, some of them being locked in a building and burned alive. One of those prisoners who survived was a Flemish combatant named Ghillebert de Lannoy (1386–1462). He provided chilling details of his own near-death experience when he surrendered to the English:

> In 1415 I was at the battle of Ruisseauville [Agincourt] where I was wounded in the knee and the head, and I laid with the dead. But when the bodies were searched through, I was taken prisoner, being wounded and helpless (*impotens*), and kept under guard for a while. I was then led to a house nearby with 10 or 12 other prisoners who were all wounded. And there, when the duke of Brabant was making a new attack, a shout went up that everyone should kill the prisoners. So that this might be effected all the quicker, they set fire to the house where we were. By the grace of God, I dragged myself a few feet away from the fire. There I was when the English returned, so I was taken prisoner again.[84]

Did Henry himself give the order to kill them, or was there some sort of miscommunication or chaotic event that led to their death? If Henry was responsible for their deaths, what precisely happened that forced him to take such deadly action against unarmed prisoners of war? When we attempt to reconstruct this chronology of events, we must also be conscious of the French resolve to capture or kill Henry himself, and to show no quarter to his troops. Any decisions that Henry made during the battle were predicated on his understanding of the dire situation that he and his men faced if the French rallied their troops with reinforcements and continued to assault the English lines that had been battered by repeated attacks. The king was faced with life-or-death decisions. And at this point in the battle, the French had not been routed, nor do they seem to have communicated through a herald that they wanted to negotiate or that they had accepted defeat. They had simply stopped sending men across the muddy field.

How and when the prisoners surrendered is difficult to know, but it is unlikely that few if any prisoners were taken in the early phases of the battle. The anonymous English cleric who wrote the *Gesta* indicates that many French attempted to surrender in the initial phases of close combat, some of them several times, but they were struck down since the English did not want to disrupt their ranks by handling prisoners.[85] But once the worst of the fighting had ended, the author of the *Gesta* indicates that prisoners were indeed taken and held for ransom. Lannoy's reference to the arrival of the Duke of Brabant with French reinforcements and Henry's fear of a major French counterattack with fresh troops provides a scenario in which Henry himself gave the order to kill the prisoners. Fearful of a new assault, and worried about the logistical challenges of maintaining a fighting formation with French prisoners in his midst, Henry ordered their deaths.

As it turned out, Anthony, Duke of Brabant (1384–1415), arrived too late to make any difference and did not engage the English in any meaningful way. Lacking his armor and heraldry, Brabant and a handful of companions rushed into the thick of the fight. He was captured wearing a herald's garb, and according to the French chronicler Edmond de Dynter (c. 1375–1448), Brabant was a casualty of Henry's order to kill the prisoners: "As a result, many princes and noblemen who were still alive as prisoners were killed. That Duke Anthony was one of these is well known, for after the battle he was found wounded only in the face and the neck."[86] At any rate, deploying newly arrived troops would have amounted to what Keegan calls the reinforcement of failure.[87] Once it became clear that there would be no counterattack, the killing must have immediately stopped, as Lannoy recalls when he was taken prisoner for the second time.

Two chroniclers—Pierre Fenin (d. 1443) and Enguerrand de Monstrelet (c. 1400–53)—indicate that the killing of prisoners was directly caused by an attack on the English baggage by a few French soldiers and low-level scavengers.[88] Monstrelet provides a more detailed account than

Fenin, identifying a large number of peasant scavengers and the theft of a large number of horses:

> Whilst the battle had been raging the English, already with the upper hand, had taken several French prisoners. News then came to the King that the French were attacking from behind and that they had already taken the pack horses and other baggage. This was indeed the case, for Robert de Bournville, Riflart de Clamace, Isembard d'Azincourt and other men-at-arms, accompanied by 600 peasants, had gone off to attack the baggage camp of the English king and had captured baggage and other things along with a large number of horses of the English whilst their keepers were involved in the battle.[89]

Monstrelet also notes that Henry was immediately alarmed by the news of this attack on the baggage, even as he watched the dispersed French soldiers before him regroup into small companies for another attack against his front line:

> As a result of this setback the English king was very concerned, for everywhere he looked in front of him the field was full of French who had taken flight but were regrouping in companies. [Fearing] lest they might attempt to form a new battle he had proclaimed in a loud voice to the sound of the trumpet that each Englishman, on pain of penalty, should kill prisoners so that they would not be able to assist their compatriots. There was immediately a great slaughter of French prisoners.[90]

Thus, in Fenin's and Monstrelet's recollection, the threat of an attack from the rear forced Henry to make this quick and desperate decision. But the author of the *Gesta*, who was himself an eyewitness, sitting atop a horse with the baggage, tells us that these were not soldiers but local thieves and scavengers. He insists that they began their looting *as soon as the battle started.* The anonymous English cleric notes that Henry had made provision for the clergy to be with the baggage as they offered prayers for his protection and success. But as they were praying,

> French pillagers were watching it [the baggage] from almost every side, intending to make an attack upon it immediately they saw both armies engage; in fact, directly battle was joined they fell upon the tail end of it where, owing to the negligence of the royal servants, the king's own baggage was, seizing on royal treasure of great value, a sword and a crown among other precious objects, as well as all the bedding.[91]

This does not appear to have been a coordinated military maneuver or attack, even though in his classic reconstruction of the battle, Keegan attributed Henry's order to massacre the prisoners to the attack on his baggage. Mortimer also believes that this was much more than an "opportunistic looting spree"; that this was a "planned attack on the English, directed by a French commander."[92] But Mortimer is also quick to add that the attack on the baggage did not lead to Henry's order to kill the captive French.

After carefully examining all of the chronicle evidence for what triggered the order to kill the French, Curry also concludes that it is "very unlikely that the killing of prisoners was occasioned by the attack on the baggage. Since the author of the *Gesta* was with the baggage, he would surely have drawn a link, but he does not do so."[93] We should also note that many modern historians consider the eyewitness testimony of the *Gesta* to be the most accurate surviving account of the battle. And when it comes to the circumstances of the killing of prisoners, the modern editors and translators of the *Gesta*, Frank Taylor and John S. Roskell, also dismiss the theory that the attack on the baggage triggered the massacre.[94]

If we rely on the accounts of eyewitness participants in the battle, giving priority to the *Gesta*, it seems that Henry thought that the battle was over when the piles of French dead began to be inspected and wounded prisoners were taken. At some point, Henry feared a counterattack and ordered their deaths. The time between the order and the moment that he realized that no attack was coming is impossible to know, but the killing obviously stopped when Henry realized that the battle had ended. We cannot know with certainty how many prisoners were taken, how many were killed, the exact mechanism for their killing, or precisely when the order was given to kill them.[95]

The author of the *Gesta* does not, however, *directly* link Henry to this order. He mentions the killing but provides an ambiguous report that begins with a religious trope, implying that it was a spontaneous act: "But then, all at once, because of what wrathfulness on God's part no one knows, a shout went up that the enemy's mounted rearguard (in incomparable number and still fresh) were re-establishing their position and line of battle in order to launch an attack on us, few and weary as we were."[96] The dukes who had been captured (Orléans and Bourbon) were spared, with a few other aristocrats, but others "were killed by the swords of their captors or of others following, lest they should involve us in utter disaster in the fighting that would ensue."[97] Since the *Gesta* was primarily a work of propaganda designed to glorify Henry, and promote his future conquest of France and the justice of his cause for war, it is not surprising that its author is silent about the precise origin of this deadly command. That unarmed prisoners were killed was undeniable, but the *Gesta*'s account provides "plausible deniability" for those who might have moral qualms about Henry's decision to massacre unarmed men.

In assessing the circumstances that led to Henry's order and its repercussions, Keegan argues that when contextualized, it is "comprehensible in harsh tactical logic; in ethical and practical terms much more difficult to understand."[98] That Henry could give such an order and have reluctant archers carry it out leads Keegan to conclude that "the battlefield itself was still regarded as a sort of moral no-man's-land and the hour of battle as a legal *dies non*."[99] Moving beyond the religious and chivalric codes that might have governed late medieval warfare, Keegan also proposes an interesting theory: that in loudly giving such an order, Henry was engaging in the equivalent of PSYOPS. As Keegan speculates, "Henry's order, rather than bring about the prisoners' massacre, was intended by its threat to terrorize them into abject inactivity.... Some would have been killed in the process, and quite deliberately, but we need not reckon their number in the thousands, perhaps not even in the hundreds."[100] Allmand comes to a similar conclusion, that the order to kill them was "an attempt to frighten them into submission, and to cause them to be herded off the field by the archers."[101] Allmand describes the event as "tragic," but thinks that the extent of the killing "has none the less probably been exaggerated."[102]

Even those modern historians who express some degree of admiration for Henry are appalled by his order to kill wounded and unarmed men. Barker interprets this order from two perspectives: one "humanitarian," and the other "military." From the first perspective, "Henry's decision was indefensible: to order the killing of wounded and unarmed prisoners in such a cold and calculated way violated every principle of decency and Christian morality. In chivalric terms, it was also reprehensible."[103] On the other hand, Barker is willing to consider the cold logic of the battlefield identified by Keegan: "In military terms, however, Henry's decision was entirely justified. The safety of his men was his overriding priority ... to be attacked on two fronts at once would spell death to the little English force."[104]

Mortimer addresses the controversy of the massacre of the French by considering arguments that are similar to Barker's, noting that some modern detractors consider this a "war crime," while others defend it as a military necessity.[105] Dismissing an attack on the baggage or the sudden appearance of a large, new French relief force, Mortimer concludes that the regrouping of French men-at-arms across the field from Henry led to this order. Henry was taken aback by the renewed activity of men he had considered defeated.[106] While carefully presenting the circumstances and purported logic of Henry's decision, Mortimer still believes that the decision "was made in haste and was to his everlasting shame.... By all the standards of the time, the killing was an ungodly act, and no way to win the love and respect of the people whom he sought to rule as king."[107]

When it comes to modern judgment about Henry's behavior with the French prisoners, other military historians such as Curry see clear parallels with the Battle of Aljubarrota (August 14, 1385), during the war between the Kingdoms of Portugal and Castile.[108] The Portuguese were victorious and preserved the independence of their kingdom. But French soldiers fighting for Portugal, who were taken prisoner and then brought behind the front line of the battle, were killed by the Castilians. According to the French chronicler Jean Froissart (c. 1337–1405), this action was later justified by King John I of Portugal (r. 1385–1433) on account of military necessity. The king's troops could not be distracted by keeping prisoners while a battle raged. Unlike Agincourt, none of the captured prisoners survived, and the death toll was reported by Froissart to be more than four thousand men-at-arms.[109] This action was not condemned by medieval chroniclers, nor has it generally attracted much attention from modern students of the Hundred Years War.

The French chroniclers writing about the killing of prisoners at Agincourt did not castigate Henry. As Curry observes, they blamed the French themselves for allowing this to happen: "In French narratives there is never opprobrium against Henry for this act but only against those who caused it to happen. Self-criticism dominates French accounts alongside acceptance of military necessity and of English political dominance after 1420."[110] Barker comes to the same conclusion: "Significantly, not one of his contemporaries, even among the French, criticised his decision."[111] Rogers makes the same argument, but he also forcefully criticizes those who would apply modern definitions of criminality in war to Henry at Agincourt:

> While it may have been an atrocity by modern laws of war, there is obviously little profit in applying the Geneva Convention to the actions of medieval kings. Even if Henry's contemporaries were appalled by the death of that many brave men, their emotion was generally one of sadness, not outrage. When one reads the full range of sources on the battle or Henry's reign, it is very striking that there is virtually *no* criticism of this action.[112]

In the final analysis, the French and Burgundian chronicles were afflicted by a "blame culture" that focused more on the needless loss of the battle by the French leadership than the command decisions of Henry.[113] And the death of the prisoners was much less attributable to English cruelty or the violation of the laws of war than it was to French sinfulness, political rivalry, and incompetence.

"God Fought for Us": Remembering a Miracle

Within four days of the battle, news of Henry's triumph at Agincourt reached London. Only six days later, Henry's regent and brother John, Duke of Bedford (1389–1435), convened Parliament at Westminster to raise more money for the continuation of Henry's war in Normandy. The euphoria over the English victory was hard to contain and in his opening speech, chancellor and bishop of Winchester, Henry Beaufort (c. 1375–1447), praised Henry's military prowess, while declaring that his stunning victory was directly attributable to God. The capture of Harfleur with the loss of so little English life was done "by God's great gift and with His grace"; the defeat of the French at Agincourt was achieved "with the Almighty's help."[114] Beaufort would specifically mention the glory of Henry at Agincourt in his opening speech to Parliament on three separate occasions: in November 1415; March 1416; and October 1416.[115] His words in the Parliament of March 1416, were even more emphatic than his speech of 1415:

> [W]hen our same most sovereign lord, within a short time after his most noble arrival near the town of Harfleur, had laid siege to it, the same town was surrendered to him; and afterwards on leaving there by land for Calais, as a result of his men who were severely weakened from lack of food, encountered a very large army and a great number of soldiers from France, accompanied by men from the adjoining regions, and fought with them, until God from his bountiful mercy gave the victory to him and the enemy had been killed and defeated— the aforesaid enterprise, by that noble beginning has been and is truly and justly clearly determined and approved by God the Almighty.[116]

Agincourt would also be remembered in the rolls of two other Parliaments that met to subsidize the continued war in France: in November of 1417, and October of 1419.[117]

The early recollections of the battle, and its promotion as the centerpiece of a fund-raising campaign to continue Henry's ambitious and costly war in France, focus sharply on Henry's courage and prowess. Henry is always center stage in these accounts, and remains the larger-than-life hero who dwarfs any of the other participants on either side of the conflict. This sentiment is passionately expressed in the words of the anonymous cleric who accompanied Henry, in the *Gesta*:

> Nor do our older men remember any prince ever having commanded his people on the march with more effort, bravery, or consideration, or having, with his own hand, performed greater feats of strength in the field. Nor, indeed is evidence to be found in the chronicles or annals of kings of which our long history makes mention, that any king of England ever achieved so much in so short a

time and returned home with so great and glorious a triumph. To God alone be the honour and glory, forever and ever. Amen.[118]

This is the hero king who was so eagerly embraced by his romantic revivalists. Unfortunately, the English sources for the battle are "top-heavy," with a disproportionate emphasis on the actions of the king. What the many front line soldiers or thousands of archers experienced or remembered of the battle is nearly impossible to know. In that sense, Henry's court propagandists got both the first and last word about how Agincourt should be remembered by his countrymen and women.

Three weeks after the battle, Henry, his men, and his stable of elite captives, whom he would hold for ransom, boarded ships in Calais and set sail for England. The return trip home was done piecemeal, as soldiers rented private ships at the king's expense, returning without any fanfare. The weather was terrible, with choppy seas and a heavy snowstorm when Henry landed in Dover.[119] As he progressed inland, Henry was given a hero's welcome by cheering crowds and was greeted by the archbishop of Canterbury, Henry Chichele (c. 1364–1443), as he entered the great cathedral. He came to pay his respects before the shrine of the martyred Saint Thomas Becket. On either side of Becket were the tombs of Edward III and his son, the Black Prince of Wales. But this constituted much more than a pious pilgrimage by a grateful king. According to Barker, Henry had come to take his rightful place among his predecessors who had won spectacular victories at Crécy and Poitiers: "Irrespective of the justice of his claims to the throne of France, no one could doubt any longer that Henry V was indeed, by the grace of God, king of England."[120]

The official celebration of Henry's victory took place in London, in the form of a great pageant that is vividly described by the anonymous author of the *Gesta*. This English cleric had been with Henry from Harfleur to Agincourt, and he now witnessed the magnificent festivities honoring Henry's success.[121] The modern editors and translators of this work consider the *Gesta* to be an eyewitness description that was probably also based on an official program for the event.[122] On November 23, 1415, the costly and elaborate pageantry began with the civic elite of London riding out of the city to greet Henry, his retinue, and his French captives, who would be paraded through the streets like prisoners in an ancient Roman triumph.[123] Replete with expensive implements, allegorical images, and repeated liturgical chants, the ceremonies stood in sharp contrast to Henry's own comportment and demeanor. The king was serene and seemingly emotionless as he humbly processed among the throngs of cheering Londoners who celebrated his great victory. The author of the *Gesta* draws this contrast in sharp relief:

> Amid these public expressions of praise and the display made by the citizens, however, the king himself, wearing a gown of purple, proceeded, not in exulted pride and with an imposing escort or impressively large retinue, but with an impassive countenance and at a dignified pace, and with only a few of the most trusted members of his household in attendance....Indeed, from his quiet demeanor, gentle pace, and sober progress, it might have been gathered that the king, silently pondering the matter in his heart, was rendering thanks to God alone, not to man.[124]

Was Henry silently giving thanks to God? Or was he consciously assuming a public posture that would project strength and virtue through humility? Was he perhaps ruminating over the difficult and costly campaign that he had just completed, and the battle that could have been a disastrous defeat that might have ended with his own death? Henry made it home alive and was now surrounded by soaring rhetoric, throngs of cheering crowds, and liturgical chants as he processed with a group of elite French prisoners in London. What he could not yet celebrate was any territorial concession from the French or any acknowledgment of his claim to the crown of France. And his experience at Harfleur did not augur well for the rapidity with which he could conquer Normandy and make good on his political claims. The future of his war in France, from a tactical and strategic sense, all came down to his experience at Harfleur, *not* Agincourt. But Henry's place in the pantheon of great and courageous commanders was secured by his destruction of the flower of French chivalry in the muddy fields of Agincourt.

Long after Henry's death, popular history would remember Henry for his fictional St. Crispin's Day speech at Agincourt, not the devastation of Harfleur that preceded it. The psychological terror and indiscriminate destruction of bombards and gunstones; the stench of human and animal debris in the unusually hot summer and fall of 1415; the deadly ravages of dysentery that spread among the English; the sobs of weeping women and children who were banished from their homes as the English occupied Harfleur; and a difficult and dangerous return trip to England after a successful siege do not fit nicely with the romantic legend of the warrior king that was revived in the nineteenth and twentieth century.

Henry's victory at Agincourt no doubt remains impressive, but it needs to be contextualized lest we uncritically embrace the Shakespearean myth of Henry being judged worthy of the crown after his slaughter of the disorganized and poorly commanded French forces that faced him in northeastern France six centuries ago. Henry was a great and courageous commander. He was also lucky, the beneficiary of bad weather and bad organization and division of command on the French side at Agincourt. He was also tenacious. The Treaty of Troyes, which recognized his right to the French throne, was a hard-fought victory built on Henry's exhausting and costly campaign of siege warfare across Normandy that eventually took his life.

What is often overlooked in modern recollections of Agincourt, however, is that Henry would never again fight in an open field battle in the remaining years of his campaign in France. For a variety of reasons—not the least being his personal safety—Henry preferred siege warfare, with its predictable pattern of encampment and bombardment of enemy fortresses. The decimation of the civilian population and the staggering loss of life due to starvation and the collateral damage of artillery bombardment are not the stuff of chivalrous romance. It is no surprise that in popular culture, Agincourt eclipses everything else involving Henry's grinding war in Normandy.

The king's order to kill prisoners and his brutal campaigns after Agincourt also opened Henry to intense criticism by his modern detractors, some of whom have gone so far as to accuse him of criminal behavior. The irony, of course, is that the young king is not widely remembered for his sieges, nor is Agincourt remembered for debates about conflicting numbers of combatants, or alleged war crimes committed by the English king. It was not by any measure a "decisive battle," since the French did not respond with offers of negotiations, a call for a truce, or any sort of territorial or political concessions. Henry would have to come back to Normandy in 1417, and begin a five-year war of conquest that eventually wore his health down to the point of death. But his carefully crafted public memory of the battle, including his role as God's just warrior king at Agincourt, was effectively historicized by his propagandists and outlived him by a full six centuries. By that measure, his promotion of "the miracle of Agincourt" remains one of the most successful political marketing campaigns in Western history. And in that sense, the Battle of Agincourt *was* decisive.

SEVEN

From Warrior King to Cradle King

The Treaty of Troyes and Henry VI

The Treaty of Troyes

The Treaty of Troyes (May 21, 1420) was the capstone of Henry's Norman campaign. The capitulation of the Norman capital city of Rouen (January 19, 1419), after a brutal six-month siege by English forces, had been a triumphant moment for the young king. Henry relished his role as conqueror and subjected the Rouennais to a carefully staged ritual of surrender, arrayed in golden robes and seated on a throne when he received the keys to the city.[1] The submission of Rouen was really of much greater significance to Henry's political goals than his victory at Agincourt four years earlier. The Norman capital was the largest city in France ever to be captured by siege in the entirety of the Hundred Years War (it may have had as many as seventy thousand inhabitants).[2] The fall of Rouen was soon followed by the English occupation of Paris and what appeared to be the end of the cursed civil war among the French that had devastated the once proud capital city. Henry topped off these triumphant moments with a full and public recognition by the Valois king of his legal right to the French monarchy. After intense negotiations that began in late 1419, the Valois court and the Burgundian prince of the blood, Duke Philip III, accepted Henry V's claim to the throne of France and recognized that of his future heirs.

The Treaty of Troyes made good on Henry's persistent and self-righteous demand for the French crown by right of succession.[3] The treaty betrothed the French king's eighteen-year-old daughter Catherine to the thirty-three-year-old Henry V; declared him the adopted son of the reigning Valois king; made him regent of the mad king Charles VI; and formally made him ruler of a joint kingdom of England and France at the death of

Charles VI, whose passing would mark the official extinction of his dynasty. And even if Henry's marriage to the Valois princess produced no male heir (fortunately for Henry it did), the treaty still kept the French succession within the legitimate male line of Henry V's family. The Estates General—representing the three estates of clergy, nobility, and people—was soon thereafter called into session by Charles VI in Paris, where it solemnly ratified the treaty. It was also ratified by Parliament when Henry returned to England about a year later. A subsequent meeting of the Estates General formally indicted and charged a group of conspirators with the murder of the Duke of Burgundy, John the Fearless. The Dauphin Charles (the Valois crown prince) was among those indicted, but he would not answer to the charges and was condemned *in absentia* and exiled from France for life.[4]

The Dauphin had constructed his own parallel government in exile in his capital city of Bourges and of course rejected out of hand both the treaty and the legal decrees of the Estates General. And as bleak as his circumstances might have appeared, Charles still had the loyalty of roughly half of the French kingdom as he plotted his next move. Despite his great diplomatic victory at Troyes, Henry was still obligated to continue his costly war against the Dauphinists, to crush once and for all any opposition to his dual monarchy. For all its pomp and symbolism, Henry's wedding day (June 2, 1420) was literally followed by his march to Sens and then Montereau, where he had to begin the conquest of other disloyal strongholds.[5] The grind of siege warfare in the latter years of Henry's reign took an enormous toll on the finances of England, not to mention on the king's physical health. And after his untimely death, some of the greatest reversals of fortune in European history soon took place and his Norman conquest would become, as Pugh concludes, a "gamble that failed," bankrupting his country and making him master of little more than a third of the modern French kingdom before his unexpected death.[6]

Henry would also face stiff opposition from his own Parliament when he attempted to fund his ongoing war. If he were now truly the regent of France and heir to the throne, this was no longer an English war of conquest but a French war of rebellion. The French over whom Henry claimed sovereignty should therefore absorb the cost of the conflict. And as Curry argues, the Treaty of Troyes had not really "ended" a war. It had mutated into a new phase of the ongoing civil war between the Armagnacs and Burgundians, with Henry and the English throwing in their lot with the Duke of Burgundy. Meanwhile, many of Henry's "French subjects" could never forget that he really governed them by right of conquest, not succession.[7] Sumption also concludes that despite Henry's legal claim to the French

The Marriage of Henry V and Catherine Valois (1420). Henry's conquest of Normandy led to the Treaty of Troyes (1420), which allowed him to marry the daughter of the French king, Charles VI. According to the treaty, Henry would serve as regent for the mad king, and when he died, Henry would be king of France, by right of succession. This dual monarchy would then pass to any of his legitimate male heirs (Smith Archive / Alamy Stock Photo).

throne, he was still effectively a conqueror and an occupier of a foreign country. And the occupation proved costly and difficult for the English, who were "everywhere overstretched. Unable to come to grips with their enemy on their own terms, they were compelled to fight an expensive war of static defense in Normandy and debilitating sieges everywhere else."[8]

Derisively called the "King of Bourges" by his enemies, Charles and his followers were much more tenacious in their rejection of the new dynastic order than Henry first imagined. The Dauphinists remained resolute in their resistance to the English king, and Henry V's alliance with Duke Philip III, who sometimes seemed to provide limited or half-hearted support to his military campaigns, proved to be a great disappointment. Within two years of his triumph at Troyes, Henry would be dead as a consequence of an illness he contracted during his grueling military campaign against the rebellious holdouts loyal to the Dauphin. His brother Thomas, Duke of Clarence, would precede him in death by a year, when the duke was killed in a disastrous battle that he impetuously fought against the Dauphinists at Baugé (March 22, 1421). Though he died having been legally recognized as joint ruler of England and France, Henry literally never wore the French crown. His newborn son Henry VI would be the only English monarch ever to have that honor, but his disastrous reign would ensure that his French coronation was an empty ritual.

The modern historiographic tradition surrounding the Treaty of Troyes has been generally hostile to Henry V's settlement with the Valois monarchy. Enthralled with her modern myth, many students of Joan of Arc view the treaty as an unfortunate detour on the road to the Dauphin's eventual coronation after her miraculous mission and victories. Sumption offers an important caveat about the danger of viewing the negotiation and ratification of the treaty through the lens of modern French patriotism:

> The pious orthodoxies of modern French historiography, which regard the treaty of Troyes as a base betrayal of their national allegiance, engineered by a foreign Queen [Isabeau of Bavaria] and a clique of traitors, did not seem as obvious to contemporary Frenchmen as it did to Jules Michelet writing in the middle of the nineteenth century in the high noon of French patriotism ... to the great council at Troyes and probably to many others in the provinces of the north, the dual monarchy was not a betrayal of France. It was a route to national survival.[9]

The role of Isabeau of Bavaria (c. 1370–1435) in the ratification of the Treaty of Troyes contributed to her modern reputation as a traitor to her own family and to France, who foisted an illegitimate settlement on her mentally ill husband.[10] The French queen was the target of a smear campaign that featured wild rumors of greed, gluttony, and promiscuity that continue to be uncritically repeated in modern academic works about Joan of Arc. In these accounts, the supposedly libidinous queen "lost" France while the young, unsullied virgin warrior "saved" it. Tracy Adams is one of the few scholars who have systematically exposed the fraudulent nature of this malignant hearsay, devoting an entire monograph to the history of the construction of the black legend of Isabeau.[11] This slander surely began in the queen's lifetime, when she was unfairly blamed for the political misfortunes that afflicted the court of her deranged husband. Before his assassination at the order of the Duke of Burgundy, John the Fearless, the schizophrenic king's younger and only brother, Louis of Orléans (1372–1407), was reputed to be one of Isabeau's lovers. This salacious gossip was eagerly marketed by the English, who later claimed that the Dauphin was the bastard child of some adulterous liaison by the queen. According to Adams, the adultery charge is pure fantasy.[12]

In addition to rumors of promiscuity, Isabeau was also accused of luxurious living and treasonous machinations, and to make her an even more hideous character, her enemies body-shamed her with descriptions of her grotesque obesity. This portrait of the queen persisted well into modernity. In her ground-breaking study, Rachel Gibbons notes: "As far as Isabeau's physiology is concerned, historians seem not to have left the morality theatre: if she is bad, she is ugly; if not so bad, she is allowed to be pretty. Surprisingly, this is not just the case in medieval works, where it could be seen as an acceptable literary device, but also in modern accounts."[13]

Jean-Marie Moeglin and Curry make a case that is similar to Sumption's, challenging the supposed treachery of the settlement at Troyes. Moeglin notes that nineteenth-century French historiography viewed the treaty through the xenophobic lens of the "liberation of France from foreigners."[14] After the rapprochement between Charles VII and the Burgundians (1435), and the eventual French victory in the war (1453), the treaty came to be remembered as an unjust effort to eradicate the kingdom of France. Moeglin challenges this simplistic reading and offers an analysis of every peace treaty ratified by the French and English throughout the course of the Hundred Years War. His detailed study shows that the concept of a "peaceful" settlement of the war between the English and French proposed by the Treaty of Troyes was not markedly different in intent and language from previous treaties, emphasizing the "greater good" of both kingdoms.[15] Curry's analysis demonstrates how the treaty emphasized the failure of previous diplomatic attempts to bring a peaceful settlement to the multiple conflicts afflicting the French nation. Henry V's chancellor, Henry

Beaufort, had famously declared in a speech before Parliament (October 1416) that the English king had been forced to make war in order to achieve a lasting peace.[16] Charles VI now made his peace with Henry, mindful, as the treaty declares, of "how much damage and sorrow had been caused by the divisions of the kingdoms to this point, not only for the kingdoms but also for the church."[17]

In the context within which it was drafted, the treaty represented a reasonable solution to the miserable conflict that seemed to have no end. The English were militarily unstoppable and poised to take France by bloody conquest. A negotiated, peaceful settlement with the English had evaded the best efforts of the French princes of the blood during the devastating civil war between the Armagnacs and Burgundians. Here was an opportunity to end the bloodshed and political disruption that had plagued France for decades. Even the French monastic chronicler from the Royal Abbey of St.-Denis, Michel Pintoin (c. 1350–1421), was willing to accept this imperfect solution for a greater good. Henry could exercise lordship over the French, so long as they could live in peace and safety.[18] And from a diplomatic standpoint, the treaty was a brilliant maneuver on the part of Henry. He had not "seized" or "usurped" the French crown. He had instead recognized that Charles VI was the legitimate king of France until his death, and he stood in the wings as regent and heir to his throne. Had Henry lived longer, he would have become king of France by right of succession.

That the court of an aged schizophrenic Valois king had been bludgeoned into conceding its crown to the Lancastrians has led to modern criticism of Henry V for his own ruthless opportunism. Such criticisms are to a considerable degree legitimate. But placed in a larger historical context, we must remember that success on the battlefield has been the *sine qua non* of a great many landmark political outcomes, from antiquity to modernity. That Henry could achieve the political settlement he desired through military coercion is unremarkable (when looking at the grand sweep of European history).

However, it did not help Henry's international stature that the pope whose election ended the Great Schism and had restored the Roman line of the papacy, Martin V (r. 1417–31), refused to recognize the Treaty of Troyes. As Harvey notes, the pope's withholding of his blessing was itself an act of political opportunism, designed to coerce the English king into rescinding the anti-papal legislation that had been passed by Parliament at the height of the Schism.[19] But beyond his attempt to restore traditional papal rights over the English church, Martin V became increasingly sympathetic to the Dauphin's cause, never condemning him personally for the outrage at

Montereau and making it clear, as Harvey emphasizes, that Charles was his "father's rightful heir," and "he never addressed Henry V as heir or regent nor Henry VI as king of France."[20] After his death, Henry V's brother and regent of France, John, Duke of Bedford (1389–1435), continued to press the pope for recognition of the treaty, to no avail.[21]

Henry's detractors have also argued that because of his mental incompetence, Charles VI could not legally disinherit his son and banish him from the throne.[22] Before their eventual truce with Charles VII, the Burgundians put this very case to the faculty of law at the prestigious University of Bologna (1435). They ruled in favor of the Dauphin. They argued that since his legitimacy was not in question and since his father was not mentally competent—something that Charles admitted in the treaty itself—the Dauphin could not be robbed of his title; nor could his father even make such a declaration because he could not simultaneously be an accuser and a judge. The elder Charles also could not dispose of the monarchy and the kingdom of France as if it were private property, with no regard to the rights of French princes of the blood to dynastic succession.[23] Soon after this ruling, the Duke of Burgundy, Philip III, and Charles VII were formally reconciled with the Treaty of Arras (September 1435).[24] The Burgundians openly broke their alliance with the incensed English and recognized the legitimacy Charles VII's monarchy, while Charles cynically disavowed the murder of John the Fearless and promised to bring his murderers to justice.

Henry VI and the Dual Monarchy

From the time of his second expedition to France (1417) to his death on French soil (August 31, 1422), Henry had spent only four months in England. Despite the glory of his much-vaunted victory at Agincourt, the conquest of Normandy and the acquisition of the French crown had proven far more difficult and costly than he had imagined. The second expedition marked a period of five full years of military campaigning for Henry. His relentless, grueling sieges finally overtook him when he died at the age of thirty-five in the castle of Bois de Vincennes, not far from Paris. The English monastic chronicler Thomas Walsingham states that he had been ill for quite some time before he "was attacked by an acute fever and overpowering dysentery."[25]

Henry's death modeled the conventions of late medieval Christian piety. He stoically contemplated his mortality, while dictating codicils to his last will and testament. He confessed his sins and received the sacraments of communion and extreme unction, surrounded by ardent supporters, as he lay dying.[26] The only disruption of this tranquil religious tableau is reported by the English chronicler known as Pseudo-Elmham, who says that before Henry died, he argued with some "malignant spirit." As he was about to breathe his last, the king cried out: "You lie, you lie! My portion is with the Lord Jesus Christ!" Then clutching a crucifix, he said, "Into your hands, O Lord, you have redeemed my end," and then he took his last breath.[27] His remains were soon transferred with great veneration to the royal abbey of St.-Denis, then Pontoise and finally to Rouen, before his body was transported across the Channel.[28] Henry was eventually laid to rest in the magnificent tomb that he had constructed in Westminster Abbey, where a staggering number of masses would be celebrated by the chantry priests that he had endowed for the repose of his soul.

Upon his death, Henry V was succeeded by his nine-month-old son Henry VI, the youngest monarch in English history.[29] The highly success-ful warrior king had been replaced by a helpless cradle king. The pro–Lan-castrian chronicler Thomas Walsingham reflected the despair that was felt in England at the news of Henry V's sudden, untimely death and the acces-sion of his infant son:

> When his [Henry V's] subjects reflected on [his] qualities and famous deeds,
> they felt great dread at the sudden, terrible change in their fortunes that
> the right hand of the Lord had brought about, and their sorrow cannot be
> described. Nor is this surprising, since instead of a puissant king and discern-
> ing lord who was splendidly equipped with all the characteristics of goodness,
> they were receiving for their king and lord his weak, infant son who was not yet
> a year old.[30]

The overall serenity of Henry V's death bed was soon followed by the tumult of his infant son's reign, a child Henry had never even met before he died. Henry VI (r. 1422–61, 70–71) was not only the youngest monarch in English history but also the only English king ever to be crowned "King of France." After Joan of Arc's successful liberation of Orléans from the English (May 1429), the Dauphin Charles was crowned in Reims (July 17, 1429), undercutting the Lancastrian claims that originated with the Treaty of Troyes. Alarmed by this unexpected turn of events, the regent of France, John, Duke of Bedford, was compelled to stage a hastily planned corona-tion of Henry VI as king of France. Bertram Wolffe argues that Bedford's hand was most definitely forced by Joan of Arc's spectacular military career. Five years after the English loss of Orléans, Bedford struggled to compre-hend the rapid decline of English fortunes in France on his watch. But he clearly attributed these reversals of fortune to the diabolical activity of the so-called virgin warrior—*la Pucelle*, as Joan of Arc styled herself—whom the English had tried and executed: "'The great stroke' upon Henry's people, he told the young king, was 'caused in great part as I trow of lack of sad belief and unlawful doubt that they had in a disciple and limb of the fiend called the Pucelle that used false enchantment and sorcery.'"[31]

Henry VI was the only English king ever to be crowned king of France, in what turned out to be a meaningless ceremony when he was all of nine years old (December 16, 1431). Unfortunately, he could not be anointed in the traditional site of French coronations, Reims Cathedral (then occupied by opposing French forces), and his regents had to settle for a liturgy in Paris. The Parisians remembered the coronation as featuring ceremonies that were too "English," a perception that was fueled by the presence of the young king's great uncle, Cardinal Henry Beaufort (1375–1447), who presided over Henry's coronation as king of France. There were also loud com-

Henry VI (r. 1422–61, 70–71). Nine months old when his father died, Henry became the youngest king in English history. He was also the only English monarch ever crowned king of France, when he was nine years of age. The living embodiment of the Treaty of Troyes, Henry VI personified its ultimate failure. Lacking his father's military skills and charisma, his reign witnessed the collapse of English power in France and a French victory in the Hundred Years War. Public order in England also collapsed and Henry was eventually overthrown and murdered (INTERFOTO / Alamy Stock Photo).

plaints about insufficient seating arrangements for French dignitaries and the terrible food that was served.[32] This recollection was an ominous harbinger of things to come. After this hastily organized ceremony, the young king never again stepped foot in France.

Henry VI was the living embodiment of the Treaty of Troyes and, in the end, personified its ultimate failure. He was about fifteen and governed with the aid of a regency council when the Treaty of Arras (1435) rejected his claim to the French throne. Within the year, he would come of age and fully assume the role of a ruling king. But *this* Henry was no match for the French and Burgundian political forces that were poised to rob him of his French inheritance. Scholars continue to debate Henry VI's long and chaotic reign.[33] Some have judged him to be an incompetent but aggressive ruler, responsible for a multitude of national and international disasters (especially the English loss of France). Others claim that he was indeed politically incompetent, but also king in name only: an "occasional" king whose decision-making was mostly driven by religious concerns; an "un-canonized saint," who prioritized his time around religious rituals and pious devotions.[34] His former chaplain and posthumous biographer, John Blacman (c. 1408–85), succinctly captures Henry's pious and pacifistic nature, declaring that the king was "more given to God and devout prayer than to handling worldly and temporal things or practising vain sports and pursuits: these he despised as trifling, and was continually occupied either in prayer or the reading of the scriptures or of chronicles."[35]

In the latter part of his long reign, Henry also became incapable of ruling when he was incapacitated by debilitating mental illness, while ruthless and unscrupulous councilors caused havoc in his name.[36] In many respects, his tragic reign mirrored the tumult, internal violence, and political conflicts of the reign of his grandfather, the mad King Charles VI. The antithesis of his warrior father, the pious Henry VI was utterly lacking in martial skills and was addled by bouts of severe mental illness, causing his monarchy to devolve into a disaster for his home country.[37] His failure as king led to the collapse of public authority in England, open rebellion against his government, and his overthrow by a Yorkist prince who had himself crowned King Edward IV (r. 1461–70, 71–83).[38] Deposed and held hostage by the new king, Henry VI eventually regained his throne after renewed conflicts among the Yorkists, only to be deposed for a second time, imprisoned and executed at the order of Edward IV. The highlight of his reign was the loss of his father's hard-won Anglo-Norman kingdom, which fomented a period of bloody civil war in England that came to be known collectively as the Wars of the Roses. Ironically, the marriage of his widowed mother Catherine to a Welsh soldier named Owen Tudor (c. 1400–61) created a new line of succession that would largely end this period of chaos and armed conflict with the accession of Henry VII (r. 1485–1509).

EIGHT

A Just and Holy Warrior?

Romanticism, Revisionism, and Judgment

After a period of revival and glorification which reached its peak in the mid-twentieth century, Henry V's military career became the subject of scholarly debate about the justice of his cause for war, the legitimacy of his religious ideology, and how he conducted himself on the battlefield. The same century that witnessed renewed nationalistic fervor over Henry's illustrious military feats also lived through two world wars whose consequences are still felt in the twenty-first century. These conflicts featured previously unimaginable levels of physical devastation and the dislocation and death of millions of combatants and civilians.

The Second World War in particular continues to evoke strong emotions about the horrors of modern warfare and the seemingly limitless depravity of humans in times of armed conflict. The war witnessed the mass deportation and extermination of millions of people declared "subhuman" by their Nazi murderers; the mass murder of Chinese civilians and the forced sexual slavery of Korean girls by the Japanese army; the firebombing of cities in Germany and Japan by British and American forces; the mass rape of women in Germany by conquering Russian armies; and the first use of nuclear weapons by the United States on civilian targets in Japan. The unprecedented level of violence and the ruthless efficiency with which the killing was done gave birth to ominous neologisms and legal definitions that continue to haunt us: "genocide," "war crimes" and "crimes against humanity."

The general public might assume that unlike modern warfare—with its weapons of mass destruction and smart technology that dehumanizes killing—its medieval predecessor was a nobler, more chivalrous affair. That is precisely how nineteenth-century romantics defined medieval combat: as a contest between gallant gentlemen who treated their vanquished foes with honor and respect. This popular view is based on the assumption that in the Middle Ages, war among Christians was strictly governed by the canonical codes of the Catholic Church and the honor of the knightly class.

However, experts on chivalric literature and culture such as Richard W. Kaeuper are quick to argue that the modern perception of the medieval warrior aristocracy is more the product of nineteenth-century imagination and fantasy than fourteenth- and fifteenth-century historical fact.[1] Kaeuper meticulously deconstructs this romantic mythology by noting that the medieval culture of chivalry "actually contributed as much to the problem of violence as it provided a solution."[2] In his comprehensive study of chivalric ideals during the Hundred Years War, Craig Taylor also cautions us against "the modern romantic vision of chivalry as the celebration of civilized warriors who treated war as a game, preferring to behave magnanimously and honourably towards vulnerable opponents rather than to secure victory at any cost."[3] Nigel Saul, who has focused his research on chivalry in England in the later Middle Ages, attributes this misconception to the nostalgic, romantic idealization of heroes from a glorious past that stood in sharp contrast to the supposed misery of modernity. He concludes that the roots of this romantic longing for knightly heroes "lay in an idealized view of the medieval past which grew up in reaction to the horrors of the grim industrialization of the time."[4]

This was, of course, the same cultural milieu that rediscovered Henry V and turned him into a larger-than-life heroic figure. And yet this "hero" behaved in ways that flagrantly defy the anachronistic, Romantic conceptions of chivalry that have often been imposed on him by his modern admirers. For example, Henry gave the order to massacre unarmed French prisoners at the Battle of Agincourt, something that even Shakespeare did not ignore. But this shocking scene was omitted from Olivier's patriotic, 1944 screen adaptation of the play that glorified the young king. Henry was also responsible for the deaths of hundreds of noncombatants who were trapped between the English army and the defenders of the Norman capital city of Rouen. These civilians—the elderly, women, and children—were dubbed "useless mouths" and had been expelled by the French garrison because they could not help defend the city when it faced the threat of famine during Henry's long blockade (July 1418–January 1419). By the end of the siege, about two hundred people a day were dying of starvation.[5]

Even some English observers in Henry's entourage felt sympathy for the scores of innocent Rouennais who were injured or killed in Henry's conquest of their city. The English poet John Page claimed to have been an eyewitness of these events.[6] While praising Henry's martial prowess, Page lamented the pitiable state of civilians who died of starvation in the large ditch between the walls of the city and the English forces that surrounded them. He vividly describes women clutching their dead babies, babies trying to suckle from their dead mothers, and orphaned children begging for bread from the English.[7] One of Henry's most vocal modern critics sees a similar disregard for the lives even of his own men by the English king. Ian Mortimer concludes that Henry "regarded the common Englishman in his army as little more than a chattel, and the French men-at-arms as enemies of God, to be treated according to God's law, not the laws of chivalry."[8]

Outside of the clamor of battle, the warrior class was also supposedly governed by a number of restrictions that involved the protection of sacred property and civilian life. While it is true that the medieval Church proscribed a number of activities in the conduct of war, especially the killing of innocents and the plunder and destruction of sacred spaces such as churches and monasteries, these prohibitions were often ignored by armies on both sides of the Hundred Years War. In the broader context of the war, such violations of established ecclesiastical rules for warfare are not all that surprising. In the early phases of the conflict, when tottering French armies could not be provoked into open field battle against the English, King Edward III (r. 1327–77) and his son, Edward the Black Prince (1330–76), regularly used terror tactics to grind down resistance to their armies. The *chevauchée*—a French term describing a swift and devastating cavalry raid—became the notorious, carefully calculated scorched-earth strategy of the English and their Gascon allies.[9] After the Black Death in the mid-fourteenth century, the seriously outnumbered English generally believed that such tactics could be as productive as full-scale battles and sieges. A wide trail of suffering was inflicted on the general French population as their villages burned and their churches and food stores were pillaged; in some cases, their women were raped and unarmed civilians were forced to buy protection or be murdered.[10]

The *chevauchée* represents a strategy of total warfare that is generally associated with modern armies. But according to Taylor, these English campaigns of terrorism unmask one of the great myths of chivalry: "Contrary to the romantic ideal of the knight as protector of women, children and the weak, medieval armies often targeted non-combatants during campaigns, while soldiers and garrisons abused the wider population during truces and breaks in the rhythm of warfare."[11] Green comes to the same conclusion, but he also notes that the Black Prince's aristocratic contemporaries saw no contradiction between having a "chivalric reputation" as a knight and devastating the lands and livelihoods of the lowest strata of the social order who were often defenseless. During the

English campaigns that preceded the stunning victory at Poitiers (1356), the Black Prince "built himself a chivalric reputation on the ashes of peasant houses; he gained renown by burning the property of those least able to defend themselves and by taking valuable prisoners."[12] The humiliation of the French monarchs, who seemed incapable of defending their realm or the people that inhabited it, could be taken as a surrogate form of victory on the battlefield.

Marauding armies engaged in these attacks enriched themselves with forage and plunder, yet military historians continue to debate the effectiveness of the *chevauchée* as part of a larger war strategy. Aside from traumatizing French civilians, the English raids had a questionable impact on the final outcome of the war. More often than not the French could not be provoked into open battle, nor were there widespread defections on their side. But is it fair to call these raids "criminal?" Was the killing of French prisoners at Agincourt or the forced starvation of civilians during the siege of Rouen a "war crime?" It remains a disputed question whether or not we should apply modern legal concepts of criminality in warfare to the activities of medieval armies or the orders of individual medieval military commanders.[13] For modern scholars, passing judgment on Henry's behavior and that of his contemporaries in times of war is a complex and challenging process that must begin with the institutional norms that supposedly governed warfare in their own day. But before we attempt to identify those standards, we should also recognize that the first fully operational code of conduct for an army in wartime was not published until 1863, at the height of the American Civil War.

Crafted at the behest of the War Department for the Union Armies, this code was compiled by the German-American political philosopher and legal scholar, Franz Lieber (c. 1798–1872).[14] Signed by Abraham Lincoln (April 24, 1863), the *Instruction for the Government of Armies of the United States in the Field* would become the basis for the legal thinking of the Hague and Geneva Conventions. The *Instruction* prohibited excessive cruelty, murder, rape, assassination, and despoliation of churches and charitable foundations (e.g., schools and museums). But portions of this code allowed for behaviors that the modern world would find difficult to accept: starvation of enemy cities to force them to surrender; surprise bombardment of enemy positions that would lead to civilian deaths; the confiscation of all moveable property in a captured area; shooting on sight of combatants not wearing a recognizable military uniform.[15] One of the Union's most successful generals, William Tecumseh Sherman (1820–91), rarely took heed of the Lieber *Instructions* while campaigning. His march through the

South and his strategy of "total warfare" mirrors the destructive force of the English and Burgundian *chevauchées* of the Hundred Years War.

For late medieval armies, the most obvious place to find the rules governing proper conduct for soldiers is the Church. It had a long and piecemeal history of attempting to regulate and control violence among Christians. For example, in the late tenth and early twelfth century, the Peace and Truce of God were promoted by ecclesiastical authorities in France to prevent private feuds from escalating into bloody, armed conflicts. This legislation also prohibited taking up arms on Sundays, Thursdays, Fridays, Saturdays, and holy feast days, as well as during Advent and Lent. This ambitious code honored days and liturgical seasons that were sacred in Christian salvation history, attempting to protect civilians and clerics from injury or death. But by the time of the Hundred Years War, the original decrees of popes and councils requiring such truce days had mostly become a dead letter.[16]

The Church had also crafted much broader theoretical criteria for waging legitimate war, with theologians identifying and defining two types of legal armed conflict: the just war (war between nations) and the holy war (war between Christians and infidels, or orthodox Christians and heretics). On the towering authority of the Latin Father of the Church, St. Augustine of Hippo (354–430), medieval Europe began to form a Christian just warfare tradition. It was predicated on Augustine's belief that war is a necessary evil, given the sinful nature of the human race.[17] Writing at a time when barbarian armies besieged the frontiers of Rome and public authority was collapsing, Augustine argued that secular rulers had a moral obligation to defend their citizens against the disruption of civic order and injury done by invading hosts. In an oft-quoted statement defining what constituted a just war, Augustine declares: "Wars can only be defined as just that avenge injuries."[18] In his comprehensive study of just war theory in the Middle Ages, Frederick Russell notes that Augustine's ideas are reflective of Marcus Cicero's concept of just war being "analogous to the pursuit of compensatory damages in private law."[19]

Of utmost importance to Augustine is the greater good of preserving the peace. The end of war *is* peace, and this Augustinian theology of warfare was the focal point of the opening speech to Parliament (October 1416) of Henry V's chancellor and bishop of Winchester, Henry Beaufort (c. 1375–1447). As Henry sought renewed funding for the continuation of his war in Normandy, Beaufort reflected on the first anniversary of the great English victory at Agincourt, chastising the French for their arrogance and obstinacy in rejecting Henry's just claims to the crown of France:

[T]hinking nothing of their said defeat or weakness [the French] have absolutely refused to reach any agreement. For which reason our said sovereign lord is again of necessity obliged to have recourse to the issue of the sword if he wishes to achieve an end, peace and termination of his just aim and quarrel, thereby fulfilling the words of the wise man who says: "Let us make wars so that we might have peace, for the end of war is peace."[20]

Building on the Augustinian theology of legitimate warfare, the renowned scholastic theologian St. Thomas Aquinas (1225–74) attempted to refine and codify a theory of just war that could be universally applied in European Christendom. Since Augustine's "doctrine" was not presented in a single, comprehensive work but scattered across a wide range of texts, Aquinas's synthesis played a critical role in helping to articulate a more coherent just war theory at the end of the Middle Ages. In his magisterial *Summa Theologiae* (c. 1265–74), Aquinas states:

[T]hree things are required for any war to be just. The first is the authority of the sovereign on whose command war is waged. Now a private person has no business declaring war.... Secondly, a just cause is required, namely that those who are attacked are attacked because they deserve it on account of some wrong they have done.... Thirdly, the right intention of those waging war is required, that is, they must intend to promote the good and to avoid evil.[21]

Aquinas reiterates Augustine's teaching—that the end or goal of war is peace—but what remains unclear is a definition of "proportionality" in the conduct of a military campaign. This is a bit surprising since, as Edward A. Synan observes, Aquinas came from a military family (his father and brothers were knights), and he sometimes used analogies from medieval weaponry or warfare to make theological points.[22] However, like other medieval theologians and canonists, Aquinas seemed to be much more concerned with *ius ad bellum* questions, while remaining vague or ambiguous on the problem of *ius in bello*, or right conduct in war.

While violence was a necessary evil for the restoration and preservation of peace, were there limits to the destructive force that could be used to bring about a war's end? Did indiscriminate bombardment of cities, with a high likelihood of civilian casualties and destruction of vital civilian infrastructure—followed by the forced exile of the civilian population—constitute a proportionate method of achieving victory? Chroniclers on opposite sides of the Hundred Years War often lamented such things, especially when they were inflicted on their own soldiers or civilians. But none of them proposed the equivalent of a Kantian categorical imperative to formulate a universal rule of criminality in war.

This lacuna in the laws of war could also be attributed to the difficulty

140

of drawing clear lines between "combatants" and "civilians" during the siege of cities, the most common form of military engagement in the English conquest of France. Defending a besieged city often became a communal enterprise, as was the case at Orléans in 1429–30. As Green argues: "During a siege the line differentiating combatants from non-combatants became even more blurred than usual. If one assisted by dousing fires, or bringing food, water or supplies to the garrison, and so helped to defend a town, was one really a non-combatant?"[23]

Despite Aquinas's efforts, and the labors of theologians and canon lawyers who studied his and Augustine's works, in the early fifteenth century there was no singular or universally applicable theology of just war that could consistently be enforced.[24] In his study of the religious ideology of chivalry, Kaeuper cautions us against assuming that there was a monolithic view of just war theory, even among medieval clerical authorities who paradoxically condemned the violence of the warrior class while also promoting holy war against infidels and heretics during the Crusades.[25] When France and England waged war against each other, there were no universally agreed upon norms or any formal treaties governing their conduct, nor was there a consistent and immediately applicable clerical definition of just war for all circumstances.[26] In a recent study of the English conduct of the Hundred Years War, Rory Cox questions the very notion that there was ever a "law of war" at the end of the Middle Ages: "If law is defined by criteria such as obligation, compliance, impartiality of application and enforceability of sanction, we must seriously doubt whether the 'laws of war' are a useful concept at all when discussing the conduct of medieval warfare."[27]

The combatants on opposite sides of the war were instead guided by an amalgamation of patristic, canonical, and scholastic theological texts from which they could pick and choose to construct their case for their own "just war."[28] The knights in the opposing armies were also heavily influenced by the codes of chivalry developed by the warrior class in their own vernacular literature.[29] Most participants in armed conflict understood that there had to be a just cause, promoted by a legitimate authority, for a war to be declared and waged. When it came to right conduct in war, the canonical texts of the Church prohibited harming or killing clerics and other non-combatants, while condemning the looting or destruction of ecclesiastical property. Henry V notably issued Ordinances of War during his campaign in Normandy, prohibiting the violation of churches, and he even publicly hanged an English archer who had stolen a pyx (a metal container that houses a consecrated host) from a Norman church.[30]

The chivalric literature that Henry V and the French men-at-arms read also spoke of proper conduct by knights in times of war, including the etiquette of surrender, the proper treatment of noble prisoners, and the ransoming of hostages. In his *Livre de chevalerie*, or the *Book of Chivalry*, one of the greatest theoreticians of chivalry, Geoffroi of Charny (1300–56), also identified "unworthy" behavior by knights. Among the "evil" deeds he condemns are highway robbery, plundering the goods of others without being attacked, and robbing churches.[31] His near contemporary, the Valois court poet Christine de Pisan (1364–1430) also denounced such activities in her treatise on the strategy and tactics of warfare, *Livre des fais d'armes et de chevalerie*, or *The Book of Deeds of Arms and of Chivalry* (1410). She presents the prevailing Christian tradition of just warfare, reflecting the views of both Augustine and Aquinas, while condemning those who would use the cover of war to engage in criminal behavior, calling them men who "misuse war."[32]

But generally speaking, much of the chivalric literature that addressed *ius in bello* questions showed little regard for the lower social classes who constituted the overwhelming majority of the population, whose lives and livelihoods were constantly disrupted by war. Late medieval chivalric texts regularly articulated concern for the proper treatment of fellow knights or aristocrats, not the social groups that were literally and figuratively beneath them.[33] Though he is describing the behavior of the English crusader-king Richard the Lionheart (r. 1189–99), John Gillingham's words are equally applicable to the conception of chivalry embraced by the late medieval warrior class, that it was "a status-specific form of humanity."[34] The poor would be abused or killed while the elite would be spared and ransomed. There were only a few notable exceptions to this line of thought. Christine de Pisan argued against the capture and imprisonment of children and old men, while also advocating for the immunity of peasant laborers and foreign students studying at a university who had not assisted the enemy.[35]

In the absence of an international regulatory body such as the United Nations, or internationally agreed upon rules for the conduct of war, such as the Geneva Conventions, who was ultimately responsible for determining the legality of a cause for war or the legality of conduct on the battlefield? The chaos of the Great Schism (1378–1417), with conflicting centers of ecclesiastical and legal authority, made it exceptionally difficult to enforce a universally accepted code of morality and conduct in warfare among Christian powers. And then, as now, the stress and trauma of prolonged sieges or campaigns made armies or individual commanders and combatants susceptible to violence beyond proportion, sometimes leading to atrocities such as the ones attributed to soldiers under the command of Henry V.

Eight. A Just and Holy Warrior?

Between the time of Augustine and the Hundred Years War, Europe had also developed a sophisticated theology of holy war during the era of the Crusades. The conceptual framework for Latin Christian holy war was first formulated by pope Urban II (r. 1088–99) at the Council of Clermont (1095).[36] This papal call to arms unleashed religiously sanctioned violence against the Muslim conquerors of what Christians called their Holy Land. The First Crusade was considered both a war of defense (of persecuted Christians in the Middle East) and a war of restitution of holy sites to their rightful owners (Christian holy places that had been unjustly conquered by Muslims). The demonization of exotic, religious "others" was much easier if they were Muslims, and clerical authorities had given their blessing to their killing with the promise of indulgences and heavenly rewards. On the other hand, a war by Christians against Christians was in a wholly different category than a war against "infidel" Muslims. Drawing the blood of a fellow Christian could be considered a mortal sin. The Council of Narbonne (1054) had, in fact, specifically prohibited and condemned the killing of Christians by other Christians. It went so far as characterizing such activity as "shedding the blood of Christ."[37]

Could a war between nation states, for the mundane purpose of defending territorial boundaries or the sovereignty of a ruler, ever be considered a "holy war"? According to Henry V, most definitely, "yes." Henry's *casus belli*, or cause for war, was political, but he firmly believed that he was enforcing the will of God and "fighting a good fight." As Kaeuper argues, the chivalric literature that combatants in the Hundred Years War imbibed can "readily blur or even eliminate the distinction between crusade and non-crusade.... Writers resolutely grasp the mantle of divine blessing provided crusaders and stretch it to cover all knights fighting good causes."[38] During the brutal English siege of Rouen, the celebrated Dominican preacher St. Vincent of Ferrer (1350–1419) chastised Henry for spilling so much Christian blood in France. In the face of the Dominican friar's attempts to dissuade Henry from continuing his war of conquest, the English king retorted that he was "the scourge of God, sent to punish the people of God for their synns."[39]

Henry's victory at Agincourt was so catastrophic for the French that even they interpreted their loss as an expression of divine wrath, a just punishment for the venality, moral degeneracy, and sinful pride of the French. The contemporary French and Burgundian chronicles did not castigate Henry for the killing of prisoners during the battle but rather focused their ire on the divided and incompetent command structure of the French aristocracy. Moreover, Henry modeled a new sort of holy war: he in effect declared his cause "holy" on his own authority. Bypassing the traditional clerical channels for the proclamation of a holy war, he appealed directly to the Judgment of God. Augustine's and Aquinas's theology of just war was elided with the papal theology of holy war, as Henry fought to defend his claim to the crown of France.[40]

Henry V was undoubtedly aware of and sometimes mindful of the theological and chivalric formulations and restrictions that governed warfare. But was Henry's war "just" by Augustine's and Aquinas's definition? His claim to the French crown was convoluted at best, and motivated by his need to unite his nation around a new, contested English dynasty that lived in the shadow of usurpation and regicide. Henry's opportunistic assertion of his "just rights" in France could only become a reality as a result of the political mayhem in the bitterly divided realm that he invaded.

There is no doubt that Henry V was controversial in his own day for his bold claims as arbiter of French monarchic power, and for how he caused streams of Christian blood to flow in the cities and fields of France to enforce his political agenda. But subjecting an iconic figure such as Henry to moral or ethical judgments is an exceptionally difficult task. The emotional and spiritual attachments that have developed from centuries of adulation and legendary treatment remain major impediments to sober analysis, even by supposedly objective historians. Still, we cannot reflexively impose on the past the modern standards regarding the conduct of war, especially the legal terminology that originated with the Nuremberg trials. On the other hand, we cannot entirely avoid making judgments about "good" or "bad" behavior in times of political upheaval or armed conflict. From the perspective of nineteenth-century Romanticism, the Hundred Years War produced its share of gallant warriors and legendary battles. But the suffering of untold thousands and the incalculable loss of life and livelihood in France are lamentable. The barbarity and violence of generations of soldiers on French soil during that long conflict—that included the massacre of unarmed men; the pillaging and destruction of religious foundations; the destruction of the fragile economies of peasant laborers; and the dislocation of thousands of innocent civilians—are as essential to the formation of our judgment of the military career of Henry V as are his heroic feats at Agincourt.

Suggestions for Further Reading

The Hundred Years War

Édouard Perroy, *The Hundred Years War*, trans. W. B. Wells (Oxford: Oxford University Press, 1951); although quite dated, Perroy's work is still considered foundational, particularly for his interpretation of the causes of the war. Alfred H. Burne, *The Agincourt War: A Military History of the Latter Part of the Hundred Years War, From 1369–1453* (Ware, UK: Wordsworth Editions, 1999; reprint of 1956 edition); this classic work provides a succinct narrative that focuses mostly on the campaigns of Henry V and Joan of Arc. Christopher Allmand, *The Hundred Years War: England and France at War c. 1300–1450* (Cambridge: Cambridge University Press, 1988); a concise and well-researched narrative by a leading authority. Desmond Seward, *The Hundred Years War: The English in France 1337–1453* (New York: Penguin Books, 1999); this succinct volume provides a good synopsis with a distinctly critical interpretation of the English conduct of the war. L.J. Andrew Villalon and Donald J. Kagay, eds., *The Hundred Years War: A Wider Focus* (Leiden: Brill, 2005); *The Hundred Years War (Part II): Different Vistas* (Leiden: Brill, 2008); two excellent collections of essays that feature a wide variety of interpretations of various aspects of the war. Juliet Barker, *Conquest: The English Kingdom of France, 1417–1450* (Cambridge, MA: Harvard University Press, 2012); this work is especially helpful for the historical context of Henry V's military career. David Green, *The Hundred Years War: A People's History* (New Haven, CT: Yale University Press, 2014); this provocative account focuses on the war's impact on various groups of participants. Jonathan Sumption, *The Hundred Years War*, 4 volumes (Philadelphia: University of Pennsylvania Press, 1991–2017); a well-crafted and highly detailed narrative, this is the longest and most thorough presentation of the war available in the English language. It is an indispensable reference guide for any phase or aspect of the Hundred Years War.

Henry V

J.H. Wylie and W.T. Waugh, *The Reign of Henry V*, 3 volumes (Cambridge: Cambridge University Press, 1914–29); although loquacious and quite dated, the exhaustive work of Wylie and Waugh still yields important documentary material for the modern student of Henry. T.B. Pugh, *Henry V and the Southampton Plot of 1415* (Gloucester, UK: Sutton, 1989); not a biography, per se, this work provides an important micro-historical analysis of Henry's early reign. Christopher Allmand, *Henry V* (New Haven, CT: Yale University Press, 1997); his expertise in the Hundred Years War makes this the most balanced and best modern scholarly biography of the king. Keith Dockray, *Warrior King: The Life of Henry V*, 2nd edition (Stroud, UK: Tempus, 2007); not really a conventional biography but a lively historiographic analysis of the evolution of Henry's image, from his own time to the modern era. John Matusiak, *Henry V* (New York: Routledge, 2013); one of the most recent works, this is a succinct and captivating narrative that addresses some of the ongoing debates about Henry's legacy, while featuring a good summary of the narrative primary sources for his reign. Anne Curry, *Henry V: Playboy Prince to Warrior King* (London: Penguin Books, 2015); a very compact biography in the Penguin Monarchs series by one of the leading authorities on Henry's military campaigns.

There are many modern studies of various aspects of Henry V's monarchy and career as a soldier. Some of the most important ones follow. Edward Powell, *Kingship, Law and Society: Criminal Justice in the Reign of Henry V* (Oxford: Clarendon Press, 1989); Gerald L. Harriss, ed., *Henry V: The Practice of Kingship*, 2nd edition (Stroud, UK: Sutton, 1993); Malcolm Mercer, *Henry V: The Rebirth of Chivalry* (Kew, UK: National Archives, 2004); Gwilym Dodd, ed., *Henry V: New Interpretations* (Woodbridge, UK: Boydell and Brewer, 2013); Malcolm Vale, *Henry V: The Conscience of a King* (New Haven, CT: Yale University Press, 2016).

The Battle of Agincourt

John Keegan, *The Face of Battle: A Study of Agincourt, Waterloo and the Somme* (New York: Penguin Books, 1978); this pioneering work still offers important insights about this legendary battle. Juliet Barker, *Agincourt: Henry V and the Battle That Made England* (New York: Little, Brown, 2006); a noted expert on the Hundred Years War provides a detailed analysis of Henry's campaign in Normandy leading up to and including the battle. Ian Mortimer, *1415: Henry V's Year of Glory* (London: Vintage Books, 2010); Mortimer's work provides a day-by-day chronological history of the Agincourt campaign. Rémy Ambühl and Craig Lambert, eds., *Agincourt in Context: War on Land and Sea* (London: Routledge, 2019); a collection of essays by experts on various topics associated with Henry's Agincourt campaign.

The foremost contemporary authority is Anne Curry. The best known of her publications are Anne Curry, *The Battle of Agincourt: Sources and Interpretation* (Woodbridge, UK: Boydell Press, 2011); a well-edited collection of primary source materials covering both sides of the battle. Curry's translations are also prefaced with citations to modern editions of the original sources. Anne Curry, *1415 Agincourt: A New History* (Stroud, UK: History Press, 2015); Anne Curry, *Great Battles: Agincourt* (Oxford: Oxford University Press, 2015); Anne Curry and Malcom Mercer, eds., *The Battle of Agincourt* (New Haven, CT: Yale University Press, 2015).

A Note About Primary Source Documents

There are numerous narrative and documentary sources associated with Henry, many of which are referenced in the body of my work and bibliography. As a rule, I have used readily available modern English translations of these texts so that the general reader will find them accessible for further reading. I have often consulted the original Latin, Middle English, and Middle French sources, and in some instances, I have provided my own translations.

Chapter Notes

Introduction

1. Thomas Carlyle, *On Heroes, Hero-Worship and the Heroic in History*, ed. for study by John Chester Adams (New York: Houghton Mifflin, 1907), 1.

2. Henry was born at Monmouth Castle in Wales (September 16, 1386). His name "Henry of Monmouth" is a modern moniker used to distinguish him from his father. After Henry IV's coronation, the younger Henry was appointed Earl of Chester, Duke of Cornwall, Prince of Wales, and Duke of Aquitaine and Lancaster. For the disputed date of his birth, see Ian Mortimer, *1415: Henry V's Year of Glory* (London: Vintage Books, 2010), 539.

3. K. B. McFarlane, *Lancastrian Kings and Lollard Knights* (Oxford: Oxford University Press, 1972), 133; Mortimer, *1415*, 551. McFarlane's admiration was preceded more than half a century earlier in the work of Charles L. Kingsford, *Henry V: The Typical Medieval Hero* (New York: F. DeFau, 1901). Yet despite his misgivings, Mortimer concedes that Henry *was* a great ruler: "He wanted to become a great king so desperately that he became one." Mortimer, *1415*, 532.

4. Keith Dockray, *Warrior King: The Life of Henry V*, 2nd ed. (Stroud, UK: Tempus, 2007), 9–75. Dockray's work provides a lively historiographic analysis of the evolution of Henry's image, from his own time to the modern era.

5. Henry's supposed "criminality" in war is a subject that is vigorously debated among modern Shakespeare scholars. See Theodor Meron, *Henry's Wars and Shakespeare's Laws: Perspectives on the Law of War in the Later Middle Ages* (Oxford: Oxford

University Press, 1993); John Sutherland and Cedric Thomas Watts, *Henry V: War Criminal? And Other Shakespearean Puzzles* (Oxford: Oxford University Press, 2000), esp. 108–16; Paola Pugliatti, *Shakespeare and the Just War Tradition* (London: Routledge, 2016); Christopher N. Warren, "*Henry V*, Anachronism and the History of International Law," in *The Oxford Handbook of English Law and Literature, 1500–1700*, ed. Lorna Hutson and Bradin Cormack (Oxford: Oxford University Press, 2017), 709–27. This topic will be explored in great detail in chapter six, on the Battle of Agincourt.

6. Charles L. Kingsford, ed., *The First English Life of Henry the Fifth, Written in 1513 by an Anonymous Author Known Commonly as The Translator of Livius* (Oxford: Oxford University Press, 1911), 131.

7. This testimony is in the chronicle of Guillaume Gruel (c. 1410–74/82). He was the servant of an eyewitness to the battle who was taken prisoner by Henry, Arthur de Richemont. Gruel says that Henry "received such a blow to his crown that he fell to his knees." Anne Curry, *The Battle of Agincourt: Sources and Interpretation* (Woodbridge, UK: Boydell Press, 2011), 184.

8. This terrible wound and its treatment will be discussed at length in chapter 2.

9. Gary Taylor, ed., *Henry V: The Oxford Shakespeare* (*Oxford World's Classics*) (Oxford: Oxford University Press, 2008), 116.

10. The expression of admiration for Henry by French chroniclers is highlighted by Nicole Pons, "Intellectual Patterns and Affective Reactions in Defence of the

Dauphin Charles, 1419–1422," in *War, Government and Power in Late Medieval France*, ed. Christopher Allmand (Liverpool: Liverpool University Press, 2000), 54–69. See also Elizabeth Pentland, "Agincourt and After—The Adversary's Perspective," in *King Henry V: A Critical Reader*, ed. Karen Britland and Line Cottegnies (London: The Arden Shakespeare, 2020), 200–20.

11. For a succinct overview of the principal biographies and chronicles of Henry's reign that appeared before Shakespeare's play, see John Matusiak, *Henry V* (New York: Routledge, 2013), 1–12. For Shakespeare's sources, see Anne Curry, *Great Battles: Agincourt* (Oxford: Oxford University Press, 2015), 78–95.

12. Lucy Wooding, *Henry VIII*, 2nd ed. (London: Routledge, 2015), 10–11.

13. Mortimer, *1415*, 551.

14. Curry, *Great Battles: Agincourt*, 111.

15. The first modern biography of Henry V was published at the turn of the eighteenth century by Thomas Goodwin, *The History of the Reign of Henry the Fifth, King of England* (London: Printed by J. D. for S. and J. Sprint, J. Robinson, J. Taylor, Andr. Bell, T. Ballard, and B. Lintott, 1704). But it was not until the first half of the nineteenth century that there was renewed, widespread interest in Henry in England. For a comprehensive historiographic analysis of this work, see Christopher Allmand, "Writing History in the Eighteenth Century: Thomas Goodwin's *The History of the Reign of Henry the Fifth* (1704)," in *Henry V: New Interpretations*, ed. Gwilym Dodd (Woodbridge, UK: Boydell and Brewer, 2013), 273–88.

16. Henry's revival came at roughly the same time as the French and North American Romantic revival of Joan of Arc. See for example: Robin Blaetz, *Visions of the Maid: Joan of Arc in American Film and Culture* (Charlottesville: University Press of Virginia, 2001).

17. "Henry V is a very favorite monarch with the English nation, and he appears also to have been a favorite with Shakespear [*sic*], who labors hard to apologize for the actions of the king....He scarcely deserves this honour. He was fond of war and low company:-we know little else of him." Cited from Taylor, *Henry V: Oxford Shakespeare*, 2.

18. James N. Loehlin, *Shakespeare in Performance, Henry V* (Manchester: Manchester University Press, 1997), 19. See also Dominique Goy-Blanquet, *Shakespeare's Early History Plays: From Chronicle to Stage* (Oxford: Oxford University Press, 2003). For an overview of the stage performances of the play in the nineteenth and twentieth century, see Taylor, *Henry V: Oxford Shakespeare*, 48–72; Anne Curry, *Great Battles: Agincourt*, 99–106; and Anne-Marie Miller-Blaise and Gisèle Venet, "Performance History," in *King Henry V: A Critical Reader*, 47–74.

19. In the screen adaptation of *Henry V*, Laurence Olivier omitted scenes from Shakespeare's play that would have been problematic for a wartime audience in 1944: the Southampton Plot before Henry's invasion of France and the massacre of unarmed French prisoners before the end of the Battle of Agincourt. Kenneth Branagh's film (1989) includes the Southampton Plot but excludes the massacre of prisoners, while the BBC *Hollow Crown* series with Tom Hiddleston (2012) excludes the Southampton Plot but adds the massacre scene. The Netflix original movie *The King* (2019) with Timothée Calamet presents a wildly fictional interpretation of Henry's early reign. It includes both the Southampton plot and Henry's order to kill the French prisoners.

20. The St. Crispin's Day speech is discussed at length and analyzed in chapter 6.

21. Curry, *Great Battles: Agincourt*, 78. See also Robert C. Woosnam-Savage, "Olivier's *Henry V* (1944): How a Movie Defined the Image of the Battle of Agincourt for Generations," in *The Battle of Agincourt*, ed. Anne Curry and Malcom Mercer (New Haven, CT: Yale University Press, 2015), 250–62.

22. Harry Geduld, *Filmguide to Henry V* (Bloomington: Indiana University Press, 1976), 53.

23. Winston S. Churchill, *A History of the English-Speaking Peoples, Volume I: The Birth of Britain* (London: Bloomsbury Academic, 2015), 249.

24. Churchill, *History of the English-Speaking Peoples*, 253.

25. For a study of the mythology surrounding Churchill as a legendary public figure, see John Ramsden, *Man of the*

Century: Winston Churchill and His Legend Since 1945 (New York: Columbia University Press, 2003).

26. McFarlane, *Lancastrian Kings and Lollard Knights*, 133.

27. Matusiak, *Henry V*, 237–38.

28. Matusiak, 239.

29. Juliet Barker, *Agincourt: Henry V and the Battle That Made England* (New York: Little, Brown, 2005), xi–xii.

30. Barker, *Agincourt*, 364.

31. Christopher Allmand, *Henry V* (New Haven, CT: Yale University Press, 1997), xix.

32. Allmand, 443.

33. Gwilym Dodd, "Preface and Acknowledgements," in *Henry V: New Interpretations*, ix.

34. Jonathan Sumption, *The Hundred Years War IV: Cursed Kings* (Philadelphia: University of Pennsylvania Press, 2017), 366.

35. Desmond Seward, *Henry V: The Scourge of God* (New York: Viking, 1988), 215; Desmond Seward, *The Hundred Years War: The English in France, 1337–1453* (New York: Atheneum, 1978/82), 153.

36. Mortimer, *1415*, 519–20.

37. Mortimer, *1415*, 537. Mortimer provides none of the details of this incident, which I have reconstructed from other sources. Seward's chapter on the siege of Meaux presents Henry in the most unflattering light. Seward, *Henry V*, 182–195. Sumption refers to an "angry and frustrated" Henry and says that at Meaux, he "was his most vindictive." Sumption, *Hundred Years War IV*, 754.

38. Sumption, *Hundred Years War IV*, 756, 774–88.

39. The Treaty of Troyes is analyzed in great detail in chapter 7.

40. Rémy Ambühl, "Henry V and The Administration of Justice: The Surrender of Meaux (May 1422)," in *Agincourt in Context: War on Land and Sea*, ed. Rémy Ambühl and Craig Lambert (London: Routledge, 2019), 75.

41. *A Parisian Journal, 1405–1499*, translated from the *Anonymous Journal d'un Bourgeois de Paris* by Janet Shirley (Oxford: Clarendon Press, 1968), 171–72. For a compelling analysis of the hyperbole and supposed dishonesty of the

French chronicle sources documenting this siege, see Boris Bove, "Deconstructing the Chronicles: Rumours and Extreme Violence During the Siege of Meaux (1421–1422)," *French History* 24 (2010): 501–23. One chronicler, Robert Blondel (1380–1460), attributed Henry V's death shortly after the fall of Meaux to his sinful pride and sacrilege. See also Ambühl, "Henry V and The Administration of Justice," in *Agincourt in Context*, 75–77.

42. Jean de Wavrin, *Recueil des croniques et anchiennes istories de la Grant Bretaigne, a present nomme Engleterre par Jehan de Waurin, seigneur du Forestel*, ed. William Hardy (London: Longman, Roberts and Green, 1868; reprint edition, 1965), 403–04; *La Chronique d'Enguerran de Monstrelet, avec pièces justificatives, 1400–1444*, ed. Louis Claude Douët-d'Arcq, Société de l'Histoire de France (Paris: Jules Renouard, 1860), 94. Ambühl, "Henry V and The Administration of Justice," in *Agincourt in Context*, 80.

43. Pierre de Fenin, *Mémoires de Pierre de Fenin: comprenant le récit des événements qui se sont passés en France et en Bourgogne sous les règnes de Charles VI et Charles VII (1407–1427)*, ed. Emelie Dupont (Paris: Jules Renouard, 1837), 173.

44. Mortimer, *1415*, 537. Mortimer's description of the execution of the trumpeter immediately precedes this quotation. Mortimer comes to an entirely opposite conclusion when he assesses the reign of Henry IV, calling him "one of the most courageous, conscientious, personally committed and energetic men ever to rule England." Ian Mortimer, *The Fears of Henry IV. The Life of England's Self-Made King* (London: Vintage Books, 2008), 353.

45. T. B. Pugh, *Henry V and the Southampton Plot of 1415* (Southampton: University Press, 1988), xiii; 145.

46. Ambühl, "Henry V and The Administration of Justice," in *Agincourt in Context*, 87.

47. There is a lively debate among Shakespeare scholars about the limits of presentist readings and critiques of the play. See Emma Smith, "The State of the Art," in *King Henry V: A Critical Reader*, 75–101.

48. Malcolm Vale, *Henry V: The Conscience of a King* (New Haven, CT: Yale

University Press, 2016), xv–xvi. This perspective is shared by Taylor, *Henry V: The Oxford Shakespeare*, 2–3.

49. Vale, *Henry V*, 264. Matusiak, *Henry V*, 239, makes similar points about Henry's successes as a ruler, and he argues that the king's military career cannot be detached from his broader objectives and reforms as ruler of England.

50. Vale, *Henry V*, 76.

51. Vale, *Henry V*, 206–13, 276. For Henry's supposed composition of liturgical pieces, see Alison K. McHardy, "Religion, Court Culture and Propaganda: The Chapel Royal in the Reign of Henry V," in *Henry V: New Interpretations*, 138–41.

52. Mortimer, *Fears of Henry IV*, 39–62.

53. Churchill, *History of the English-Speaking Peoples*, 253.

54. Anne Curry, ed., *Agincourt 1415: Henry V, Sir Thomas Erpingham and the Triumph of the English Archers* (Stroud, UK: Tempus, 2000), 9.

55. Curry, *Agincourt 1415*, 9.

56. Allmand, *Henry V*, 34.

57. Anne Curry, *Henry V: Playboy Prince to Warrior King*. (London: Penguin Books, 2015), 12.

Chapter One

1. John Aberth, *From the Brink of the Apocalypse: Confronting Famine, War, Plague and Death in the Later Middle Ages*, 2nd ed. (London: Routledge, 2010). See also Charles T. Wood, *Joan of Arc and Richard III: Sex, Saints, and Government in the Middle Ages* (New York: Oxford University Press, 1988); though dated, Wood's study offers a vibrant analysis of the various crises of authority that afflicted the governments of England and France during the Hundred Years War.

2. For a short history of the Avignon Papacy, see Edwin Mullins, *The Popes of Avignon: A Century of Exile* (New York: BlueBridge, 2008). For a comprehensive study, see Joëlle Rollo-Koster, *Avignon and its Papacy (1309–1417): Popes, Institutions, and Society* (Lanham, MD: Rowman and Littlefield, 2015).

3. For a recent comprehensive study, see Unn Falkeid, *The Avignon Papacy Contested: An Intellectual History From Dante to Catherine of Siena* (Cambridge, MA: Harvard University Press, 2017).

4. For a good overview of the Schism, see Joëlle Rollo-Koster, *Raiding Saint Peter: Empty Sees, Violence, and The Initiation of the Great Western Schism (1378)* (Leiden: Brill, 2008), 167–225. See also Joëlle Rollo-Koster and Thomas M. Izbicki, eds., *A Companion to the Great Western Schism (1378–1417)* (Leiden: Brill, 2009).

5. For Henry's complex relationship with the pope who ended the Schism, see Margaret M. Harvey, "Martin V and Henry V," *Archivum Historiae Pontificiae* 24 (1986): 49–70; Margaret M. Harvey, *England, Rome and the Papacy, 1417–1464: The Study of a Relationship* (Manchester: Manchester University Press, 1993).

6. The Treaty of Troyes (1420), which Martin V refused to honor, is discussed at length in chapter 7.

7. Helen Castor, *She-Wolves: The Women Who Ruled England Before Elizabeth* (New York: Harper Perennial, 2012), 231–321.

8. For good recent biographies, see Ian Mortimer, *The Perfect King: The Life of Edward III, Father of the English Nation* (London: Vintage Books, 2008); Ormrod, *Edward III*. For a comprehensive treatment of this phase of the Hundred Years War, see Jonathan Sumption, *The Hundred Years War I: Trial by Battle* (Philadelphia: University of Pennsylvania Press, 1990); *The Hundred Years War II: Trial by Fire* (Philadelphia: University of Pennsylvania Press, 2001).

9. David Green, *The Hundred Years War: A People's History* (New Haven, CT: Yale University Press, 2014), 185. For a detailed analysis of the rediscovered Salic Law and its polemical life in the fifteenth century, see Craig Taylor, "The Salic Law, French Queenship, and the Defense of Women in the Late Middle Ages," *French Historical Studies* 29 (2006): 543–64; Daisy Delogu, *Allegorical Bodies: Power and Gender in Late Medieval France* (Toronto: University of Toronto Press, 2015), 125–66.

10. Sumption, *Hundred Years War I*, 84.

11. The etymology of this family name comes from Henry II's father, Geoffrey of Anjou, who sported the *planta genista* (the yellow broom blossom) in his cap. Dan

Notes—Chapter One

Jones, *The Plantagenets: The Warrior Kings and Queens Who Made England* (New York: Penguin Books, 2012), 1.

12. The term "Angevin" was first used in the nineteenth century to describe the English kings who claimed direct sovereignty over French lands by their association with Eleanor of Aquitaine and her husband Henry II. This included Henry II, his sons Richard I and John, and his grandson Henry III. See Kate Norgate, *England Under the Angevin Kings*, vol. 1 (London: Macmillan, 1887). For recent histories, see John Gillingham, *The Angevin Empire* (London: Arnold, 2001); Richard Huscroft, *Tales From the Long Twelfth Century: The Rise and Fall of the Angevin Empire* (New Haven, CT: Yale University Press, 2017).

13. For the complex relationship between Philip II and Richard I, see John D. Hosler, *The Siege of Acre, 1189–1191. Saladin, Richard the Lionheart, and the Battle That Decided the Third Crusade* (New Haven, CT: Yale University Press, 2018).

14. Richard was suppressing a rebellion by the Viscount of Limoges, asserting his rights as Duke of Aquitaine and Normandy and Count of Anjou. The castle was poorly defended and Richard was walking around its perimeter when he was hit by the crossbow bolt. Jones, *The Plantagenets*, 130–31.

15. For the circumstances of Richard's death and the treatment of his wound, see John Gillingham, *Richard I* (New Haven, CT: Yale University Press, 1999), 323–24. Mount notes that there were allegations of a poisonous arrow being used, but modern forensic analysis of his remains ruled out poisoning. He died of a fatal, gangrenous infection. Toni Mount, *Medieval Medicine: Its Mysteries and Science* (Stroud, UK: Amberley, 2015), 172–75.

16. Jones, *The Plantagenets*, 140–80. See also Dan Jones, *Magna Carta: The Birth of Liberty* (New York: Penguin Books, 2016).

17. Jones, *The Plantagenets*, 179–80; John France, "The Battle of Bouvines 27 July 1214," in *The Medieval Way of War: Studies in Medieval Military History in Honor of Bernard S. Bachrach*, ed. Gregory I. Halfond (Farnham, UK: Ashgate, 2015), 251–71.

18. Jones, *The Plantagenets*, 290–92.

19. For the requirement of homage to the French king for the English monarchy's ancestral lands in France, see Ormrod, *Edward III*, 26–34.

20. For the complex proximate events that started the war, see Ormrod, *Edward III*, 189–96.

21. For the evolution of Edward's claim to the French crown and the aftermath of Crécy, see Ormrod, *Edward III*, 212–98. For an anthology of primary sources for the legendary battle, see Michael Livingston and Kelly DeVries, eds., *The Battle of Crécy: A Casebook* (Liverpool: Liverpool University Press, 2015). For a micro-historical analysis of the battle, see David Nicolle, *Crécy 1346: Triumph of the Longbow* (Oxford: Osprey, 2000).

22. Sumption, *The Hundred Years War I*, 68.

23. For a general presentation of his life, see Michael Jones, *The Black Prince: England's Greatest Medieval Warrior* (New York: Pegasus Books, 2018).

24. Ormrod, *Edward III*, 352; David Nicolle, *Poitiers 1356: Capture of a King* (Oxford: Osprey, 2004); David Green, *The Battle of Poitiers 1356* (Stroud, UK: Tempus, 2008).

25. Green, *The Hundred Years War*, 43–46. The origin of the name of the rebellion is obscure. "Jacques Bonhomme" could be a generic reference for the peasants, "Jacques everyman." The only named leader in the contemporary chronicles is Guillaume Cale. See Samuel Kline Cohn Jr., *Lust for Liberty: The Politics of Social Revolt in Medieval Europe, 1200–1425* (Cambridge, MA: Harvard University Press, 2006), 34–35, 196.

26. Pre-plague England had a population of roughly five to six million, while France's population was roughly fifteen to sixteen million. Sumption, *Hundred Years War I*, 10.

27. Françoise Autrand, *Charles V: Le Sage* (Paris: Fayard, 1994); Jeannine Quillett, *Charles V: Le roi lettré* (Paris: Perrin, 2002). For a good English introduction to the reigns of both kings, see Françoise Autrand, "France Under Charles V and Charles VI," in *The New Cambridge Medeival History, Volume 6, c. 1300–1415*, ed. Michael Jones (Cambridge: Cambridge University Press, 2000), 422–41.

28. The sack of Limoges continues to be the focus of academic debate. The contemporary chronicler Jean Froissart (c. 1337–1405) indicates that several thousand people, including civilians, were massacred. Most modern scholars see this as exaggerated hyperbole. The city no doubt was sacked and devastated by the English, but Froissart's numbers are more than likely greatly inflated for rhetorical effect. The casualties probably numbered in the hundreds, not thousands. Jonathan Sumption, *Hundred Years War III: Divided Houses* (Philadelphia: University of Pennsylvania Press, 2009), 83. See also Ormrod, *Edward III*, 507–08; Jones, *The Black Prince*, 405–08.

29. Ormrod, *Edward III*, 472–75. For a detailed analysis of the economic consequences of the Hundred Years War for the English economy, see Bruce M. S. Campbell, *The Great Transition: Climate, Disease and Society in the Late-Medieval World* (Cambridge: Cambridge University Press, 2016), 134–82.

30. A detailed analysis is presented by C. J. Phillpotts, "The Fate of the Truce of Paris, 1396–1415," *Journal of Medieval History* 24 (1998): 61–80.

31. Juliet Barker, *England Arise: The People, the King and the Great Revolt of 1381* (London: Abacus, 2014); Dan Jones, *Summer of Blood: England's First Revolution* (New York: Penguin Books, 2016). For an analysis within the context of Richard's reign, see Nigel Saul, *Richard II* (New Haven, CT: Yale University Press, 1997), 56–82. Laura Ashe argues that "Peasant Rebellion" is probably a misnomer, since this revolt had support across all levels of English society and was led by ambitious and well-educated individuals. Laura Ashe, *Richard II: A Brittle Glory* (London: Penguin Books, 2016), 39–40.

32. Saul, *Richard II*, 345.

33. Not long after his own coronation, Henry IV put down a failed rebellion against his new regime. According to Saul, as long as Richard II lived, the imprisoned former king remained a serious challenge to the new Lancastrian ruler's authority. While there are conflicting theories about Richard's cause of death, Henry IV undoubtedly bore responsibility for it. See Saul, *Richard II*, 424–27.

34. Sumption, *Hundred Years War IV*, 46.

35. The plot is also called the Cambridge Plot since it was apparently led by Richard Conisburgh (1385–1415), the Earl of Cambridge. The principal conspirators were executed in Southampton, hence the more commonly used "Southampton Plot."

36. Allmand, *Henry V*, 74–78. Barker, *Agincourt*, 77–82.

37. Henry V's father, Henry Bolingbroke (1367–1413) was the son of John of Gaunt (1340–99), son of Edward III.

38. Pugh, *Henry V*, xii.

39. Allmand, *Henry V*, 74–78.

40. Curry, *Henry V*, 57–58.

41. Paul Strohm, *England's Empty Throne: Usurpation and the Language of Legitimation, 1399–1422*, 2nd ed. (Notre Dame, IN: University of Notre Dame Press, 2006), 89.

42. *Gesta Henrici Quinti: The Deeds of Henry the Fifth*, trans. and ed. F. Taylor and J. S. Roskell (Oxford: Oxford University Press, 1975), 19.

43. Strohm, *England's Empty Throne*, 93.

44. Anne Curry, *1415 Agincourt: A New History* (Stroud, UK: History Press, 2105), 59.

45. For the tumultuous reign of Charles VI, see R. C. Famiglietti, *Royal Intrigue. Crisis at the Court of Charles VI, 1392–1420* (New York: AMS Press, 1986); Bernard Guenée, *Un roi et son historien. Vingt études sure le règne de Charles VI et la "Chronique du Réligieux de Saint-Denis"* (Paris: Diffusion de Boccard, 1999); Bernard Guenée, *La folie de Charles VI: roi bien-aimé* (Paris: CNRS, 2004).

46. Elisabeth von Wittelsbach, better known by her French name, Isabeau of Bavaria, has been unfairly maligned in modern academic literature. For a systematic deconstruction of this black legend, see Tracy Adams, *The Life and Afterlife of Isabeau of Bavaria* (Baltimore: Johns Hopkins University Press, 2010).

47. Famiglietti documents this incident and offers a detailed analysis of the nature of Charles' mental illness, making a case for schizophrenia. Famiglietti, *Royal Intrigue*, 1–21.

48. Tracy Adams, *Christine de Pizan and the Fight for France* (Philadelphia:

University of Pennsylvania Press, 2014), 4–5. The same point is made by Famiglietti, *Royal Intrigue*, xi.

49. Jonathan Sumption, *The Hundred Years War IV: Cursed Kings* (Philadelphia: University of Pennsylvania Press, 2017), 576–78. Pierre Goubert, *The Course of French History*, trans. Maarten Ultee (London: Routledge, 1991), 62. Goubert gives a figure of more than forty thousand deaths. For a comprehensive study of medieval Paris, see Simone Roux, *Paris in the Middle Ages*, trans. Jo Ann McNamara (Philadelphia: University of Pennsylvania Press, 2009).

50. *A Parisian Journal, 1405–1449*, 155, 157. For a study of English occupation, see Raymond Reagan Butler, *Is Paris Lost? The English Occupation, 1422–1436* (Staplehurst, UK: Spellmont, 2003).

51. For a good overview of the political tumult in France that preceded Joan's mission, see Helen Castor, *Joan of Arc: A History* (New York: Harper, 2015), 19–86.

52. Sumption, *Hundred Years War IV*, 543.

53. The authoritative biography in English is by Richard Vaughn, *John the Fearless: The Growth of Burgundian Power* (London: Longmans, 1966; reprint, Woodbridge, UK: Boydell Press, 2002). The best overall recent treatment of the ravages of Charles VI's madness and the bloody feud between the Orléanists and Burgundians can be found in Sumption, *Hundred Years War IV*.

54. Vaughn, *John the Fearless*, 45.

55. For a detailed analysis of John's military career, see Kelly DeVries, "John the Fearless' Way of War," in *Reputation and Representation in Fifteenth Century Europe*, ed. Douglas Biggs, Sharon D. Michalove, and Albert Compton Reeves (Leiden: Brill, 2004), 39–55.

56. Vaughn, *John the Fearless*, 70–71; Adams, *The Life and Afterlife of Isabeau*, 21–22.

57. Adams, *The Life and Afterlife of Isabeau*, 24.

58. Vaughn provides the most detailed account, with a thorough evaluation of the primary sources. Vaughn, *John the Fearless*, 263–86. See also Sumption, *Hundred Years War IV*, 649–54.

59. Vaughn, *John the Fearless*, 283.

60. Sumption, *Hundred Years War IV*, 654. Vale, *Charles VII*, 14.

61. For a detailed summary of the negotiations that led to the treaty and its ratification, see Sumption, *Hundred Years War IV*, 655–700. For a translation of the original Latin text, see Pierre Chaplais, ed., *English Medieval Diplomatic Practice: Part I Documents and Interpretations* (London: Her Majesty's S.O., 1982), 629–36. See also Anne Curry, "Two Kingdoms, One King: The Treaty of Troyes (1420) and the Creation of a Double Monarchy of England and France," in *Contesting the Kingdoms: France and England 1420–1700*, ed. G. Richardson (Aldershot, UK: Ashgate Press, 2008), 23–41.

62. The French word *Dauphin* means "dolphin" in English and was the term used to designate the heir to the French throne, beginning in the mid-fourteenth century. Charles V (r. 1364–80) was the first crown prince to use that designation before he became king. The heraldic symbol of the crown prince was a dolphin and the fleur-de-lis, the traditional symbol of the French monarchy.

63. There are numerous biographies of Joan, but the best study of her life in the context of the Hundred Years War is Castor, *Joan of Arc: A History*. For a good analysis and English translation of the major portions of the condemnation trial, see Daniel Hobbins, *The Trial of Joan of Arc* (Cambridge, MA: Harvard University Press, 2005).

Chapter Two

1. Strohm, *England's Empty Throne*, 153.

2. Sumption, *Hundred Years War IV*, 366; Curry, *Henry V*, 33.

3. Matusiak, *Henry V*, 74.

4. *Chronica Maiora of Thomas Walsingham*, 389. The contemporary English chronicler Adam Usk (1352–1430) recalls that even though it was April, there was a "driving snow which covered the country's mountains, burying men and animals and houses, and, astonishingly, even inundating the valleys and the fenlands, creating great danger and much loss of life." *The Chronicle of Adam Usk*, 243.

5. Strohm, *England's Empty Throne*, 212.

6. Matusiak, *Henry V*, 10. In the introduction to his biography, he offers a good overview of this literature and the relative strengths and weaknesses of each chronicle.

7. *Chronica Maiora of Thomas Walsingham*, 445.

8. Sumption, *Hundred Years War IV*, 369. See also Matusiak, *Henry V*, 8. *Chronique du Réligieux de Saint-Denys (1380–1422)*, ed. F. Bellaguet (Paris: Imprimerie de Crapelet, 1852), 6: 480–81.

9. Vale, *Henry V*, 127. Vale's source is L. Mirot, "Le Procès de Maître Jean Fusoris, chanoine de Notre-Dame de Paris (1415–1416): épisode de négociations franco-anglaises durant la guerre de Cent ans," *Mémoires de la Société de l'histoire de Paris et de l'Île de France* 17 (1900): 175. The cathedral chapter of Notre Dame where Fusoris was a canon did not have enough evidence to prove his guilt, but enough to make him spend the rest of his life in confined exile. He still continued to practice his craft, including the manufacture of astronomical instruments. See S. H. Cuttler, *The Law of Treason and Treason Trials in Later Medieval France* (Cambridge: Cambridge University Press, 2003), 71–72. For a study of the role of astrology at the English court, see Hilary M. Carey, *Courting Disaster: Astrology at the English Court and University in the Later Middle Ages* (New York: Palgrave Macmillan, 1992).

10. Allmand, *Henry V*, 61.

11. Curry, *Henry V*, 32. In the work of the contemporary anonymous chronicler wrongly identified as Thomas Elmham (c. 1364–1427?), there is a description of Henry's physique. Pseudo-Elmham, *Thomae de Elmham Vita et Gesta Henrici Quinti Anglorum Regis*, ed. Thomas Hearne (Oxford: E Theatro Sheldoniano, 1727), 12.

12. "*Guerre sans feu ne valoit rien, non plus que andouilles sans moustarde.*" Jean Juvénal des Ursins, *Histoire de Charles VI*, ed. J. A. C. Buchon (Paris: Choix de chroniques et mémoires sur l'histoire de France 4, 1841), 565. This could very well be an apocryphal tale since it is not attested in other sources.

13. A detailed description of his tomb with excellent images can be found on the official Westminster Abbey webpage: https://www.westminster-abbey.org/abbey-commemorations/royals/henry-v-and-catherine-de-valois

14. Saul, *Richard II*, 450.

15. https://www.npg.org.uk/collections/search/portrait/mw03074/King-Henry-V. The National Portrait Gallery website identifies it as a late sixteenth- or early seventeenth-century painting.

16. https://www.royalcollection.org.uk/collection/403443/henry-v-1387-1422. The website dates the oil painting from c. 1504–20 and notes that it was the work of a Flemish or British painter working for the royal court.

17. Sumption, *Hundred Years War IV*, 366.

18. For a detailed account of the Percy rebellion and the Battle of Shrewsbury, see Chris Given-Wilson, *Henry IV* (New Haven, CT: Yale University Press, 2016), 216–32.

19. For a succinct overview of the causes of the rebellion, see Sumption, *Hundred Years War IV*, 109–15.

20. His father Henry Earl of Northumberland was not convicted of treason, since he had not directly participated in the rebellion, but he was stripped of his offices. He participated in the failed rebellion of archbishop of York, Thomas Scrope (1405) and fled to Scotland. He died at the Battle of Bramham Moor (1408), the last battle of the Percy rebellion against Henry IV. See Sumption, *Hundred Years War IV*, 224–25.

21. Allmand, *Henry V*, 26. Given-Wilson, *Henry IV*, 226. A vivid description of this injury can be found in the contemporary chronicle of Pseudo-Elmham. *Vita et Gesta Henrici Quinti*, 7. Arner examines the chronicle accounts of his wounding and seriously challenges the truthfulness of these often-repeated claims in modern academic works, that Henry continued to fight courageously. Timothy D. Arner, "The Disappearing Scar of Henry V: Triage, Trauma, and the Treatment of Henry's Wounding at the Battle of Shrewsbury," *Journal of Medieval and Early Modern Studies* 49 (2019): 347–76, esp. 349–53. Livingston notes that even though the surgeon who treated Henry's wound referred to it as being on the "left side" of his face, he more

than likely described where it was located from his *own* perspective: John Bradmore's "left" is Henry's "right." Michael Livingston, "'The Depth of Six Inches': Prince Hal's Head-Wound at the Battle of Shrewsbury," in *Wounds and Wound Repair in Medieval Culture*, ed. Larissa Tracy and Kelly DeVries (Leiden: Brill, 2015), 229.

22. Livingston, "'The Depth of Six Inches,'" 219.

23. Sheila L. Lang, "The *Philomena* of John Bradmore and Its Middle English Derivative: A Perspective on Surgery in Late Medieval England" (PhD thesis, St. Andrew's University, 1999), 65–66. For an analysis of this surgical procedure, see R. Theodore Beck, *The Cutting Edge: Early History of the Surgeons of London* (London: Lund Humphries, 1974), 117–18; H. Cole and T. Lang, "The Treating of Prince Henry's Arrow Wound, 1403," *Journal of the Society of Archer Antiquaries* 46 (2003): 95–101; Livingston, "'The Depth of Six Inches,'" 215–31.

24. Arner, "The Disappearing Scar of Henry V," 354–55.

25. Livingston, "'The Depth of Six Inches,'" 225–27.

26. Richard was suppressing a rebellion by the Viscount of Limoges, asserting his rights as Duke of Aquitaine and Normandy and Count of Anjou. The Castle was poorly defended and Richard was walking around its perimeter when he was hit by the crossbow bolt. Jones, *The Plantagenets*, 130–31.

27. For the circumstances of Richard's death and the treatment of his wound, see Gillingham, *Richard I*, 323–324. Mount notes that there were allegations of a poisonous arrow being used, but modern forensic analysis of his remains ruled out poisoning. He died of a fatal, gangrenous infection. Mount, *Medieval Medicine*, 172–75.

28. Arner, "The Disappearing Scar of Henry V," 347.

29. Mortimer, *1415*, 26.

30. Vale, *Henry V*, 262

31. Vale, *Henry V*, 263.

32. Sumption, *Hundred Years War IV*, 413.

33. Livingston, "'The Depth of Six Inches,'" 218–19.

34. Henry's father, Henry Bolingbroke,

was the eldest son of John of Gaunt (1340–99), the third son of the legendary warrior king Edward III (r. 1327–77). His mother was the second daughter of a powerful magnate, Humphrey (1341–73), 7th Earl of Hereford, Essex, and Northampton. Henry V was therefore the great-grandson of Edward III, the English monarch who claimed the French crown through his mother, Isabella, the daughter of the French king Philip IV, when the Capetian dynasty died out in the male line of succession in 1328.

35. For a good historiographic essay on the modern literature covering Henry IV's life and reign, see Mortimer, *The Fears of Henry IV*, 1–12.

36. Joanna was the daughter of Charles II (r. 1349–87), king of Navarre, and Joan Valois, the daughter of French King Jean II (r. 1350–64). Her grandfather Jean II was famously captured by the English at the Battle of Poitiers (1356) and was held hostage in England for several years, where he eventually died. Joanna was widowed with eight children after her marriage to the Duke of Brittany, John IV (r. 1365–99).

37. Given-Wilson, *Henry IV*, 234–35.

38. Given-Wilson, 421.

39. For Richemont's tumultuous career in service of the Dauphin, see Vale, *Charles VII*, 35–41; Kelly DeVries, *Joan of Arc: A Military Leader* (Stroud, UK: Sutton, 2003), 108–14. For his experience at Agincourt and his description of the battle, see Anne Curry, *Great Battles: Agincourt* (Oxford and New York: Oxford University Press, 2015), 70.

40. Anne Curry, *The Battle of Agincourt: Sources and Interpretation* (Woodbridge, UK: Boydell Press, 2011), 184.

41. Curry, 185.

42. Barker, *Conquest*, 121–22.

43. Strohm, *England's Empty Throne*, 153–72. Given-Wilson, *Henry IV*, 523. Matusiak, *Henry V*, 198. For a detailed study of this strange series of events, see A. R. Meyers, "The Captivity of a Royal Witch: The Household Accounts of Queen Joan of Navarre, 1419–21," *Bulletin of the John Rylands Library* 24 (1940): 262–84. Meyers notes that she lived a very comfortable life in captivity.

44. For what little we know of his childhood, see Allmand, *Henry V*, 7–15;

Malcolm Mercer, *Henry V: The Rebirth of Chivalry* (Kew, UK: The National Archives), 5–6; Teresa Cole, *The Life of the Warrior King and the Battle of Agincourt* (Stroud, UK: Amberley, 2015), 11–30; Matusiak, *Henry V*, 21–44.

45. For the context of Henry's formal education as a prince, see Nicholas Orme, *From Childhood to Chivalry: The Education of English Kings and Aristocracy, 1066–1530* (London: Routledge, 2017).

46. Vale, *Henry V*, 206–213.

47. Barker, *Agincourt*, 174–75. For a discussion of the role that Vegetius played in late medieval warfare, see Craig Taylor, *Chivalry and the Ideals of Knighthood in France During the Hundred Years War* (Cambridge: Cambridge University Press, 2013), 255–75. For the Latin text, see Flavius Vegetius Renatus, *Epitoma rei militaris*, ed. M. D. Reeve (Oxford: Oxford University Press, 2004). For an English translation, see *Vegetius: Epitome of Military Science*, trans. N. P. Milner, 2nd ed. (Liverpool: Liverpool University Press, 1996). For a comprehensive study of its use in medieval warfare, see Christopher Allmand, *The De re militari of Vegetius: The Reception, Transmission and Legacy of a Roman Text in the Middle Ages* (Cambridge: Cambridge University Press, 2014).

48. The best recent biography is by Nigel Saul, *Richard II*.

49. For a clear presentation of the chronology of events that led to Henry's overthrow of Richard, see Saul, *Richard II*, 405–34.

50. Ashe, *Richard II*, 39–40.

51. For an engaging overview of the rebellion, see Barker, *England Arise: The People, the King and the Great Revolt*; Jones, *Summer of Blood: England's First Revolution*. For an analysis of the rebellion within the context of Richard's reign, see Saul, *Richard II*, 56–82.

52. Mortimer, *Fears of Henry IV*, 19.

53. Nigel Saul, *The Three Richards* (London: Bloomsbury, 2006), 94.

54. Saul, *Richard II*, 439.

55. For the complicated turn of events involving the Appellants, including Richard's brief imprisonment and the condemnation of his councilors by the so-called Merciless Parliament, see Saul, *Richard II*, 148–204.

56. Bertram Wolffe, *Henry VI* (New Haven, CT: Yale University Press, 2001), 25.

57. The official Lancastrian account of these events is known as the "Record and Process." For the Latin and English documents, see *The Deposition of Richard II: "The Record and Process of the Renunciation and Deposition of Richard II" (1399) and Related Writings*, ed. David R. Carlson, Toronto Medieval Latin Texts 29 (Toronto: Pontifical Institute of Mediaeval Studies, 2007).

58. Mortimer, *Fears of Henry IV*, 188; 192.

59. *Chronica Maiora of Thomas Walsingham*, 317.

60. Mortimer, *Fears of Henry IV*, 21–22. Mortimer offers a detailed analysis of the various theories of what accounted for Richard's death. He calls Henry's act a "political assassination" (p. 218), rather than a personal vendetta. Saul is more hesitant about establishing as fact precisely how Richard died. Saul, *Richard II*, 426.

61. Saul, *Richard II*, 419. Frederick was constantly at war with the papacy over his domains in Italy and was excommunicated a total of four times. This was part of an ongoing saga involving the hegemony of the popes over their territorial claims in Italy.

62. *Deposition of Richard II*, 29–54.

63. *The Chronicle of Adam Usk*, 63. For the text of the deposition at the Council of Lyons, see *Liber Sextus* 2.14.1–2, in *Corpus Iuris Canonici*, ed. A. Friedberg (Leipzig: Bernhard Tauchnitz, 1881), 2: 1007–11.

64. Laura Ashe, *Richard II*, 3–4.

65. Edward the Black Prince of Wales (1330–76) was heir to the throne, but died at the age of forty-five, one year before his own father Edward III died. For John of Gaunt, this created a crisis of succession that needed a legal solution from the dying king Edward III. A charter was drawn up, only a portion of which survives in a mutilated fourteenth-century copy. Mortimer notes that it clearly "nullified the rights of the Mortimer family and recognized John of Gaunt as next in line after Richard II. It also meant that Henry, after his father, was third in line for the throne." Mortimer, *Fears of Henry IV*, 32.

66. This argument was based on simplifying the succession as a *male-only*

prerogative, which had been changed by Edward I (r. 1272–1307), who stipulated that succession could pass through male and female heirs. This would undermine any other contrary claims made by the deposed Richard or his relatives, and to Henry's mind, solidify his claim. Mortimer, *Fears of Henry IV*, 184–85.

67. *Deposition of Richard II*, 58.

68. *Deposition of Richard II*, 9.

69. Pugh, *Henry V and the Southampton Plot*, 7.

70. Ashe, *Richard II*, 102.

71. *Chronica Maiora of Thomas Walsingham*, 394.

72. Strohm, *England's Empty Throne*, 117–18.

73. *Chronica Maiora of Thomas Walsingham*, 428.

74. The etymology of this term of derogation is unclear. "Lollard" is supposed to have come from the Middle Dutch word *lollaerd*, which means "mumbler" or "mutterer." For Wycliffe and Lollardy in general, see J. I. Catto, "Wyclif and Wycliffism at Oxford, 1356–1430," in *The History of the University of Oxford, II. Late Medieval Oxford*, ed. J. I. Catto and T. A. R. Evans (Oxford: Oxford University Press, 1992), 175–262; Kantik Gosh, *The Wycliffite Heresy: Authority and the Interpretation of Texts* (Cambridge: Cambridge University Press, 2009). For Henry V and the persecution of Lollards, see Maureen Jurkowski, "Henry V's Suppression of the Oldcastle Revolt," in *Henry V: New Interpretations*, ed. Gwilym Dodd, 103–30.

75. *The Chronicle of Adam Usk, 1377–1421*, ed. and trans. Chris Given-Wilson (Oxford: Clarendon Press, 1997), 123.

76. Strohm, *England's Empty Throne*, 182. For a comprehensive study, see Peter McNiven, *Heresy and Politics in the Reign of Henry IV: The Burning of John Badby* (Woodbridge, UK: Boydell Press, 1987).

77. The proposal for abdication was made by young Henry and the king's half-brother, Thomas Beaufort, Duke of Exeter. Given-Wilson, *Henry IV*, 495. There is no doubt that the king was gravely ill. Given-Wilson has carefully examined contemporary sources and concludes that Henry IV suffered with a number of afflictions: psoriasis, a prolapsed rectum, coronary thrombosis, poor blood circulation, and gangrenous skin ulcers. Given-Wilson, *Henry IV*, 533.

78. *Chronicle of Adam of Usk*, 243.

79. Given-Wilson, *Henry IV*, 512. See also Sumption, *Hundred Years War IV*, 306–31.

80. Given-Wilson, *Henry IV*, 504.

81. Allmand, *Henry V*, 57–58. Given-Wilson, *Henry IV*, 505. The source is *First English Life of Henry the Fifth*, 11–13. The testimony came from James Earl of Ormond. Some modern scholars have said that he claimed to be an eyewitness to this event, which cannot be confirmed.

82. *La Chronique d'Enguerran de Monstrelet, avec pièces justificatives, 1400–1444*, ed. Louis Claude Doüet-d'Arcq (Paris: Renouard, 1858), 2: 338–39.

83. Allmand, *Henry V*, 58; Given-Wilson, *Henry IV*, 2. See also Sumption, *Hundred Years War IV*, 331.

Chapter Three

1. Sumption, *Hundred Years War IV*, 44. For a good explanation of the profound differences between English and French theories of monarchic power in the late medieval period, see Green, *Hundred Years War*, 104–24.

2. For a detailed study of Henry IV's burial of Richard, see Joel Burden, "How do You Bury a Deposed King? The Funeral of Richard II and the Establishment of Lancastrian Royal Authority in 1400," in *Henry IV: The Establishment of the Regime, 1399–1406*, ed. Gwilym Dodd and Douglas Biggs (York: York Medieval Press, 2003), 35–54.

3. The best all-around analysis of the political motivations for Henry's reburial of Richard is by Strohm, *England's Empty Throne*, 101–27. For the expenses paid for the procession and funeral, see 115.

4. Given-Wilson, *Henry IV*, 521; Mortimer, *Fears of Henry IV*, 219. The chantries are noted in *First English Life of Henry the Fifth*, 21–22.

5. Saul, *Richard II*, 427–28. See also Given-Wilson, *Henry IV*, 521–22.

6. Strohm, *England's Empty Throne*, 117.

7. Sumption, *Hundred Years War IV*, 464.

8. Sumption, 465.

9. A detailed analysis of the history of this peace is presented by C. J. Phillpotts, "The Fate of the Truce of Paris, 1396–1415," *Journal of Medieval History* 24 (1998): 61–80.

10. Isabella's tragedies did not end until her death. On her return to France, she married Charles, Duke of Orléans. But she died in childbirth at the age of nineteen when their daughter Joan was born. An accomplished poet, Charles was one of the many noblemen who fought at Agincourt and was captured and held hostage in England for twenty-four years before his release. His daughter Joan married Jean II, Duke of Alençon, who famously fought with Joan of Arc as one of her most favored comrades-in-arms.

11. Sumption, *Hundred Years War IV*, 49–52, 61–63.

12. F. Taylor, "The Chronicle of John Streeche for the Reign of Henry V (1414–1422)," *Bulletin of the John Rylands Library* 16 (1932): 150. Not much is known about Streeche, who was an Augustinian canon and chronicler of the reigns of both Henry IV and Henry V. He was a contemporary of both kings.

13. Taylor, *Henry V*, 116.

14. Barker, *Agincourt*, 69.

15. Sumption, *Hundred Years War IV*, 374.

16. Curry, *Great Battles: Agincourt*, 16.

17. Curry, *Henry V*, 54–55.

18. Mortimer, *1415*, 133.

19. This challenge to a trial by combat is reported in the *Gesta Henrici Quinti*, 59. Barker, *Agincourt*, 99–102. For the full text of his message to the Dauphin, see Mortimer, *1415*, 387–89.

20. Sumption, *Hundred Years War IV*, 422–28; Mortimer, *1415*, 276–77.

21. Curry, *Henry V*, 52.

22. Barker has Henry Beaufort giving this speech, while Sumption follows the account of Enguerrand de Monstrelet, who has Chichele speaking. Barker, *Agincourt*, 121.

23. *La Chronique d'Enguerran de Monstrelet*, 3: 74.

24. Sumption, *Hundred Years War IV*, 427. Accounts of this embassy can be found in *Chronique du Réligieux de Saint-Denys*

(1380–1422), 5: 512–25; *Chronique d'Enguerran de Monstrelet*, 3: 72–75. The angry speech cited by Sumption comes from Juvénal des Ursins (1388–1473) and Jean de Waurin (c. 1390–1474), and he thinks that these reports are reliable. Pugh thinks it unlikely that such a scene ever took place. Pugh, *Southampton Plot*, 60.

25. *Gesta Henrici Quinti*, 17–19.

26. Sumption, *Hundred Years War IV*, 640. The Dauphin Louis also died within a few months of Henry's victory, adding more drama to the chaos surrounding the mad King Charles VI. He was succeeded by his younger brother John, Duke of Touraine, who died in 1419 at the age of eighteen. His younger brother, Charles, became the next Dauphin and was crowned King Charles VII (1429), thanks to Joan of Arc.

27. *First English Life of Henry the Fifth*, 131.

28. P. J. P. Goldberg, ed., *Richard Scrope: Archbishop, Rebel, Martyr* (Donington, UK: Shaun Tyas, 2007). For the political consequences of Scrope's execution, see J. W. McKenna, "Popular Canonization as Political Propaganda: The Cult of Archbishop Scrope," *Speculum* 45 (1970): 608–23.

29. Sumption, *Hundred Years War IV*, 166–70.

30. Given-Wilson, *Henry IV*, 269. See also Mortimer, *Fears of Henry IV*, 297–99.

31. Given-Wilson, *Henry IV*, 270.

32. Given-Wilson, 277.

33. A good analysis of Henry's relationship with the Norman church can be found in Vale, *Henry V*, 175–86.

34. For the history of monasteries in medieval England, see David Knowles, *The Religious Orders in England II: The End of the Middle Ages* (Cambridge: Cambridge University Press, 1955). The best succinct analysis of the connection between the Brigittines and the English monarchy is by Nancy Bradley Warren, "Kings, Saints and Nuns: Gender, Religion and Authority in the Reign of Henry V," *Viator* 30 (1999): 307–22. See also F. R. Johnston, "The English Cult of St. Bridget of Sweden," *Analecta Bollandiana* 103 (1985): 75–93; Carol Heffernan, "The Revelations of St. Bridget of Sweden in Fifteenth-Century England," *Neophilologus* 101 (2017): 337–49.

35. Warren, "Kings, Saints and Nuns,"

315. For the full text of Henry's will, see Thomas Rymer, *Foedera, conventiones et litterae et cujuscunque generis acta publica inter Reges Angliae* (London: Jacob Tonson, 1729), 9: 289–92.

36. *The Revelations of St. Birgitta of Sweden, Volume 2, Liber Caelestis Bks IV–V*, trans. Denis Michael Searby, with introduction and notes by Bridget Morris (Oxford: Oxford University Press, 2008), 184–86. For a good synopsis of St. Bridget's life and her revelations, see the introduction of this work.

37. *Revelations of St. Birgitta of Sweden, Volume 2*, 186.

38. Knowles, *Religious Orders in England II*, 175; Neil Becket, "St. Bridget, Henry V and Syon Abbey," *Studies in St. Bridget and the Brigittine Order 2*, ed. James Hogg, Analecta Carthusiana 35 (1993), 127; cited by Warren, "Kings, Saints and Nuns," 315.

39. *Gesta Henrici Quinti*, 186. J. W. McKenna, "Popular Canonization as Political Propaganda," 615. Knowles, *Religious Orders in England II*, 175–82.

40. Knowles, *Religious Orders in England II*, 181. In his chronicle, Adam Usk notes that Henry endowed these houses "with the possession of monks from France," without providing any real details. *The Chronicle of Adam Usk*, 253.

41. Knowles, *Religious Orders in England II*, 175.

42. Knowles, 180. The pro-Lancastrian chronicler Thomas Walsingham describes at length the foundation of Syon and explains the Brigittine rule and governance structure of the monastery. *Chronica Maiora of Thomas Walsingham*, 398.

43. Vale, *Henry V*, 142. Vale is quoting J. Catto, "Religious Change Under Henry V," in *Henry V: The Practice of Kingship*, ed. Gerald L. Harriss, 2nd ed. (Stroud, UK: Sutton, 1993), 110–11.

44. Warren, "Kings, Saints and Nuns," 316. As Wolffe notes in his biography of his son and successor, Henry VI (r. 1422–61, 1470–71), the usurpation of his grandfather was remembered throughout his own long and tumultuous reign. Wolffe, *Henry VI*, 18.

45. For the difficult relationship between Henry V and Martin V, see K. B. McFarlane, "Henry V, Bishop Beaufort and the Red Hat, 1417–1421," *English Historical Review*

60 (1945): 316–48; Margaret M. Harvey, "Martin V and Henry V," *Archivum Historiae Pontificiae* 24 (1986): 49–70; Margaret M. Harvey, *England, Rome and the Papacy, 1417–1464: The Study of a Relationship* (Manchester: Manchester University Press, 1993).

46. *Chronica Maiora of Thomas Walsingham*, 440. For a brief synopsis of this meeting, see Knowles, *The Religious Orders in England II*, 182–84.

47. The Latin term *praemunire* originally meant "to fortify." But the Act of Parliament used the term to mean a writ of summons to appear before an English magistrate. For a detailed study of the legislation and its use by the English monarchy, see W. T. Waugh, "The Great Statute of Praemunire," *The English Historical Review* (1922): 173–205. See also Frederick Daniel Gosling, "Church State and Reformation: The Use and Interpretation of *Praemunire* From Its Creation to the English Break With Rome" (PhD thesis, University of Leeds, 2016), 83–97. For Henry's aggressive control of the English Church, see Vale, *Henry V*, 161–203.

Chapter Four

1. Barker, *Agincourt*, 360–61. Barker's text has been modernized from the original Middle English. Two early manuscripts preserving the carol come from the early fifteenth and mid-fifteenth century. The earliest is Cambridge, Trinity College, MS O.3.58, http://trin-sites-pub.trin.cam.ac.uk/james/viewpage.php?index=749. The second is Oxford, Bodleian Library, MS Arch Selden B.26, fols. 3r–33v, http://image.ox.ac.uk/show?collection=bodleian&manuscript=msarchseldenb26.

An excellent review of the text, music and debates about its origin can be found in Vale, *Henry V*, 214–16, and Helen Deeming, "The Sources and Origin of the Agincourt Carol," *Early Music* 35 (2007): 23–36. While dispelling one of the myths long associated with this piece—that it was spontaneously sung by the English after their victory—modern research on its authorship and place of composition remains inconclusive. Vale suggests that it might have been composed for Henry's triumphant entry into London after he had won the battle (November 23, 1415). Also useful for understanding the religious ideology of the carol is Wolfgang G. Müller, "The Battle of Agincourt in Carol and Ballad," *Fifteenth Century Studies* 8 (1983): 159–78.

2. McHardy posits that the author of this important text might have been Henry's confessor, the erudite Carmelite priest Stephen Patrington (died 1417). Patrington was an Oxford-educated, anti-Wycliffite theologian who was made bishop of St. David's and then appointed to the bishopric of Chichester shortly before he died. He was also present at the Council of Constance. McHardy, "Religion, Court Culture and Propaganda: The Chapel Royal in the Reign of Henry V," in *Henry V: New Interpretations*, 142–53.

3. *Gesta Henrici Quinti*, 79.

4. "Liber Metricus de Henrico Quinto," in *Memorials of Henry the Fifth, King of England*, ed. C. A. Cole (London: Rolls Series, 1858), 113–24.

5. Curry, *Battle of Agincourt: Sources*, 45.

6. *Gesta Henrici Quinti*, 83.

7. *Chronica Maiora of Thomas Walsingham 1376–1422*, 445–46.

8. *Gesta Henrici Quinti*, 186. J. W. McKenna, "Popular Canonization as Political Propaganda," 615. Knowles, *Religious Orders in England II*, 175–82.

9. For the history of chantries in England, see the important pioneering work of Kathleen L. Wood-Legh, *Perpetual Chantries in Britain* (Cambridge: Cambridge University Press, 1965). For more recent work, see Julian M. Luxford and John McNeill, *The Medieval Chantry in England* (Leeds: British Archaeological Association, 2011); Marie-Helene Rousseau, *Saving the Souls of Medieval London: Perpetual Chantries at St. Paul's Cathedral, c. 1200–1548* (London: Routledge, 2016).

10. Taylor, *Henry V*, 220–21.

11. *Chronica Maiora of Thomas Walsingham*, 440. For a brief synopsis of this meeting, see Knowles, *Religious Orders in England II*, 182–84.

12. Knowles, *Religious Orders in England II*, 183.

13. The academic literature on the medieval Mass is voluminous. Representative works include Miri Rubin, *Corpus Christi:*

The Eucharist in Late Medieval Culture (Cambridge: Cambridge University Press, 1991); Enrico Mazza, *The Celebration of the Eucharist: The Origin of the Rite and the Development of Its Interpretation*, trans. Matthew J. O'Connell (Collegeville, MN: Liturgical Press, 1999). For the later medieval period, there is no finer study than Eamon Duffy's *The Stripping of the Altars: Traditional Religion in England, 1400–1580*, 2nd ed. (New Haven, CT: Yale University Press, 2005).

14. Vale, *Henry V*, 129; 159.

15. *Gesta Henrici Quinti*, 155.

16. Vale, *Henry V*, 138.

17. McHardy, "Religion, Court Culture and Propaganda," in *Henry V: New Interpretations*, 131.

18. McHardy, 141.

19. Matusiak, *Henry V*, 82.

20. For a comprehensive study of this important religious movement that originated in the Netherlands, see John Van Engen, *Sisters and Brothers of the Common Life: The Devotio Moderna and the World of the Later Middle Ages* (Philadelphia: University of Pennsylvania Press, 2014).

21. For the context of Henry's religious devotions, see Duffy, *Stripping of the Altars*.

22. *Gesta Henrici Quinti*, 83.

23. *Gesta Henrici Quinti*, 89.

24. McHardy, "Religion, Court Culture and Propaganda," 135.

25. Vale, *Henry V*, 182–183. For the full text of these papal privileges, see Rymer, *Foedera*, 9: 615–16.

26. *Chronica Maiora of Thomas Walsingham*, 445.

27. An early fifteenth-century manuscript (ECR 59) containing copies of the documents was rediscovered at Eton College in 1978. This school was founded by Henry's son and successor, Henry VI (1440). An analysis and transcription of the Latin texts can be found in Patrick Strong and Felicity Strong, "The Last Will and Codicils of Henry V," *English Historical Review* 96 (1981): 79–102.

28. Rymer, *Foedera*, 9: 289. In the will from 1421, he changed his title to "*Henricus, Dei gratia rex Anglie, heres et regens regni Francie et dominus Hibernie*," or "Henry, King of England by the grace of God, heir and regent for the King of France

and lord of Ireland." This is obviously on account of the ratification of the Treaty of Troyes (1420), which named Henry regent and then king of France when Charles VI died. Strong and Strong, "The Last Will and Codicils of Henry V," 89.

29. Vale, *Henry V*, 240–41. Vale is quoting McFarlane, *Lancastrian Kings and Lollard Knights*, 132. At the end of the Latin text, there is an English note: "This is my last will subscribed with my own hand R. H. Jesu Mercy and Gremercy Ladie Marie help." Rymer, *Foedera*, 9: 293.

30. Vale, *Henry V*, 251.

31. Rymer, *Foedera*, 9: 289, 290.

32. Caroline Walker Bynum, *Holy Feast and Holy Fast: The Religious Significance of Food to Medieval Women* (Berkeley: University of California Press, 1987), 54–55; Caroline Walker Bynum, *Wonderful Blood: Theology and Practice in Late Medieval Northern Germany and Beyond* (Philadelphia: University of Pennsylvania Press, 2007), 87.

33. The Feast of Corpus Christi (1264) offers the most dramatic example of the host as a "seen" relic. For a detailed study of the evolution of the feast, see Barbara R. Walters, Vincent J. Corrigan, and Peter T. Ricketts, eds., *The Feast of Corpus Christi* (Philadelphia: University of Pennsylvania Press, 2006).

34. Juliet Barker, *Agincourt*, 277.

35. *Gesta Henrici Quinti*, 68–69.

36. Mortimer, *1415*, 212, 523.

37. Wylie and Waugh, *Reign of Henry V*, 1: 475. For detailed inventory and study of these items, see Jenny Stratford, "'Par le special commandement du roy.' Jewels and Plate Pledged for the Agincourt Expedition," in *Henry V: New Interpretations*, 157–70.

Chapter Five

1. Malcom Vale offers the most recent analysis of Henry's literary tastes. Vale, *Henry V*, esp. 205–39.

2. Vale, *Henry V*, 127. For Vale's primary source, see note 9 in chapter 2.

3. *Chronica Maiora of Thomas Walsingham 1376–1422*, 445–46.

4. Barker, *Agincourt*, 362.

5. Mortimer, *1415*, 532. A similar view is expressed by J. I. Catto, "The Burden and Conscience of Government in the Fifteenth Century," *Transactions of the Royal Historical Society* 17 (2007): 98.

6. This work was formerly attributed to Thomas Elmham (c. 1364–1427), an English monk who accompanied Henry on his Agincourt campaign. He wrote a verse life of Henry, *Liber metricus de Henrico V*, but he is no longer considered the author of the *Vita et Gesta*.

7. Curry, *Henry V*, 32. *Thomae de Elmham Vita et Gesta*, 12.

8. "I haue hearde of credible report, this noble prince, Kinge Henrie the Fifte, obserued so constantly that from the death of the Kinge his Father vntill the marriage of himself he neuer lo had knowledge carnally of weomen." *First English Life of Henry V*, 5.

9. The mother is unknown, but Henry IV had an illegitimate son named Edmund Le Boorde (1401–19). Mortimer, *Fears of Henry IV*, 372.

10. Mortimer, *1415*, 49–50.

11. Anne Curry, "The Military Ordinances of Henry V: Texts and Contexts," in *War, Government and Aristocracy in the British Isles, c. 1150–1500: Essays in Honor of Michael Prestwich*, ed. Chris Given-Wilson, Ann Kettle and Len Scales (Woodbridge, UK: Boydell Press, 2008), 214–49. Curry notes (p. 237) that "it is not possible at this stage to date with certainty any of the surviving texts of military ordinances for the reign of Henry V."

12. *Gesta Henrici Quinti*, 26–27.

13. Curry, "Military Ordinances of Henry V," 227.

14. Curry, "Military Ordinances of Henry V," 249; context is 232. This ordinance is also noted in Francis Grose, *Military Antiquities Respecting a History of the English Army From the Conquest to the Present Time* (London: I. Stockdale, 1812), 2:68.

15. Jean Chartier, *Chronique de Charles VII, Roi de France*, ed. A. Vallet de Viriville (Paris: P. Jannet, 1858), 123.

16. Mortimer, *1415*, 35.

17. Mortimer, 34.

18. Curry, *Henry V*, 62. In fact, Henry had already put forth this theological argument in a letter he sent to King Charles VI, roughly a month before his invasion of

France. See *La Chronique d'Enguerran de Monstrelet*, 3:78–81.

19. McHardy, "Religion, Court Culture and Propaganda," in *Henry V: New Interpretations*, 136. *Gesta Henrici Quinti*, 50. Though this parallels the siege of Jericho in Joshua chapter 6, McHardy observes that the account in the *Gesta* provides no biblical reference for this procession.

20. Barker, *Agincourt*, 174–75.

21. *Chronica Maiora of Thomas Walsingham*, 406.

22. Barker, *Agincourt*, 174; Curry, *Henry V*, 62–63.

23. *Gesta Henrici Quinti*, 34–35.

24. *New American Bible*, United States Conference of Catholic Bishops, https://bible.usccb.org/bible/deuteronomy/20.

25. *Gesta Henrici Quinti*, 35–37.

26. Curry, *Henry V*, 63.

27. Curry, 62.

28. Taylor, *Chivalry and the Ideals of Knighthood*, 182. For a general history of medieval siege warfare, see Sean McGlynn, *By Sword and Fire: Cruelty and Atrocity in Medieval Warfare* (London: Weidenfeld and Nicolson, 2008), 141–94.

29. *Chronicle of Adam Usk, 1377–1421*, 255. Ormrod, *Edward III*, 292. For a study of Henry's rituals of surrender and formal entrance into defeated cities, see Neil Murphy, "Ceremony and Conflict in Fifteenth-Century France: Lancastrian Ceremonial Entries into French Towns, 1415–1431," *Explorations in Renaissance Culture* 39 (2013): 113–33.

30. Ormrod, *Edward III*, 292.

31. Barker, *Agincourt*, 196–97.

32. Sumption, *Hundred Years War IV*, 533–34.

33. Seward, *Henry V*, 105. Mortimer states that Henry gave the order for the slaughter of eighteen hundred men when the city fell. Mortimer, *1415*, 536. See also Matusiak, *Henry V*, 176. The contemporary source for Henry's order was the Venetian chronicler Antonio Morosini (c. 1365–1433). Léon Dorez, and Germain Lefèvre-Pontalis, eds., *Chronique d'Antonio Morosini: extraits relatifs à l'histoire de France* (Paris: Librairie Renouard, H. Laurens succ., 1899), 2: 146–49. Even one of the greatest modern historians of Henry's reign and an admirer of the king, W. T.

Waugh, expressed his great discomfort as an Englishmen when narrating the horrible events that transpired with the fall of Caen. Wylie and Waugh, *Reign of Henry V*, 3: 61.

34. Sumption, *Hundred Years War IV*, 534.

35. For an excellent analysis of the text, debates about its authorship, and its value as a historical source, see Bellis, *John Page's The Siege of Rouen*. For a detailed study of Rouen under English occupation, see Paul Le Cacheux, ed., *Rouen au temps de Jeanne d'Arc pendant l'occupation anglaise (1419–1449)* (Paris: Picard, 1931).

36. Bellis, *John Page's The Siege of Rouen*, 26.

37. Bellis, 22.

38. *First English Life of Henry the Fifth*, 131. After spending several hours arguing in private with Henry, St. Vincent apparently changed his mind on the justice of the king's war in France. This story comes late in the source tradition and may be apocryphal.

39. Jonathan Riley-Smith, *The First Crusade and the Idea of Crusading* (Philadelphia: University of Pennsylvania Press, 1986), 142.

40. The academic literature on the Crusades is vast. Among the best recent works are Thomas Asbridge, *The Crusades: The Authoritative History of the War for the Holy Land* (New York: Harper Collins, 2010); Thomas Madden, *The Concise History of the Crusades*, 3rd student ed. (Lanham, MD: Rowen and Littlefield, 2014).

41. Despite the supposed religious nature of this war—and there is no doubt that Henry Bolingbroke viewed it as a holy war—this may have been more of a political war between rival family members in the Lithuanian royal family. Henry attempted to participate in another crusade in Lithuania, but after a peace settlement and with nothing else to do in Eastern Europe, he successfully undertook a long pilgrimage to Jerusalem. See Mortimer, *Fears of Henry IV*, 94–95, 104–05.

42. Important recent works on the topic include Malcolm Barber, "The Albigensian Crusades: Wars Like Any Other?" in *Dei gesta per Francos: Crusade Studies in Honor of Jean Richard*, ed. Michel Balard, Benjamin Z. Kedar, and Jonathan Riley-Smith

(Aldershot, UK: Ashgate, 2001), 45–56; Mark Gregory Pegg, *A Most Holy War:The Albigensian Crusade and the Battle for Christendom* (Oxford: Oxford University Press, 2008); Jonathan Sumption, *The Albigensian Crusade* (London: Faber and Faber, 2011).

43. The Cathars derived their name from the Latin term *Cathari*, or "the pure ones," although this is not a name that they themselves used. They were dualists who believed that the body and physical creation were evil and they sought to purify their souls by renouncing procreation. They seemed to have had some beliefs in common with the early Christian heresy of Gnosticism, but they called themselves "true Christians" and rejected clerical authority and the sacraments. They are also known as Albigensians since one of their earliest strongholds was the French city of Albi in the south of France.

44. There are wildly conflicting numbers of casualties given in the contemporary chronicles (some saying that twenty thousand were killed, which is probably an exaggeration). There is no known reliable number of deaths.

45. Green, *Hundred Years War*, 245.

46. Richard W. Kaeuper, *Holy Warriors: The Religious Ideology of Chivalry* (Philadelphia: University of Pennsylvania Press, 2009), 95–96.

47. Ormrod, *Edward III*, 282.

48. For a detailed discussion of this legislation and what stood behind it, see Finbarr McAuley, "Canon Law and the End of the Ordeal," *Oxford Journal of Legal Studies* 26 (2006): 473–513.

Chapter Six

1. Taylor, *Henry V*, 228.

2. Taylor, 229–30.

3. Curry notes that the many chronicle accounts of Henry's words are literary constructions modeled on biblical texts, or copied from sermon literature or from each other. Anne Curry, "The Battle Speeches of Henry V," *Reading Medieval Studies* 34 (2008): 77–97.

4. *Gesta Henrici Quinti*, 79; for Hungerford's identity see, p. 78, n. 2. In the *Liber*

Metricus de Henrico Quinto, or *The Metrical Life of Henry the Fifth* (c. 1418), English monastic chronicler Thomas Elmham records a similar exchange. "Liber Metricus de Henrico Quinto," in *Memorials of Henry the Fifth, King of England*, 113–24.

5. Taylor, *Henry V*, 258.

6. Curry, *Battle of Agincourt: Sources*, 164.

7. *Chronica Maiora of Thomas Walsingham*, 413.

8. There are obvious logistical problems with depicting a battle of such numbers and magnitude on a relatively small stage. The vital role of the archers in the victory would also be difficult to stage. For an analysis of the "conspicuous absence" of archers in Shakespeare's play, see Evelyn Tribble, "Where Are the Archers in Shakespeare?" *ELH* 82 (2015): 789–814.

9. In 2015, to mark the 600th anniversary of the battle a special commemorative service was held in Westminster Abbey that included readings from Shakespeare's *Henry V*. Karen Britland and Line Cottegnies, "Introduction," in *King Henry V: A Critical Reader*, 3.

10. An excellent review of the text, music, and debates about the carol's origin can be found in Vale, *Henry V*, 214–16, and Deeming, "The Sources and Origin of the Agincourt Carol," 23–36. Vale suggests that it might have been composed for Henry's triumphant entry into London, after he had won the battle (November 23, 1415). Also useful for understanding the religious ideology of the carol is Müller, "The Battle of Agincourt in Carol and Ballad," 159–78.

11. There are some modern historians who think otherwise. See Clifford Rogers, "Henry V's Military Strategy in 1415," in *The Hundred Years War: A Wider Focus*, 399–427.

12. Barker, *Agincourt*, 82–143. For a detailed analysis of a neglected component of Henry's war in Normandy, see Craig Lambert, "Henry V and the Crossing to France: Reconstructing Naval Operations for the Agincourt Campaign, 1415," in *Agincourt in Context: War on Land Sea*, ed. Ambühl and Lambert, 24–39.

13. For the modern debate about the discovery of the supposed plot, see the introduction.

14. Mortimer, *1415*, 212; 523. Stratford, "'Par le special commandement du roy': Jewels and Plate Pledged for the Agincourt Expedition," in *Henry V: New Interpretations*, 157–70.

15. *Gesta Henrici Quinti*, 39–41.

16. Barker, *Agincourt*, 175. For detailed study of the critical importance of artillery at Harfleur, see Dan Spencer, "'The Scourge of Stones': English Gunpowder Artillery at the Siege of Harfleur," in *Agincourt in Context*, 59–73.

17. *Chronica Maiora of Thomas Walsingham*, 406.

18. Barker, *Agincourt*, 197.

19. *Gesta Henrici Quinti*, 55.

20. Curry, *Henry V*, 63.

21. *Gesta Henrici Quinti*, 45.

22. Barker, *Agincourt*, 205.

23. Barker, *Agincourt*, 205.

24. Anne Curry, "After Agincourt, What Next? Henry V and the Campaign of 1416," *Fifteenth Century England* 7 (2007): 29.

25. Spencer, "'The Scourge of Stones':" 69. Sumption calls the siege of Harfleur "an artillery battle interrupted by periodic assaults." Sumption, *Hundred Years War IV*, 436.

26. Clifford J. Rogers, "The Battle of Agincourt," in *Hundred Years War II*, 40.

27. *Gesta Henrici Quinti*, 61.

28. Sumption, *Hundred Years War IV*, 441.

29. Ormrod, *Edward III*, 290–92.

30. Curry, *Great Battles: Agincourt*, 8. A more detailed chronology and analysis can be found in Curry, *1415 Agincourt: A New History* (Stroud, UK: History Press, 2015). Allmand also provides a succinct and well documented account of the siege of Harfleur and the Agincourt campaign. See Allmand, *Henry V*, 61–101.

31. Curry, *Battle of Agincourt: Sources*, 43.

32. Mortimer, *1415*, 406.

33. Rogers entertains the possibility that he was actually "hoping for a battle with the French, and expected to win regardless of the numerical odds against him." Rogers, "Henry V's Military Strategy in 1415," in *Hundred Years War: Wider Focus*, 410.

34. Curry, *Battle of Agincourt: Sources*, 184. No other chronicle makes references to Henry's body-doubles, so it is difficult to

ascertain the validity of this claim. Interestingly, the *First English Life* (p. 54) notes that Henry had no fear of being identified by his splendid helmet, crown, or heraldry: "he feared not to be knowne of his adversaries."

35. Barker, *Conquest*, 121–122.

36. Rogers, "The Battle of Agincourt," in *Hundred Years War II*, 67.

37. Barker, *Agincourt*, 323.

38. Keegan, *The Face of Battle: A Study of Agincourt, Waterloo and the Somme* (New York: Penguin Books, 1978), 78–116. The most methodical point-by-point analysis of every aspect of the battle is Rogers, "The Battle of Agincourt," in *Hundred Years War II*, 37–132.

39. Keegan, *Face of Battle*, 85.

40. Allmand, *Henry V*, 90.

41. Curry, *Battle of Agincourt: Sources*, 24.

42. Keegan, *Face of Battle*, 90. Keegan provides many precise details about distances and ranges for longbows and crossbows in his reconstruction of the battle.

43. Mortimer, *1415*, 426.

44. Curry, *1415 Agincourt*, 160.

45. Curry, *Battle of Agincourt: Sources*, 46.

46. Recorded by the contemporary English chronicler Thomas Elmham. Curry, *Battle of Agincourt: Sources*, 44. As Sumption notes, the use of sharpened stakes, archers, and dismounted knights were tactics that the English learned in their wars with the Scots in the fourteenth century. Sumption, *Hundred Years War I*, 65–67.

47. Matthew Bennett, "The Battle of Agincourt," in *The Battle of Agincourt*, ed. Anne Curry and Malcolm Mercer (New Haven, CT: Yale University Press, 2015), 105. This is confirmed by the *Gesta Henrici Quinti*, 68–71.

48. Curry, *Great Battles: Agincourt*, 25.

49. *Chronica Majora of Thomas Walsingham*, 411.

50. Rogers, "The Battle of Agincourt," in *Hundred Years War II*, 44, 74.

51. Rogers, 73.

52. Curry, *Battle of Agincourt: Sources*, 46.

53. Barker, *Agincourt*, 279. See also Allmand, *Henry V*, 91; this is recorded by one of the late fifteenth-century manuscripts of the *Brut Chronicle*.

54. Curry, *Battle of Agincourt: Sources*, 60.

55. Rogers, "The Battle of Agincourt," in *Hundred Years War II*, 64.

56. Curry, *Battle of Agincourt: Sources*, 130.

57. Barker, *Agincourt*, 86.

58. *Gesta Henrici Quinti*, 89.

59. *Gesta Henrici Quinti*, 91.

60. *Chronica Majora of Thomas Walsingham*, 411.

61. Curry, *Battle of Agincourt: Sources*, 11–13.

62. Curry, *Great Battles: Agincourt*, 32.

63. Curry, *1415, Agincourt*, 9.

64. Taylor, *Henry V*, 239.

65. Curry, *1415 Agincourt*, 288–97; Curry, *Battle of Agincourt: Sources*, 11–13.

66. Keegan, *Face of Battle*, 87.

67. Barker, *Agincourt*, 264. Rogers, "Henry V's Military Strategy in 1415," in *Hundred Years War: Wider Focus*, 399; Rogers, "The Battle of Agincourt," in *Hundred Years War II*, 107.

68. Rogers, "The Battle of Agincourt," 57.

69. Mortimer, *1415*, 421, 566.

70. Curry, *1415 Agincourt*, 13.

71. For a useful study of this subject, see M. Cassidy-Welch, "Grief and Memory After the Battle of Agincourt," in *Hundred Years War II*, 133–50. For the glorification of French chivalry at Agincourt in the Burgundian chronicles, see Georges Le Brusque, "Chronicling the Hundred Years War in Burgundy and France in the Fifteenth Century," in *Writing War: Medieval Literary Responses to Warfare*, ed. Corinne Saunders, Françoise Le Saux, and Neil Thomas (Cambridge: D.S. Brewer, 2004), 80–81.

72. Sumption, *Hundred Years War IV*, 461.

73. Barker, *Agincourt*, 321. The Dauphin Louis's death within a few months of Agincourt added more drama to the chaos surrounding the mad King Charles VI. He was succeeded by his younger brother, John, Duke of Touraine, who died in 1419, at the age of eighteen. His younger brother Charles became the next Dauphin and was crowned King Charles VII, thanks to Joan of Arc. Sumption, *Hundred Years War IV*, 640.

74. An exception is Guillame Gruel (c. 1410–74/82), who served Arthur de Richemont (1393–1458), one of Henry's most famous captives at Agincourt. Gruel noted the narrow confines of the battlefield and the devastation caused by the archers as major reasons for the loss. See Le Brusque, "Chronicling the Hundred Years War," in *Writing War*, 88–89. Honig also notes that the medieval narrative sources generally lacked our interest in the precise details of battle upon which modern military history is predicated (e.g., accurate numbers, troop dispositions, and casualties). Jan W. Honig, "Reappraising Late Medieval Strategy: The Example of the 1415 Agincourt Campaign," *War in History* 19 (2012): 129.

75. A lost manuscript copy of the original plan, drafted under the supervision of Marshall Boucicaut, was discovered in an archive in the 1980s. See Christopher J. Phillpotts, "The French Battle Plan During the Agincourt Campaign," *English Historical Review* 99 (1984): 59–66.

76. Rogers, "The Battle of Agincourt," *Hundred Years War II*, 69.

77. Barker, *Agincourt*, 251.

78. Mortimer, *1415*, 434.

79. Curry, *Agincourt: Great Battles*, 20.

80. Contamine argues that the existence of the *oriflamme* cannot be reliably documented until the reign of Louis VI (r. 1108–37). For a detailed study of its history, see Philippe Contamine, "L'Oriflamme de Saint-Denis aux XIVe et XVe siècles. Étude de symbolique religieuse et royale," *Annales de l'Est* 7 (1973): 179–244.

81. Green, *Hundred Years War*, 220. Geoffroi de Charny, *A Knight's Own Book of Chivalry*, trans. Elspeth Kennedy, with an introduction by Richard W. Kaeuper (Philadelphia: University of Pennsylvania Press, 2005).

82. Barker, *Agincourt*, 288.

83. Given-Wilson and Bériac claim that the presence of the *oriflamme* does not exonerate Henry for killing prisoners. Men on the battlefield were fair game for death, but men who had surrendered did not fall under the penalty of death symbolized by the banner. Chris Given-Wilson and Françoise Bériac, "Edward III's Prisoners of War: The Battle of Poitiers and

Its Context," *English Historical Review* 116 (2001): 803.

84. Curry, *Battle of Agincourt: Sources*, 475.

85. *Gesta Henrici Quinti*, 91.

86. Curry, *Battle of Agincourt: Sources*, 174.

87. Keegan, *Face of Battle*, 106.

88. Curry, *Battle of Agincourt: Sources*, 118. Thomas Walsingham also makes a brief comment about the attack on the baggage but does not mention the killing of prisoners. *Chronica Majora of Thomas Walsingham*, 413.

89. Curry, *Battle of Agincourt: Sources*, 162–63.

90. Curry, 163.

91. *Gesta Henrici Quinti*, 85.

92. Mortimer, *1415*, 444.

93. Curry, *Agincourt*, 214.

94. *Gesta Henrici Quinti*, xxxvi.

95. Curry, *Agincourt: Great Battles*, 35. Sumption gives a number of about seven hundred, but cites no specific source. Sumption, *Hundred Years War IV*, 458.

96. *Gesta Henrici Quinti*, 91.

97. *Gesta Henrici Quinti*, 93.

98. Keegan, *Face of Battle*, 109.

99. Keegan, 109. Keegan's Latin phrase is a truncated form of *Dies non juridicum*, "a day where there is no legal activity" or a "day when courts do not sit."

100. Keegan, 112.

101. Allmand, *Henry V*, 95.

102. Allmand, 95.

103. Barker, *Agincourt*, 289.

104. Barker, 289.

105. Mortimer, *1415*, 447.

106. Mortimer, 452.

107. Mortimer, 453.

108. Curry, *Agincourt: Great Battles*, 33. See also Keegan, *Face of Battle*, 85. For the importance of this battle, see J. G. Monteiro, "The Battle of Aljubarrota (1385): A Reassessment," *Journal of Medieval Military History* 7 (2009): 75–103. For a comprehensive analysis of this battle and the killing of prisoners in the Hundred Years War, see Andy King, "'Then a Great Misfortune Befell Them': The Laws of War on Surrender and the Killing of Prisoners in the Hundred Years War," in *Agincourt in Context*, 106–17.

109. King, "'Then a Great Misfortune Befell Them,'" 109–10.

110. Curry, *Agincourt: Great Battles*, 72. See also Sumption, *Hundred Years War IV*, 461.

111. Barker, *Agincourt*, 292.

112. Rogers, "The Battle of Agincourt," in *Hundred Years War II*, 99–100. Taylor rightly points out that by modern conventions, such behavior is abhorrent, but by medieval standards—even among the French chroniclers—such an order in the heat of battle was acceptable. Craig Taylor, "Henry V, Flower of Chivalry," in *Henry V: New Interpretations*, 234–36. For a deeper analysis of the conflict between "anachronists" who condemn Henry's actions and "historicists" who avoid making legal judgements about his order, see Warren, "Henry V, Anachronism and the History of International Law," *The Oxford Handbook of English Law and Literature, 1500–1700*, 709–27.

113. Elizabeth Pentland offers a fresh analysis of French literary reactions to Agincourt, describing in detail a "literature of consolation" that offered comfort to the bereaved women who lived with the aftermath of the battle. See Pentland, "Agincourt and After—The Adversary's Perspective," in *King Henry V: A Critical Reader*, 200–20.

114. Chris Given-Wilson, ed. and trans., *The Parliament Rolls of Medieval England 1275–1504, vol. IX: Henry V, 1413–1422* (Woodbridge, UK: Boydell Press, 2012), 115.

115. *Parliament Rolls IX,* 115, 135, 177–78.

116. *Parliament Rolls IX,* 135.

117. *Parliament Rolls,* 207, 231.

118. *Gesta Henrici Quinti*, 101.

119. Barker, *Agincourt*, 329.

120. Barker, 329–30.

121. *Gesta Henrici Quinti*, 101–13. For a good reconstruction and analysis of pageants in medieval London, see Nicola Coldstream, "Pavilion'd in Splendour: Henry V's Agincourt Pageants," *Journal of the British Archeological Association* 165 (2012): 153–71.

122. *Gesta Henrici Quinti*, xxxvi.

123. Barker and Mortimer offer highly detailed accounts of the entire event. Barker, *Agincourt*, 330–36; Mortimer, *1415*, 479–85.

124. *Gesta Henrici Quinti*, 113.

Chapter Seven

1. Seward, *Henry V*, 119.
2. Curry, *Henry V*, 85. See also Curry, "Les villes normandes et l'occupation anglaise: l'importance du siege de Rouen (1418–1419)," in *Les villes normandes au moyen age*, ed. Pierre Bouet and François Neveux (Caen: Presses Universitaires de Caen, 2006), 109–23. Sumption has a permanent population of twenty thousand to twenty-five thousand inhabitants. Sumption, *Hundred Years War IV*, 584.
3. An excellent summary can be found in Sumption, *Hundred years War IV*, 655–700. See also Allmand, *Henry V*, 143–50. For a translation of the original Latin text, see Pierre Chaplais, ed., *English Royal Documents: King John—Henry VI, 1199–1461* (Oxford: Clarendon Press, 1971), 629–36. Delogu offers an important study of the redefinition French monarchic succession as a result of the Treaty. Daisy Delogu, *Allegorical Bodies: Power and Gender in Late Medieval France* (Toronto: University of Toronto Press, 2015), 127–66.
4. Sumption, *Hundred Years War IV*, 716. Vale, *Charles VII*, 31–32.
5. Allmand, *Henry V*, 151–52.
6. Pugh, *Southampton Plot*, 138.
7. Curry, *Henry V*, 97; Curry, *Great Battles: Agincourt*, 8.
8. Sumption, *Hundred Years War IV*, 766.
9. Sumption, *Hundred years War IV*, 696. His reference is to the French nationalist historian Jules Michelet (1798–1874), who wrote a multi-volume history of France and was almost single-handedly responsible for the Romantic revival of the study of Joan of Arc. See Jacques Barzun, "Jules Michelet and Romantic Historiography," in *European Writers: The Romantic Century*, ed. Jacques Barzun (New York: Charles Scribner's Sons, 1985), 571–606.
10. Tracy Adams, *The Life and Afterlife of Isabeau of Bavaria* (Baltimore: Johns Hopkins University Press, 2010), 35–36.
11. Adams, *Life and Afterlife of Isabeau*, xv, 42–43. See also Rachel Gibbons, "Isabeau of Bavaria, Queen of France (1385–1422): The Creation of a Historical Villainess," *Transactions of the Royal Historical Society* 6 (1996): 51–73.

12. Adams, *Life and Afterlife of Isabeau*, xv.
13. Gibbons, "Isabeau of Bavaria," 55.
14. Jean-Marie Moeglin, "Récrire l'histoire de la Guerre de Cent Ans. Une relecture historique et historiographique du traité de Troyes (21 mai 1420)," *Revue historique* 2012/4 (no. 664): 914.
15. Moeglin, "Récrire l'histoire de la Guerre de Cent Ans," 903–06.
16. Given-Wilson, *Parliament Rolls of Medieval England IX*, 178.
17. Curry, *Henry V*, 78, 92. The translated text is cited from Curry, "Two Kingdoms, One King: The Treaty of Troyes (1420)," in *Contesting the Kingdoms*, 23–41.
18. *Chronique du Réligieux de Saint-Denys (1380–1422)*, ed. and trans. Louis Bellaguet (Paris: Imprimerie de Crapelet, 1854; reprint edition, Paris: Éditions du Comité des travaux historiques et scientifiques, 1994), 6:162.
19. Harvey, "Martin V and Henry V," 51.
20. Harvey, 69.
21. Thomas Izbicki, "The Canonists and the Treaty of Troyes," in *Proceedings of the Fifth International Congress of Medieval Canon Law, Held in 1976*, ed. Stephen Kuttner and Kenneth Pennington (Vatican City: Biblioteca ApostolicaVaticana, 1980), 425–34.
22. Pons provides an important context for polemical debates about the Dauphin's rights and the dual monarchy. Nicole Pons, "Intellectual Patterns and Affective Reactions in Defence of the Dauphin Charles, 1419–1422," in *War, Government and Power*, ed. Christopher Allmand, 54–69. See also Izbicki, "The Canonists and the Treaty of Troyes," 433.
23. Vale, *Charles VII*, 32. Curry, *Henry V*, 93. Curry cites a passage in which Charles states, "we are hindered in such a way that we cannot personally attend to the disposition of the business of the realm."
24. The definitive study is by Jocelyne Gledhill Dickinson, *The Congress of Arras 1435: A Study in Medieval Diplomacy* (Oxford: Oxford University Press, 1955).
25. *Chronica Maiora of Thomas Walsingham 1376–1422*, 445. See also *Chronique du Réligieux de Saint-Denys*, 6: 480. The French chronicler says he died from an "abdominal flux." The anonymous author of the *Journal*

d'un Bourgeois de Paris notes that there was an outbreak of smallpox in the unusually hot summer that Henry died; he even states that Henry himself caught it. *A Parisian Journal, 1405–1449*, 177.

26. *Chronica Maiora of Thomas Walsingham*, 445.

27. *Thomae de Elmham Vita et Gesta*, 334. This work was formerly attributed to Thomas Elmham (c. 1364–1427), an English monk who accompanied Henry on his Agincourt campaign. He wrote a verse life of Henry, *Liber metricus de Henrico V*, but he is no longer considered to be the author of the *Vita and Gesta Henrici V*.

28. *A Parisian Journal, 1405–1499*, 178. For the iconography of his funeral procession and its relation to his reputation as a knight, see Craig Taylor, "Henry V, Flower of Chivalry," in *Henry V: New Interpretations*, 217–22. For the most comprehensive study of Henry's funerary rituals and the construction of his tomb, see W. H. St. John Hope, "The Funeral, Monument and Chantry Chapel of Henry V," *Archeologia* 65 (1913–14): 129–86.

29. Henry III (r. 1216–72) became king at age nine, while Richard II (r. 1377–99) was ten when he was crowned king.

30. *Chronica Maiora of Thomas Walsingham,* 446.

31. Bertram Wolffe, *Henry VI* (New Haven, CT: Yale University Press, 2001), 55.

32. *A Parisian Journal, 1405–1449*, 271–72.

33. This scholarly debate is reviewed by John L. Watts in his forward to the biography of the king by Bertram Wolffe, *Henry VI*. See also J. L. Watts, *Henry VI and the Politics of Kingship* (Cambridge: Cambridge University Press, 1996). This debate continues in the most recent appraisals of his reign: David Grummitt, *Henry VI* (Abingdon, UK: Routledge, 2015); James Ross, *Henry VI: A Good, Simple and Innocent Man* (London: Penguin Books, 2016).

34. Ross, *Henry VI*, 39–40.

35. *Henry the Sixth, a Reprint of John Blacman's Memoir, With Translation and Notes*, ed. M. R. James (Cambridge: Cambridge University Press, 1919), 25. For his afterlife as a popular saint and miracle-worker, see Grummitt, *Henry VI*, 232–47.

36. As a medical doctor with expertise in mental illness, Bark makes a forceful case for Henry VI suffering from schizophrenia. Nigel Bark, "Did Schizophrenia Change the Course of English History? The Mental Illness of Henry VI," *Medical Hypotheses* 59, no. 4 (2002): 416–21.

37. Seward, *The Hundred Years War*, 235.

38. Dan Jones, *The Hollow Crown: The Wars of the Roses and the Rise of the Tudors* (London: Faber and Faber, 2014), 363.

Chapter Eight

1. Richard W. Kaeuper, *Medieval Chivalry* (Cambridge: Cambridge University Press, 2016), 15–22. Le Brusque does note, however, that some medieval chroniclers, particularly those working in the "Burgundian school" of historiography, glorified war and chivalry as "beautiful" things. Le Brusque, "Chronicling the Hundred Years War," in *Writing War*, 80.

2. Kaeuper, *Holy Warriors*, 5.

3. Taylor, *Chivalry and the Ideals of Knighthood*, 16. For a good historiographic analysis that focuses on cultural values as they relate to warfare in the Middle Ages, see Kelly De Vries, "Medieval Warfare and the Value of Human Life," in *Noble Ideals and Bloody Realities: Warfare in the Middle Ages*, ed. Niall Christie and Maya Yazigi (Leiden: Brill, 2006), 27–55.

4. Nigel Saul, *For Honor and Fame: Chivalry in England 1066–1500* (London: Pimlico, 2012), vii.

5. Sumption, *Hundred Years War IV*, 601.

6. For an excellent analysis of the text, debates about its authorship, and its value as a historical source, see Bellis, *John Page's The Siege of Rouen*.

7. Bellis, *John Page's The Siege of Rouen*, 26.

8. Mortimer, *1415*, 544.

9. Kelly DeVries, *Joan of Arc: A Military Leader* (Stroud, UK: Sutton, 2003), 11–12. See also Sumption, *Hundred Years War III*, 187–96. Sumption points out that these raids, while terrifying and destructive, were more symbolic than anything else; they were largely ineffective in altering

the outcome of the war. Sumption, *Hundred Years War IV*, 416. This type of warfare also had roots in the twelfth century, when English King Henry II (r. 1154–89) terrorized rebellious French territories in his Angevin empire. See Gillingham, *Richard I*, 93–94.

10. See Seward, *Hundred Years War*, 84–5, 172–79. He is especially critical of the "criminality" of these raids. But Ormrod shows how these raids eventually forced the hand of the French King Jean II to do battle with disastrous consequences at Poitiers (1356). Ormrod, *Edward III*, 347–55.

11. Taylor, *Chivalry and the Ideals of Knighthood*, 178.

12. Green, *Hundred Years War*, 32–33. See also Clifford J. Rogers, "By Fire and Sword: *Bellum Hostile* and 'Civilians' in the Hundred Years War," in *Civilians in the Path of Wars*, ed. Mark Grimsley and Clifford J. Rogers (Lincoln: University of Nebraska Press, 2002), 33–78. For a detailed study of the Black Prince's activity before the Battle of Poitiers, see Peter Hoskins, *In the Steps of the Black Prince: The Road to Poitiers, 1355–1356* (Woodbridge, UK: Boydell Press, 2013).

13. Allmand argues against making rash judgments that would apply modern standards to medieval conflicts. Allmand, "Introduction," in *Henry V: New Interpretations*, 8. See also Christopher Allmand, "War and the Non-Combatant in the Middle Ages," in *Warfare: A History*, ed. Maurice Keen (Oxford: Oxford University Press, 1999), 253–73. The French historian Contamine makes a similar case. See Philippe Contamine, "La Théologie de la guerre à la fin du Moyen Age: La Guerre de Cent ans fut-elle une guerre juste?" in *Jeanne d'Arc, Une époque, un rayonnement (Colloque d'histoire médiévale, Orléans Octobre 1979)* (Paris: CNRS, 1982), 9–21.

14. Dietrich Schindler and Jiri Toman, *The Laws of Armed Conflicts: A Collection of Conventions, Resolutions and Other Documents*, 4th rev. ed. (Leiden: Martinus Nijhoff, 2004), 3–20.

15. Art. 17, Art. 19, Art. 31, Art. 83, Schindler and Toman, *The Laws of Armed Conflicts*, 6–7, 11–13.

16. For succinct history of this early peace movement, see Geoffrey Koziol,

The Peace of God (Leeds: Arc Humanities Press, 2018). See also Matthew Strickland, *War and Chivalry: Conduct and Perception of War in England and France, 1066–1217* (Cambridge: Cambridge University Press, 1996); Allmand, "War and the Non-Combatant in the Middle Ages," esp. 255–59.

17. Frederick H. Russell, *The Just War in the Middle Ages* (Cambridge: Cambridge University Press, 1975), 16. For a more recent study, see Alex Bellamy, *Just Wars: From Cicero to Iraq* (Cambridge: Polity Press, 2006).

18. Augustine, *Quaestiones in Heptateuchum*, 6.10, ed. J. Zycha, *Corpus Scriptorum Ecclesiasticorum Latinorum* 28.2 (Prague, Vienna, Leipzig: F. Tempsky, 1895), 428. See Russell, *Just War*, 18.

19. Russell, *Just War*, 19.

20. Given-Wilson, *Parliament Rolls of Medieval England IX*, 178. The speech is in Anglo-Norman French, but the quotation is in Latin: "Bella faciamus, ut pacem habeamus, quia finis belli, pax."

21. Thomas Aquinas, *Summa Theologiae, Volume 35, Consequences of Charity (2a2ae. 34–36)*, ed. and trans. by Thomas Heath (New York: McGraw-Hill and Eyre and Spottiswoode, 1972), 80–84.

22. Edward A. Synan, "St. Thomas Aquinas and the Profession of Arms," *Mediaeval Studies* 50 (1988): 404–37.

23. Green, *Hundred Years War*, 55.

24. Keen notes that even if there were a universal code, no one had the authority to enforce it. Maurice H. Keen, *The Laws of War in the Late Middle Ages* (London: Routledge, 2016), 7.

25. Kaeuper, *Holy Warriors*, 10–17.

26. Kaeuper, 11; Kaeuper, *Medieval Chivalry*, 10.

27. Rory Cox, "A Law of War? English Protection and Destruction of Ecclesiastical Property During the Fourteenth Century," *English Historical Review* 128 (2013): 417.

28. For expert analysis of this subject, see Russell, *The Just War in the Middle Ages*; James Turner Johnson, *The Just War Tradition and the Restraint of War* (Princeton, NJ: Princeton University Press, 1981); David Whetham, *Just Wars and Moral Victories: Surprise, Deception and the Normative Framework of European War in the*

Notes—Chapter Eight

Later Middle Ages (Leiden: Brill, 2009); Michael S. Bryant, *A World History of War Crimes: From Antiquity to the Present* (London: Bloomsbury Academic, 2016). Though her primary focus is on Joan, the work of Pinzino is also an important contribution to this overall topic. See Jane Marie Pinzino, "Just War, Joan of Arc and the Politics of Salvation," in *The Hundred Years War: A Wider Focus*, ed. L. J. Andrew Villalon and Donald Kagay (Leiden: Brill, 2005), 365–96.

29. Kaeuper offers a compelling analysis of the various strands of piety in the chivalric literature of the warrior elite. Kaeuper, *Holy Warriors*, esp. chapters 5 and 6.

30. Curry, "The Military Ordinances of Henry V," in *War, Government and Aristocracy*, 214–49. The story of the pyx thief being hanged is in the anonymous chronicle of an English cleric who accompanied Henry on his campaign. *Gesta Henrici Quinti*, 68–69.

31. Geoffroi de Charny, *A Knight's Own Book of Chivalry*, 96–97. For an analysis of the work, see Kaeuper, *Holy Warriors*, 42–51.

32. Christine de Pisan, *The Book of Deeds of Arms and of Chivalry*, trans. Sumner Willard, edited with an introduction by Charity Cannon Willard (University Park: Pennsylvania State University Press, 1999), 14.

33. Taylor, *Chivalry and the Ideals of Knighthood*, 228. According to Le Brusque, clerical chroniclers were more apt to chastise and criticize the warrior aristocracy for the suffering and tribulation they imposed on the defenseless peasants. Le Brusque, "Chronicling the Hundred Years War," 82.

34. Gillingham, *Richard I*, 261.

35. Christine de Pisan, *The Book of Deeds of Arms*, 171–73, 176–78.

36. For the theoretical underpinnings of Christian holy war, see Jonathan Riley-Smith, *The First Crusade and the Idea of Crusading* (Philadelphia: University of Pennsylvania Press, 1986); Jay Rubenstein, *Armies of Heaven: The First Crusade and the Quest for Apocalypse* (New York: Basic Books, 2011).

37. Ernst-Dieter Hehl, "War, Peace and the Christian Order," in *The New Cambridge Medieval History IV, c. 1024–c.1198, Part I*, ed. David Luscombe and Jonathan Riley-Smith (Cambridge: Cambridge University Press, 2004), 191.

38. Kaeuper, *Holy Warriors*, 104.

39. *First English Life of Henry the Fifth*, 131. After spending several hours arguing in private with Henry, St. Vincent apparently changed his mind on the justice of the king's war in France. This story comes late in the source tradition and may be apocryphal.

40. For a study of the development of religious nationalism in the age of Henry V, see Norman Housely, *Religious Warfare in Europe 1400–1536* (Oxford: Oxford University Press, 2002).

Bibliography

Primary Sources

Aquinas, Thomas. *Summa Theologiae, Volume 35, Consequences of Charity (2a2ae. 34–36).* Translated and edited by Thomas Heath. New York: McGraw-Hill and Eyre and Spottiswoode, 1972.

Augustine. *Quaestiones in Heptateuchum.* Edited by J. Zycha. *Corpus Scriptorum Ecclesiasticorum Latinorum* 28.2. Prague: F. Tempsky, 1895.

Basin, Thomas. *Histoire de Charles VII.* Translated and edited by Charles Samaran. 2 vols. Paris: Société d'édition Les Belles Lettres, 1933–44.

Bellis, Joanna, ed. *John Page's The Siege of Rouen, Edited From London, British Library MS Egerton 1995.* Heidelberg: Universitätsverlag Winter, 2015.

The Brut; or, the Chronicles of England. Edited by Friedrich W. D. Brie. London: Early English Text Society, 1906–08.

Carlson, David R., ed. *The Deposition of Richard II: "The Record and Process of the Renunciation and Deposition of Richard II" (1399), and Related Writings.* Toronto Medieval Latin Texts. Toronto: Pontifical Institute of Mediaeval Studies, 2007.

Chaplais, Pierre. *English Royal Documents: King John—Henry VI, 1199–1461.* Oxford: Clarendon Press, 1971.

Chartier, Jean. *Chronique de Charles VII, Roi de France.* Edited by A. Vallet de Viriville. Paris: P. Jannet, 1858; reprint edition, Nendeln: Kraus Reprint, 1979.

Christine de Pisan. *The Book of Deeds of Arms and of Chivalry.* Translated by Sumner Willard. Edited by Charity Cannon Willard. University Park: Pennsylvania State University Press, 1999.

The Chronica Maiora of Thomas Walsingham, 1376–1422. Translated by David Preest. With introduction and notes by James G. Clark. Woodbridge, UK: Boydell Press, 2005.

The Chronicle of Adam Usk, 1377–1421. Edited and translated by Chris Given-Wilson. Oxford: Clarendon Press, 1997.

The Chronicles of Enguerrand de Monstrelet, Containing an Account of the Cruel Civil Wars Between the Houses of Orleans and Burgundy. 2 vols. Translated by Thomas Johns. London: Stanley Paul, 1913.

Chronique d'Arthur de Richemont par Guillaume Gruel. Edited by Achille La Vavasseur. Paris: Librarie Renouard, 1890.

La Chronique d'Enguerran de Monstrelet, avec pièces justificatives, 1400–1444. Edited by Louis Claude Douët-d'Arcq, Société de l'Histoire de France. 4 vols. Paris: Jules Renouard, 1858–62.

Curry, Anne. *The Battle of Agincourt: Sources and Interpretation.* Woodbridge, UK: Boydell Press, 2011.

De Fenin, Pierre. *Mémoires de Pierre de Fenin: comprenant le récit des événements qui se sont passés en France et en Bourgogne sous les règnes de Charles VI et Charles VII (1407–1427).* Edited by Emelie Dupont. Paris: Jules Renouard, 1837.

De Wavrin, Jean. *Chronicles and Memorials of Great Britain and Ireland During the Middle Ages.* Translated by William Hardy and L. C. P. Hardy. London: Public Record Office, 1887.

De Wavrin, Jean. *Recueil des croniques et anchiennes istories de la Grant Bretaigne, à présent nommé Engleterre par Jehan de Waurin, seigneur du Forestel.* Edited by William Hardy. London: Longman, Roberts and Green, 1868; reprint edition, Nendeln: Kraus Reprint, 1965.

Bibliography

Elmham, Thomas. "Liber Metricis de Henrico Quinto." In *Memorials of Henry the Fifth, King of England*. Edited by C. A. Cole. London: Rolls Series, 1858.

Geoffroi de Charny. *A Knight's Own Book of Chivalry*. Translated by Elspeth Kennedy. With an introduction by Richard W. Kaeuper. Philadelphia: University of Pennsylvania Press, 2005.

Gesta Henrici Quinti: The Deeds of Henry the Fifth. Translated and edited by F. Taylor and J. S. Roskell. Oxford: Oxford University Press, 1975.

Henry the Sixth, a Reprint of John Blacman's Memoir, With Translation and Notes. Edited by M. R. James. Cambridge: Cambridge University Press, 1919.

Jean Juvénal des Ursins. *Histoire de Charles VI*. Edited by J. A. C. Buchon. Paris: Choix de chroniques et mémoires sur l'histoire de France 4, 1841.

Journal d'un Bourgeois de Paris de 1405 à 1449. Edited by Colette Beaune. Paris: Le Livre de Poche, 1990.

Kingsford, Charles L., ed. *The First English Life of Henry the Fifth, Written in 1513 by an Anonymous Author Known Commonly as The Translator of Livius*. Oxford: Oxford University Press, 1911.

A Parisian Journal, 1405–1449. Translated from the *Anonymous Journal d'un Bourgeois de Paris* by Janet Shirley. Oxford: Clarendon Press, 1968.

The Parliament Rolls of Medieval England 1275–1504, vol. IX: Henry V, 1413–1422. Edited and translated by Chris Given-Wilson. Woodbridge, UK: Boydell Press, 2012.

Pintoin, Michel. *Chronique du Réligieux de Saint-Denys (1380–1422)*. Edited and translated by Louis Bellaguet. 6 vols. Paris: Imprimerie de Crapelet, 1839–1854; reprint edition, Paris: Éditions du Comité des travaux historiques et scientifiques, 1994.

Pseudo-Elmham. *Thomae de Elmham Vita et Gesta Henrici Quinti Anglorum Regis*. Edited by Thomas Hearne. Oxford: E Theatro Sheldoniano, 1727.

The Revelations of St. Birgitta of Sweden, Volume 2, Liber Caelestis Books IV–V. Translated by Denis Michael Searby. With introduction and notes by Bridget Morris. Oxford: Oxford University Press, 2008.

Rymer, Thomas. *Foedera, conventiones et litterae et cujuscunque generis acta publica inter Reges Angliae*. Vol. 9. London: Jacob Tonson, 1729.

Schindler, Dietrich, and Jiri Toman. *The Laws of Armed Conflicts: A Collection of Conventions, Resolutions and Other Documents*. 4th rev. ed. Leiden: Martinus Nijhoff, 2004.

Streeche, John. "The Chronicle of John Streeche for the Reign of Henry V (1414–1422)." Edited by F. Taylor. *Bulletin of the John Rylands Library* 16 (1932): 137–87.

Taylor, Gary, ed. *Henry V: The Oxford Shakespeare*. Oxford World's Classics. Oxford: Oxford University Press, 2008.

The True Chronicles of Jean Le Bel, 1290–1360. Translated by Nigel Bryant. Woodbridge, UK: Boydell and Brewer, 2011.

Secondary Sources

Aberth, John. *From the Brink of the Apocalypse: Confronting Famine, War, Plague and Death in the Later Middle Ages*. 2nd ed. London: Routledge, 2010.

Adams, Tracy. *Christine de Pizan and the Fight for France*. Philadelphia: University of Pennsylvania Press, 2014.

Adams, Tracy. *The Life and Afterlife of Isabeau of Bavaria*. Baltimore: Johns Hopkins University Press, 2010.

Allmand, Christopher. *The De re militari of Vegetius: The Reception, Transmission and Legacy of a Roman Text in the Middle Ages*. Cambridge: Cambridge University Press, 2014.

Allmand, Christopher. "The English and the Church in Lancastrian Normandy." In *England and Normandy in the Middle Ages*, 288–97. Edited by David Bates and Anne Curry. London: Hambledon Press, 1994.

Allmand, Christopher. *Henry V*. New Haven, CT: Yale University Press, 1997.

Allmand, Christopher. *The Hundred Years War: England and France at War c. 1300–1450*. Cambridge: Cambridge University Press, 1988.

Allmand, Christopher. *Lancastrian*

Bibliography

Normandy, 1415–1450. The History of a Medieval Occupation. Oxford: Oxford University Press, 1983.

Allmand, Christopher. "War and the Non-Combatant in the Middle Ages." In *Medieval Warfare: A History*, 253–73. Edited by Maurice Keen. Oxford: Oxford University Press, 1999.

Allmand, Christopher. *War, Government and Power in Late Medieval France.* Liverpool: Liverpool University Press, 2000.

Allmand, Christopher. "Writing History in the Eighteenth Century: Thomas Goodwin's *The History of the Reign of Henry the Fifth* (1704)." In *Henry V: New Interpretations*, 273–88. Edited by Gwilym Dodd. Woodbridge, UK: Boydell and Brewer, 2013.

Ambühl, Rémy. *Prisoners of War in the Hundred Years War: Ransom Culture in the Late Middle Ages.* Cambridge: Cambridge University Press, 2015.

Ambühl, Rémy, and Craig L. Lambert, eds. *Agincourt in Context: War on Land and Sea.* London: Routledge, 2019.

Arner, Timothy D. "The Disappearing Scar of Henry V: Triage, Trauma, and the Treatment of Henry's Wounding at the Battle of Shrewsbury." *Journal of Medieval and Early Modern Studies* 49 (2019): 347–76.

Asbridge, Thomas. *The Crusades: The Authoritative History of the War for the Holy Land.* New York: HarperCollins, 2010.

Ashe, Laura. *Richard II: A Brittle Glory.* Penguin Monarchs. London: Penguin Books, 2016.

Aston, Margaret, and Colin Richmond, eds. *Lollardy and the Gentry in the Later Middle Ages.* New York: St. Martin's Press, 1997.

Autrand, Françoise. *Charles V: Le Sage.* Paris: Fayard, 1994.

Autrand, Françoise. "France Under Charles V and Charles VI." In *The New Cambridge Medieval History, Volume 6, c. 1300–1415*, 422–41. Edited by Michael Jones. Cambridge: Cambridge University Press, 2000.

Bark, Nigel. "Did Schizophrenia Change the Course of English History? The Mental Illness of Henry VI." *Medical Hypotheses* 59, no. 4 (2002): 416–21.

Barker, Juliet. *Agincourt: Henry V and the Battle That Made England.* New York: Little, Brown, 2006.

Barker, Juliet. *Conquest: The English Kingdom of France, 1417–1450.* Cambridge, MA: Harvard University Press, 2012.

Barker, Juliet. *England Arise: The People, the King and the Great Revolt of 1381.* London: Abacus, 2014.

Barzun, Jacques. "Jules Michelet and Romantic Historiography." In *European Writers: The Romantic Century*, 571–606. Edited by Jacques Barzun. New York: Charles Scribner's Sons, 1985.

Baume, Andrew J. L. "Soldats et paysans en Normandie, 1419–1449." *Annales de Normandie, séries des Congrés des Sociétés historiques et archéologique de Normandie* 3 (1998): 275–82.

Becket, Neil. "St. Bridget, Henry V and Syon Abbey." *Studies in St. Bridget and the Brigittine Order 2.* Edited by James Hogg. *Analecta Carthusiana* 35 (1993): 125–50.

Bellamy, Alex. *Just Wars: From Cicero to Iraq.* Cambridge: Polity Press, 2006.

Bellis, Joanna. *The Hundred Years War in Literature, 1337–1600.* Cambridge: D. S. Brewer, 2016.

Bennett, M. "Legality and Legitimacy in War and Its Conduct, 1350–1650." In *European Warfare, 1350–1750*, 264–77. Edited by Frank Tallett and D. J. B. Trim. Cambridge: Cambridge University Press, 2010.

Bennett, Matthew. "The Battle of Agincourt." In *The Battle of Agincourt*, 90–109. Edited by Anne Curry and Malcolm Mercer. New Haven, CT: Yale University Press, 2015.

Blumenfeld-Kosinski, Renate. *Poets, Saints and Visionaries of the Great Schism, 1378–1417.* University Park: Pennsylvania State University Press, 2006.

Bove, Boris. "Deconstructing the Chronicles: Rumours and Extreme Violence During the Siege of Meaux (1421–1422)." *French History* 24 (2010): 501–23.

Brantley, Jessica. *Reading in the Wilderness: Private Devotion and Public Performance in Late Medieval England.* Chicago: University of Chicago Press, 2008.

Britland, Karen, and Line Cottegnies, eds. *Henry V: A Critical Reader.* Arden Early

Bibliography

Modern Drama Guides. London: The Arden Shakespeare, 2020.

Burden, Joel. "How do You Bury a Deposed King? The Funeral of Richard II and the Establishment of Lancastrian Royal Authority in 1400." In *Henry IV: The Establishment of the Regime, 1399–1406*, 35–54. Edited by Gwilym Dodd and Douglas Biggs. York: York Medieval Press, 2003.

Burne, Alfred H. *The Agincourt War: A Military History of the Latter Part of the Hundred Years War, From 1369–1453*. Ware, UK: Wordsworth Editions, 1999; reprint of 1956 edition.

Carey, Hilary M. *Courting Disaster: Astrology at the English Court and University in the Later Middle Ages*. New York: Palgrave Macmillan, 1992.

Cassidy-Welch, M. "Grief and Memory After the Battle of Agincourt." In *The Hundred Years War (Part II): Different Vistas*, 133–50. Edited by L. J. Andrew Villalon and Donald J. Kagay. Leiden: Brill, 2008.

Castor, Helen. *Joan of Arc: A History*. New York: Harper, 2015.

Castor, Helen. *She-Wolves: The Women Who Ruled England Before Elizabeth*. New York: Harper Perennial, 2012.

Catto, J. I. "The Burden and Conscience of Government in the Fifteenth Century." *Transactions of the Royal Historical Society* 17 (2007): 83–99.

Catto, J. I. "Wyclif and Wycliffism at Oxford, 1356–1430." In *The History of the University of Oxford, II: Late Medieval Oxford*, 175–262. Edited by J. I. Catto and T. A. R. Evans. Oxford: Oxford University Press, 1992.

Cazelles, Raymond. *Société politique, noblesse et couronne sous Jean le Bon et Charles V*. Geneva: Droz, 1982.

Christie, Niall, and Maya Yazigi, eds. *Noble Ideals and Bloody Realities: Warfare in the Middle Ages*. Leiden: Brill, 2006.

Churchill, Winston S. *A History of the English-Speaking Peoples, Volume I: The Birth of Britain*. London: Bloomsbury Academic, 2015.

Clarke, Maude Violet, and V. H. Galbraith. "The Deposition of Richard II." *Bulletin of the John Rylands Library* 14 (1930): 125–81.

Cohn, Samuel Kline, Jr. *Lust for Liberty: The Politics of Social Revolt in Medieval Europe, 1200–1425*. Cambridge, MA: Harvard University Press, 2006.

Coldstream, Nicola. "Pavilion'd in Splendour: Henry V's Agincourt Pageants." *Journal of the British Archeological Association* 165 (2012): 153–71.

Cole, H., and T. Lang. "The Treating of Prince Henry's Arrow Wound, 1403." *Journal of the Society of Archer Antiquaries* 46 (2003): 95–101.

Cole, Teresa. *Henry V: The Life of the Warrior King and the Battle of Agincourt*. Stroud, UK: Amberley Publishing, 2015.

Contamine, Philippe. "France et Bourgogne, l'historiographie du XVe et la paix d'Arras (1435)." In *Arras et la diplomatie européenne, XVe–XVIe siècles*, 81–100. Edited by Denis Clauzel, Charles Giry-Deloison, and Christophe Leduc. Artois: Artois Presses Universitaires, 1999.

Contamine, Philippe. *La guerre de Cent ans*. Paris: Presses universitaire de France, 2016.

Contamine, Philippe. "La Théologie de la guerre à la fin du Moyen Age: La guerre de Cent ans fut-elle une guerre juste?" In *Jeanne d'Arc, Une époque, un rayonnement (Colloque d'histoire médiévale, Orléans Octobre 1979)*, 9–21. Paris: CNRS, 1982.

Contamine, Philippe. *La vie quotidienne pendant la guerre de Cent ans*. Paris: Hachette, 1976.

Contamine, Philippe. "L'Oriflamme de Saint-Denis aux XIVe et XVe siècles. Étude de symbolique religieuse et royale." *Annales de l'Est* 7 (1973): 179–244.

Contamine, Philippe. *War in the Middle Ages*. Translated by Michael Jones. Oxford: Blackwell, 1984.

Copeland, Rita. *Pedagogy, Intellectuals, and Dissent in the Later Middle Ages: Lollardy and Ideas of Learning*. Cambridge: Cambridge University Press, 2005.

Cox, Rory. "A Law of War? English Protection and Destruction of Ecclesiastical Property During the Fourteenth Century." *English Historical Review* 128 (2013): 381–417.

Curry, Anne. "After Agincourt, What Next? Henry V and the Campaign of 1416."

Bibliography

Fifteenth Century England 7 (2007): 23–51.

Curry, Anne. "The Battle Speeches of Henry V." *Reading Medieval Studies* 34 (2008): 77–97.

Curry, Anne. *1415 Agincourt: A New History.* Stroud, UK: History Press, 2015.

Curry, Anne. *Great Battles: Agincourt.* Oxford: Oxford University Press, 2015.

Curry, Anne. *Henry V: Playboy Prince to Warrior King.* Penguin Monarchs. London: Penguin Books, 2015.

Curry, Anne. "The Military Ordinances of Henry V: Texts and Contexts." In *War, Government and Aristocracy in the British Isles, c. 1150–1500: Essays in Honor of Michael Prestwich,* 214–49. Edited by Chris Given-Wilson, Ann Kettle, and Len Scales. Woodbridge, UK: Boydell Press, 2008.

Curry, Anne. "Two Kingdoms, One King: The Treaty of Troyes (1420) and the Creation of a Double Monarchy of England and France." In *Contesting the Kingdoms: France and England 1420–1700,* 23–41. Edited by G. Richardson. Aldershot, UK: Ashgate Press, 2008.

Curry, Anne. "Les villes normandes et l'occupation anglaise: l'importance du siege de Rouen (1418–1419)." In *Les villes normandes au moyen age,* 109–23. Edited by Pierre Bouet and François Neveux. Caen: Presses Universitaires de Caen, 2006.

Curry, Anne, and Malcolm Mercer, eds. *The Battle of Agincourt.* New Haven, CT: Yale University Press, 2015.

Cuttler, S. H. *The Law of Treason and Treason Trials in Later Medieval France.* Cambridge: Cambridge University Press, 2003.

Deeming, Helen. "The Sources and Origin of the Agincourt Carol." *Early Music* 35 (2007): 23–36.

Delogu, Daisy. *Allegorical Bodies: Power and Gender in Late Medieval France.* Toronto: University of Toronto Press, 2015.

DeVries, Kelly. *Joan of Arc: A Military Leader.* Stroud, UK: Sutton, 2003.

DeVries, Kelly. "John the Fearless' Way of War." In *Reputation and Representation in Fifteenth Century Europe,* 39–55. Edited by Douglas Biggs, Sharon D. Michalove, and Albert Compton Reeves. Leiden: Brill, 2004.

De Vries, Kelly. "Medieval Warfare and the Value of Human Life." In *Noble Ideals and Bloody Realities: Warfare in the Middle Ages,* 27–55. Edited by Niall Christie and Maya Yazigi. Leiden: Brill, 2006.

Dockray, Keith. *Warrior King: The Life of Henry V.* 2nd ed. Stroud, UK: Tempus, 2007.

Dodd, Gwilym, ed. *Henry V: New Interpretations.* Woodbridge, UK: Boydell and Brewer, 2013.

Dodd, Gwilym, and Douglas Biggs, eds. *Henry IV: The Establishment of the Regime 1399–1406.* York: York Medieval Press, 2003.

Duffy, Eamon. *The Stripping of the Altars: Traditional Religion in England, 1400–1580.* 2nd ed. New Haven, CT: Yale University Press, 2005.

Falkeid, Unn. *The Avignon Papacy Contested: An Intellectual History From Dante to Catherine of Siena.* Cambridge, MA: Harvard University Press, 2017.

Famiglietti, R. C. *Royal Intrigue: Crisis at the Court of Charles VI, 1392–1420.* New York: AMS Press, 1986.

Fletcher, C., J. P. Genet, and J. Watts, eds. *Government and Political Life in England and France, c. 1300–1500.* Cambridge: Cambridge University Press, 2015.

Forrest, Ian. *The Detection of Heresy in Late Medieval England.* Oxford: Oxford University Press, 2005.

Friel, Ian. *Henry V's Navy: The Sea Road to Agincourt and Conquest, 1413–1422.* Stroud, UK: History Press, 2015.

Fryde, Edmund B. *The Great Revolt of 1381.* London: Historical Association, 1981.

Geduld, Harry. *Filmguide to Henry V.* Bloomington: Indiana University Press, 1976.

Gibbons, Rachel. "Isabeau of Bavaria, Queen of France (1385–1422): The Creation of an Historical Villainess." The Alexander Prize Essay. *Transactions of the Royal Historical Society,* 6th series, vol. 6 (1996): 51–73.

Gillingham, John. *Richard I.* New Haven, CT: Yale University Press, 1999.

Girardot, Alain. "La guerre au XIVe siècle: La devastation, ses modes et ses degrés." *Bulletin de la société d'histoire et d'archéologie de la Meuse* 30–31 (1994–95): 1–32.

Bibliography

Given-Wilson, Chris. *Chronicles: The Writing of History in Medieval England*. London: Hambeldon, 2004.

Given-Wilson, Chris. *Henry IV*. New Haven, CT: Yale University Press, 2016.

Gledhill Dickinson, Jocelyne. *The Congress of Arras 1435: A Study in Medieval Diplomacy*. Oxford: Oxford University Press, 1955.

Goldberg, P. J. P., ed. *Richard Scrope: Archbishop, Rebel, Martyr*. Donington, UK: Shaun Tyas, 2007.

Goodman, Anthony. *John of Gaunt: The Exercise of Princely Power in Fourteenth-Century Europe*. Abingdon, UK: Routledge, 2016.

Gosh, Kantik. *The Wycliffite Heresy: Authority and the Interpretation of Texts*. Cambridge: Cambridge University Press, 2009.

Gosling, Frederick Daniel. "Church State and Reformation: The Use and Interpretation of *Praemunire* From Its Creation to the English Break With Rome." PhD thesis, University of Leeds, 2016.

Goubert, Pierre. *The Course of French History*. Translated by Maarten Ultee. London: Routledge, 1991.

Goy-Blanquet, Dominique. *Shakespeare's Early History Plays: From Chronicle to Stage*. Oxford: Oxford University Press, 2003.

Gransden, Antonia. *Historical Writing in England c. 1307 to the Early Sixteenth Century*. 2nd ed. London: Routledge, 2000.

Green, David. *The Battle of Poitiers 1356*. Stroud, UK: Tempus, 2008.

Green, David. *Edward the Black Prince: Power in Medieval Europe*. Harlow, UK: Pearson/Longman, 2007.

Green, David. *The Hundred Years War: A People's History*. New Haven, CT: Yale University Press, 2014.

Griffiths, Ralph. *The Reign of King Henry VI*. Stroud, UK: Sutton, 2004.

Grummitt, David. *Henry VI*. Abingdon, UK: Routledge, 2015.

Guenée, Bernard. *La folie de Charles VI: roi bien-aimé*. Paris: CNRS, 2004.

Guenée, Bernard. *Un meurtre, une société: l'assassinat du duc d'Orléans, 23 novembre 1407*. Paris: Gallimard, 1992.

Guenée, Bernard. *Un roi et son historien.*

Vingt etudes sur le règne de Charles VI et la "Chronique du Réligieux de Saint-Denis." Paris: Diffusion de Boccard, 1999.

Harriss, Gerald L. *Shaping the Nation, England 1360-1461*. Oxford: Clarendon Press, 2008.

Harriss, Gerald L., ed. *Henry V: The Practice of Kingship*. 2nd edition. Stroud, UK: Sutton, 1993.

Harvey, Margaret M. *England, Rome and the Papacy, 1417-1464: The Study of a Relationship*. Manchester: Manchester University Press, 1993.

Harvey, Margaret M. "Martin V and Henry V." *Archivum Historiae Pontificiae* 24 (1986): 49-70.

Heffernan, Carol. "The Revelations of St. Bridget of Sweden in Fifteenth-Century England." *Neophilologus* 101 (2017): 337-49.

Hehl, Ernst-Dieter. "War, Peace and the Christian Order." In *The New Cambridge Medieval History IV, c. 1024-c.1198, Part I*, 185-228. Edited by David Luscombe and Jonathan Riley-Smith. Cambridge: Cambridge University Press, 2004.

Hicks, M. A. *The Wars of the Roses*. New Haven, CT: Yale University Press, 2010.

Honig, Jan W. "Reappraising Late Medieval Strategy: The Example of the 1415 Agincourt Campaign." *War in History* 19 (2012): 123-51.

Hoskins, Peter. *In the Steps of the Black Prince: The Road to Poitiers, 1355-1356*. Woodbridge, UK: Boydell Press, 2013.

Housely, Norman. *Religious Warfare in Europe 1400-1536*. Oxford: Oxford University Press, 2008.

Izbicki, Thomas. "The Canonists and the Treaty of Troyes." In *Proceedings of the Fifth International Congress of Medieval Canon Law, Held in 1976*, 425-34. Edited by Stephen Kuttner and Kenneth Pennington. Vatican City: Biblioteca Apostolica Vaticana, 1980.

Jackson, Richard A. *"Vive le Roi!" A History of the French Coronation Ceremony From Charles V to Charles X*. Chapel Hill: University of North Carolina Press, 1984.

Jacob, E. F. *Henry V and the Invasion of France*. New York: ACLS History E-Book Project (1946), 2005.

Johnston, F. R. "The English Cult of St.

Bibliography

Bridget of Sweden." *Analecta Bollandiana* 103 (1985): 75–93.

Jones, Dan. *The Hollow Crown: The Wars of the Roses and the Rise of the Tudors*. London: Faber and Faber, 2014.

Jones, Dan. *The Plantagenets: The Warrior Kings and Queens Who Made England*. New York: Penguin Books, 2012.

Jones, Dan. *Summer of Blood: England's First Revolution*. New York: Penguin Books, 2016.

Jones, Michael. *The Black Prince: England's Greatest Medieval Warrior*. New York: Pegasus Books, 2018.

Jones, W. R. "The English Church and Royal Propaganda During the Hundred Years War." *Journal of British Studies* 19 (1979): 18–30.

Jurkowski, Maureen. "Henry V's Suppression of the Oldcastle Revolt." In *Henry V: New Interpretations*, 103–30. Edited by Gwilym Dodd. Woodbridge, UK: Boydell and Brewer, 2013.

Kaeuper, Richard W. *Chivalry and Violence in Medieval Europe*. Oxford: Oxford University Press, 1999.

Kaeuper, Richard W. *Holy Warriors: The Religious Ideology of Chivalry*. Philadelphia: University of Pennsylvania Press, 2009.

Kaeuper, Richard W. *Medieval Chivalry*. Cambridge: Cambridge University Press, 2016.

Keegan, John. *The Face of Battle: A Study of Agincourt, Waterloo and the Somme*. New York: Penguin, 1978.

Keen, Maurice. *Chivalry*. London: Folio Society, 2010.

Keen, Maurice. *The Laws of War in the Late Middle Ages*. London: Routledge, 2016.

King, Andy. "'Then a Great Misfortune Befell Them': The Laws of War on Surrender and the Killing of Prisoners in the Hundred Years War." *Journal of Medieval History* (2017): 106–17.

Kingsford, Charles L. "The Early Biographies of Henry V." *English Historical Review* 25 (1910): 58–92.

Kingsford, Charles L. *Henry V: The Typical Medieval Hero*. New York: F. DeFau, 1901.

Knecht, R. J. *The Valois Kings of France, 1328–1589*. London: Bloomsbury, 2007.

Knowles, David. *The Religious Orders in England II: The End of the Middle Ages*. Cambridge: Cambridge University Press, 1955.

Koziol, Geoffrey. *The Peace of God*. Leeds: Arc Humanities Press, 2018.

Lang, Sheila L. "The *Philomena* of John Bradmore and Its Middle English Derivative: A Perspective on Surgery in Late Medieval England." PhD thesis, St. Andrew's University, 1999.

Le Brusque, Georges. "Chronicling the Hundred Years War in Burgundy and France in the Fifteenth Century." In *Writing War: Medieval Literary Responses to Warfare*, 77–92. Edited by Corinne Saunders, Françoise Le Saux, and Neil Thomas. Cambridge: D.S. Brewer, 2004.

Little, Roger G. *The Parlement of Poitiers: War, Government and Politics in France, 1418–1436*. London: Humanities Press, 1984.

Livingston, Michael. "'The Depth of Six Inches': Prince Hal's Head-Wound at the Battle of Shrewsbury." In *Wounds and Wound Repair in Medieval Culture*, 215–31. Edited by Larissa Tracy and Kelly DeVries. Leiden: Brill, 2015.

Livingston, Michael, and Kelly DeVries, eds. *The Battle of Crécy: A Casebook*. Liverpool: Liverpool University Press, 2015.

Loehlin, James N. *Shakespeare in Performance: Henry V*. Manchester: Manchester University Press, 1997.

Luxford, Julian M., and John McNeill. *The Medieval Chantry in England*. Leeds: British Archaeological Association, 2011.

Matusiak, John. *Henry V*. London: Routledge, 2013.

May, Larry. *War Crimes and Just War*. Cambridge: Cambridge University Press, 2007.

McAuley, Finbarr. "Canon Law and the End of the Ordeal." *Oxford Journal of Legal Studies* 26 (2006): 473–513.

McFarlane, K. B. "Henry V, Bishop Beaufort and the Red Hat, 1417–1421." *English Historical Review* 60 (1945): 316–48.

McFarlane, K. B. *Lancastrian Kings and Lollard Knights*. Oxford: Oxford University Press, 1972.

McGlynn, Sean. *By Sword and Fire: Cruelty and Atrocity in Medieval Warfare*. London: Weidenfeld and Nicolson, 2008.

McHardy, Alison K. "Religion, Court

Bibliography

Culture and Propaganda: The Chapel Royal in the Reign of Henry V." In *Henry V: New Interpretations*, 131–56. Edited by Gwilym Dodd. Woodbridge, UK: Boydell and Brewer, 2013.

McKenna, J. W. "Henry VI of England and the Dual Monarchy: Aspects of Royal Propaganda 1422–1432." *Journal of the Warburg and Courtauld Institutes* (1965): 145–162.

McKenna, J. W. "Popular Canonization as Political Propaganda: The Cult of Archbishop Scrope." *Speculum* 45 (1970): 608–23.

McNiven, Peter. *Heresy and Politics in the Reign of Henry IV: The Burning of John Badby*. Woodbridge, UK: Boydell Press, 1987.

Mercer, Malcolm. *Henry V: The Rebirth of Chivalry*. Kew, UK: National Archives, 2004.

Meron, Theodor. *Henry's Wars and Shakespeare's Laws: Perspectives on the Law of War in the Later Middle Ages*. Oxford: Oxford University Press, 1993.

Meyers, A. R. "The Captivity of a Royal Witch: The Household Accounts of Queen Joan of Navarre, 1419–21." *Bulletin of the John Rylands Library* 24 (1940): 262–84.

Meyerson, Mark D., Daniel Thiery, and Oren Falk, eds. *"A Great Effusion of Blood?" Interpreting Medieval Violence*. Toronto: University of Toronto Press, 2004.

Mirot, L. "Le Procès de Maître Jean Fusoris, chanoine de Notre-Dame de Paris (1415–1416): épisode de négociations franco-anglaises durant la guerre de Cent ans." *Mémoires de la Société de l'histoire de Paris et de l'Île de France* 17 (1900): 137–287.

Moeglin, Jean-Marie. "Récrire l'histoire de la Guerre de Cent Ans. Une relecture historique et historiographique du traité de Troyes (21 mai 1420)." *Revue historique* 2012/4 (no. 664): 887–919.

Monteiro, J. "The Battle of Aljubarrota (1385): A Reassessment." *Journal of Medieval Military History* 7 (2009): 75–103.

Mortimer, Ian. *The Fears of Henry IV: The Life of England's Self-Made King*. London: Vintage Books, 2008.

Mortimer, Ian. *1415: Henry V's Year of Glory*. London: Vintage Books, 2010.

Mortimer, Ian. *The Perfect King: The Life of Edward III, Father of the English Nation*. London: Vintage Books, 2008.

Mount, Toni. *Medieval Medicine: Its Mysteries and Science*. Stroud, UK: Amberley, 2015.

Müller, Wolfgang G. "The Battle of Agincourt in Carol and Ballad." *Fifteenth Century Studies* 8 (1983): 159–78.

Murphy, Neil. "Ceremony and Conflict in Fifteenth-Century France: Lancastrian Ceremonial Entries into French Towns, 1415–1431." *Explorations in Renaissance Culture* 39 (2013): 113–33.

Newhall, R. A. *The English Conquest of Normandy, 1416–1424: A Study in Fifteenth-Century Warfare*. Cambridge, MA: Harvard University Press, 1924.

Nicolle, David. *Crécy 1346: Triumph of the Longbow*. Oxford: Osprey, 2000.

Nicolle, David. *Poitiers 1356: Capture of a King*. Oxford: Osprey, 2004.

Orme, Nicholas. *From Childhood to Chivalry: The Education of English Kings and Aristocracy, 1066–1530*. London: Routledge, 2017.

Ormrod, W. Mark. *Edward III*. New Haven, CT: Yale University Press, 2013.

Perroy, Édouard. *La guerre de Cent ans*. Paris: Gallimard, 1945.

Perroy, Édouard. *The Hundred Years War*. Translated by W. B. Wells. Oxford: Oxford University Press, 1951.

Phillpotts, C. J. "The Fate of the Truce of Paris, 1396–1415." *Journal of Medieval History* 24 (1998): 61–80.

Phillpotts, C. J. "The French Battle Plan During the Agincourt Campaign." *English Historical Review* 99 (1984): 59–66.

Pinzino, Jane Marie. "Just War, Joan of Arc and the Politics of Salvation." In *The Hundred Years War: A Wider Focus*, 365–96. Edited by L. J. Andrew Villalon and Donald Kagay. Leiden: Brill, 2005.

Pons, Nicole. "Intellectual Patterns and Affective Reactions in Defence of the Dauphin Charles, 1419–1422." In *War, Government and Power in Late Medieval France*, 54–69. Edited by Christopher Allmand. Liverpool: Liverpool University Press, 2000.

Powell, Edward. *Kingship, Law and Society: Criminal Justice in the Reign of Henry V*. Oxford: Clarendon Press, 1989.

Bibliography

Pugh, T. B. *Henry V and the Southampton Plot of 1415*. Southampton, UK: Southampton University Press, 1988.

Pugliatti, Paola. *Shakespeare and the Just War Tradition*. London: Routledge, 2016.

Puiseaux, Léon. *Siège et prise de Caen par les Anglais en 1417: épisode de la guerre de Cent ans*. Caen: Le Gost-Clérisse, 1858.

Quillett, Jeannine. *Charles V: Le roi lettré*. Paris: Perrin, 2002.

Riley-Smith, Jonathan. *The First Crusade and the Idea of Crusading*. Philadelphia: University of Pennsylvania Press, 1986.

Rogers, Clifford J. "The Age of the Hundred Years War." In *Medieval Warfare: A History*, 136–60. Edited by Maurice Keen. Oxford: Oxford University Press, 1999.

Rogers, Clifford J. "The Battle of Agincourt." In *The Hundred Years War II: Different Vistas*, 37–132. Edited by L. J. Andrew Villalon and Donald J. Kagay. Leiden: Brill, 2008.

Rogers, Clifford J. "By Fire and Sword: *Bellum Hostile* and 'Civilians' in the Hundred Years War." In *Civilians in the Path of Wars*, 33–78. Edited by Mark Grimsley and Clifford J. Rogers. Lincoln: University of Nebraska Press, 2002.

Rogers, Clifford J. "Henry V's Military Strategy in 1415." In *The Hundred Years War: A Wider Focus*, 399–427. Edited by L. J. Andrew Villalon and Donald J. Kagay. Leiden: Brill, 2005.

Rollo-Koster, Joëlle. *Avignon and Its Papacy (1309–1417): Popes, Institutions, and Society*. Lanham, MD: Rowman and Littlefield, 2015.

Rollo-Koster, Joëlle. *Raiding Saint Peter: Empty Sees, Violence, and the Initiation of the Great Western Schism (1378)*. Leiden: Brill, 2008.

Rollo-Koster, Joëlle, and Thomas M. Izbicki, eds. *A Companion to the Great Western Schism (1378–1417)*. Leiden: Brill, 2009.

Ross, James. *Henry VI: A Good, Simple and Innocent Man*. London: Penguin Books, 2016.

Rousseau, Marie-Helene. *Saving the Souls of Medieval London: Perpetual Chantries at St. Paul's Cathedral, c.1200–1548*. London: Routledge, 2016.

Roux, Simone. *Paris in the Middle Ages*. Translated by Jo Ann McNamara. Philadelphia: University of Pennsylvania Press, 2009.

Rubin, Miri. *Corpus Christi: The Eucharist in Late Medieval Culture*. Cambridge: Cambridge University Press, 1991.

Russell, Frederick H. *The Just War in the Middle Ages*. Cambridge: Cambridge University Press, 1975.

St. John Hope, W. H. "The Funeral, Monument and Chantry Chapel of Henry V." *Archeologia* 65 (1913–14): 129–86.

Sales, G. O. "The Deposition of Richard II: Three Lancastrian Narratives." *Bulletin of the Institute of Historical Research* 54 (1981): 257–70.

Saul, Nigel. *For Honor and Fame: Chivalry in England 1066–1500*. London: Pimlico, 2012.

Saul, Nigel. *Richard II*. New Haven, CT: Yale University Press, 1997.

Seward, Desmond. *Henry V: The Scourge of God*. New York: Viking, 1988.

Seward, Desmond. *The Hundred Years War: The English in France 1337–1453*. New York: Penguin Books, 1999.

Smith, Emma, ed. *King Henry V: Shakespeare in Production*. Cambridge: Cambridge University Press, 2002.

Stratford, Jenny. "'Par le special commandement du roy.' Jewels and Plate Pledged for the Agincourt Expedition." In *Henry V: New Interpretations*, 157–70. Edited by Gwilym Dodd. Woodbridge, UK: Boydell and Brewer, 2013.

Strohm, Paul. *England's Empty Throne. Usurpation and the Language of Legitimation, 1399–1422*. 2nd ed. Notre Dame, IN: University of Notre Dame Press, 2006.

Strong, Patrick, and Felicity Strong, eds. "The Last Will and Codicils of Henry V." *English Historical Review* 96 (1981): 79–102.

Sumption, Jonathan. *The Albigensian Crusade*. London: Faber and Faber, 2011.

Sumption, Jonathan. *The Hundred Years War*. 4 vols. Philadelphia: University of Pennsylvania Press, 1991–2017.

Sutherland, John, and Cedric Thomas Watts. *Henry V: War Criminal? And Other Shakespearean Puzzles*. Oxford: Oxford University Press, 2000.

Synan, Edward A. "St. Thomas Aquinas and the Profession of Arms." *Mediaeval Studies* 50 (1988): 404–37.

Bibliography

Taylor, Craig. *Chivalry and the Ideals of Knighthood in France During the Hundred Years War.* Cambridge: Cambridge University Press, 2013.

Taylor, Craig. "Edward III and the Plantagenet Claim to the French Throne." In *The Age of Edward III*, 155–69. Edited by James Bothwell. Woodbridge, UK: Boydell and Brewer, 2001.

Taylor, Craig. "Henry V, Flower of Chivalry." In *Henry V: New Interpretations*, 217–47. Edited by Gwilym Dodd. Woodbridge, UK: Boydell and Brewer, 2013.

Taylor, Craig. "The Salic Law, French Queenship, and the Defense of Women in the Late Middle Ages." *French Historical Studies* 29 (2006): 543–64.

Taylor, John. *English Historical Literature in the Fourteenth Century.* Oxford: Oxford University Press, 1987.

Thompson, Guy Llewelyn. *Paris and Its People Under English Rule: The Anglo-Burgundian Regime 1420–1436.* Oxford: Oxford University Press, 1991.

Toureille, Valérie. *Le drame d'Azincourt. Histoire d'une étrange défaite.* Paris: Albin Michel, 2015.

Trim, D. J. B., ed. *The Chivalric Ethos and the Development of Military Professionalism.* Leiden: Brill, 2003.

Vale, Malcolm. *Charles VII.* Berkeley: University of California Press, 1974.

Vale, Malcolm. *Henry V: The Conscience of a King.* New Haven, CT: Yale University Press, 2016.

Vale, Malcolm. *War and Chivalry: Warfare and Aristocratic Culture in England, France and Burgundy at the End of the Middle Ages.* Athens: University of Georgia Press, 1981.

Van Engen, John. *Sisters and Brothers of the Common Life: The Devotio Moderna and the World of the Later Middle Ages.* Philadelphia: University of Pennsylvania Press, 2014.

Vaughn, Richard. *John the Fearless: The Growth of Burgundian Power.* London: Longmans, 1966; reprint, Woodbridge, UK: Boydell, 2002.

Villalon, L. J. Andrew, and Donald J. Kagay, eds. *The Hundred Years War: A Wider Focus.* Leiden: Brill, 2005.

Villalon, L. J. Andrew, and Donald J. Kagay, eds. *The Hundred Years War (Part II): Different Vistas.* Leiden: Brill, 2008.

Wagner, John A. *Encyclopedia of the Hundred Years War.* Westport, CT: Greenwood Press, 2006.

Warren, Christopher N. "*Henry V*, Anachronism and the History of International Law." In *The Oxford Handbook of English Law and Literature, 1500–1700*, 709–27. Edited by Lorna Hutson and Bradin Cormack. Oxford: Oxford University Press, 2017.

Warren, Nancy Bradley. "Kings, Saints and Nuns: Gender, Religion and Authority in the Reign of Henry V." *Viator* 30 (1999): 307–22.

Watts, J. L. *Henry VI and the Politics of Kingship.* Cambridge: Cambridge University Press, 1996.

Waugh, W. T. "The Great Statute of Praemunire." *The English Historical Review* (1922): 173–205.

Whetham, David. *Just Wars and Moral Victories: Surprise, Deception and the Normative Framework of European War in the Later Middle Ages.* Leiden: Brill, 2009.

Wolffe, Bertram. *Henry VI.* New Haven, CT: Yale University Press, 2001.

Woosnam-Savage, Robert C. "Olivier's *Henry V* (1944): How a Movie Defined the Image of the Battle of Agincourt for Generations." In *The Battle of Agincourt*, 250–62. Edited by Anne Curry and Malcom Mercer. New Haven, CT: Yale University Press, 2015.

Wright, Nicholas. *Knights and Peasants: The Hundred Years War in the French Countryside.* Woodbridge, UK: Boydell and Brewer, 2000.

Wylie, J. H., and W. T. Waugh. *The Reign of Henry V.* 3 vols. Cambridge: Cambridge University Press, 1914–29.

Index

Numbers in *bold italics* indicate pages with illustrations

Index

Index